THE BECOMING CHURCH

THE
BECOMING CHURCH

John Adair

Foreword by
the Archbishop of Canterbury

LONDON
SPCK

First published 1977
SPCK
Holy Trinity Church
Marylebone Road
London NW1 4DU

Text set in 11/12 pt Photon Times, printed by photolithography,
and bound in Great Britain at The Pitman Press, Bath

ISBN 0 281 02964 4

Contents

Foreword

There are several things which make me grateful for the opportunity of writing a Foreword to this book. One of them is that I have had the privilege of the friendship of its author for a good many years and, when I was Archbishop of York, welcomed the help which his Report on the diocese gave to our work, help which, I believe, is still being felt. I have followed the activities of Dr Adair, and not least his writings, with appreciative interest.

Then, I am grateful because this book comes from the pen of a man who, himself a committed and practising Christian, dares to look at the Church with unblinkered eyes—he faces the facts—and at the same time with faith and hope. He writes as one theologically competent who has already put his sociological expertise at the disposal of the Church. He knows where his hope is founded. Thus: 'Although some theologians and secular well-wishers have attempted to lighten the ship of the Church by throwing overboard the person of Christ, he is still with us'. 'The Church can be held to rest upon the unchanged, unchanging, and unchangeable original identity of Jesus Christ.'

Against that background, he ventures to look boldly into the future. He would assume the mantle of the futurologist—'What will the Church be like in ten years' time? What ought the Church to become by then?' These are no easy questions to answer. Theological, historical, sociological, political, creative perspectives must all be given their place in seeking clues. There is the unpredictability of the open seas, and the Church must not seek the comfort and predictability of the well-girt harbour.

There is realism in this book. Dr Adair knows, from close experience of them, the perplexities which beset the modern Christian disciple. But there is also vision. The decline in the number of the clergy 'is full of creative possibilities'. The parochial system 'has countless opportunities for communication, community, experience, growth, and love'. So has the Deanery—but its potential has yet to be realized and exploited. The author would like to see clergy from other parts of the Anglican Communion working in this country in large numbers for a period of, say, two or three years each. How right he is! Experience on a small scale in the diocese of Canterbury has proved how infinitely enriching the presence of a priest from overseas can be.

So one could go on. Enough has been said to show that in this book we have food for much thought, experimentation, venturing. It is to be hoped that the book will be widely read and carefully studied by clergy and laity alike.

DONALD CANTUAR:

Acknowledgements

Thanks are due to the following for permission to quote from copyright sources:

Basil Blackwell (Publisher) and Bernard Babington Smith: 'Purpose and Choice' by Bernard Babington Smith, in *Sociology, Theology and Conflict*, ed. D. E. H. Whiteley and R. Martin.

Church Times: the editorial 'Synod's tasks', in the *Church Times*, 7 November 1975, and (by permission also of Mrs Margaret Duggan) 'Many good future priests in the colleges', *Church Times*, 16 January 1976, and 'Top thinking at Windsor Castle', *Church Times*, 27 February 1976, both by Margaret Duggan.

The Gallup Poll: *Religion in America*, 1971, The Gallup Poll Index, No. 70, 1971.

A. W. Gottschalk: 'Adult Education in the Church of England: a Preliminary Study' by A. W. Gottschalk, Department of Adult Education, University of Nottingham, September 1968.

Hodder & Stoughton Ltd: *The Impatience of a Parson*, by H. R. L. Sheppard.

Canon T. G. King and the Central Readers' Board: *Readers: A Pioneer Ministry*, by T. G. King.

Lutterworth Press and The Westminster Press: *A Theology of the Laity*, by Hendrik Kraemer, © Hendrik Kraemer, 1958. Used by permission.

Macmillan, London and Basingstoke: *Function, Purpose and Powers*, by D. M. Emmet.

John Murray (Publishers) Ltd: 'Slough' from *Collected Poems*, by John Betjeman; and *The Life and Correspondence of Arthur Penrhyn Stanley, D.D.*, by R. E. Prothero.

The Observer: 'Nothing left but faith?' by Bryan Wilson, in *The Observer*, 2 March 1976.

Oxford University Press: 'The Testament of Beauty' from *The Poetical Works of Robert Bridges*.

Penguin Books Ltd: *The English Church: A New Look*, ed. Leslie S. Hunter (1966), copyright © Leslie S. Hunter, 1966, p. 81. Reprinted by permission of Penguin Books Ltd.

The Society for Promoting Christian Knowledge: *Ministry and Ordination*: A Statement agreed by the Anglican–Roman Catholic International Commission; 'A Staff College for the Church of England' by John Adair, in *Theology*, May 1962; 'The Doctrine of Vocation' by John Adair, in *Theology*, July 1964; and (by permission also of Professor G. W. H. Lampe) 'Secularization in the New Testament and the Early Church' by G. W. H. Lampe, in *Theology*, April 1968.

The Reverend B. D. A. Spurry: 'How can the Reader play a more effective part in the total pattern of the Church's ministry?' by B. D. A. Spurry (research study, 1969).

Times Newspapers Ltd: 'Synod misgivings about Baptism and Confirmation' by the *Times* Religious Correspondent, in *The Times*, 23 February 1974; the obituary of R. C. Hutchinson in *The Times*, 5 July 1975; 'Synod fulfils some intentions' by Clifford Longley in *The Times*, 7 July 1975, and (by permission also of The Most Reverend Derek Worlock) 'Fewer priests do not mean a decline in achievement' by Derek Worlock, in *The Sunday Times*, 24 May 1975.

The Standing Committee of the General Synod of the Church of England: *Future Business of the Synod*, GS 96, Report of the Standing Committee, General Synod (1972).

The Sunday Telegraph: 'Subtle rules of Church unity game' by Douglas Brown, in *The Sunday Telegraph*, 7 May 1972.

The Reverend David Wasdell: Urban Church Project, Workpaper 1: *Let My People Grow*.

Thanks are also due to the Church Commissioners for supplying the statistics on pp. 126–7 showing the deployment of the full-time parochial ministry at 1 August 1976.

Introduction

'Looking at the situation in the round, it is difficult to avoid the feeling that the Church of England is on the brink of crisis. It is, in a rather frightening way, a microcosm of British society—unsure of its position, reluctant and ill-equipped to keep pace with a changing environment, and internally divided to a point where sectarian interests are allowed to outweigh the common good.' With these words an anonymous writer summarized a major series of seven articles on the Church of England, entitled 'Christians Asleep', which *The Times* published in 1966. 'There is little discipline, little loyalty—perhaps the church is too vague and loose an organization to inspire them. It sometimes seems, in the words of Tennyson, that 'the churchmen fain would kill their church'. But perhaps one should remember that all these troubles spring from the diversity of the Church of England, and that this quality, plus its national genius for compromise, has kept it alive for a thousand years.' It is perhaps not surprising that a bishop felt moved to write in response a book entitled *What's Right with the Church of England?*

Since 1966 other writers have used the language of crisis, either about the Church of England as a whole or about some of its activities, such as church schools, theological colleges, finance, or the statistics of membership. The crisis atmosphere permeated the report *Partners in Ministry* (1967) from the Commission on the Deployment and Payment of the Clergy, and such books as *Crisis in Confirmation* (1967). With this sense of either one great but hydra-headed crisis, or a nest of little venemous crises, there marches an uneasy awareness that the Church of England as a body is not in the right shape to respond to them. For example, Trevor Beeson, a parish clergyman, in *The Church of England in Crisis* (1973) took the rejection of the scheme to unite the Established Church and the Methodist Church, and the failure to carry out the radical structural reforms outlined in the report on the deployment of the ministry of 1967, as two glaring examples of the unwillingness of the leadership to measure up to these problems and the power of the various ecclesiastical parties to frustrate any drive for reform.

The Church of England is sometimes compared to a living organic body. On this analogy, some diagnosticians judge it to be wasting away as a slow disease grows almost imperceptibly within its frame. To support their case they point to general factors, such as the effects of secularization in society and the decline in Christian belief, which they see measured in those ominous symptoms, the 'statistics of decline'. In order to achieve a decisive change for the better they urge that major decisions should be taken about the deployment of the clergy, the reform of decision-making at the centre, unity schemes and the selection of episcopal leaders. But decisions are like surgical operations: the sprawling body, already incapacitated by old age and crippled by arthritis, rejects the proposed transplants or amputations. It prefers medicines, well watered down, the medicines of coloured and flavoured compromises.

Other physicians report, to the contrary, that the body is in good health and is even growing. The crisis lies outside it, in the world. First, there is the disease of unbelief. This deadly ailment might take a turn for the better; they point to some dubious signs for hope: the 'Jesus movement', the renewal of intellectual interest in religion, the spread of pentecostalism and—more recently—the 'charismatic movement'. On the other hand, the progress of atheism and agnosticism may lead to a collapse of Western civilization. While this external disease wastes away the Church's ministry and membership, a second social disease—inflation—attacks its material pillars and rafters. Such observers argue that there is nothing wrong with the body of the Church itself: indeed, the diverse parties within it are advanced as signs of vitality and good health. Moreover, both the ills of unbelief and inflation are not confined to these islands: they affect all the Churches. Reorganizing the Church, and all the other panaceas, will not alter the progress of these two universal scourges.

The truth, I believe, lies between these two extremes. The Church of England, like all Churches, is experiencing the effects of a variety of changes in its social, cultural, and economic environment. It is not in the grip of a single crisis in the sense that it is passing a decisive turning point in its life. Rather, it is a process of developing or becoming in relation to a perception of its environment which includes a sense of God at work in, through, and for the secular order. The full implications of that theological revolution in outlook, which has influenced both the direction of Western society and the Churches within it, have yet to be worked out in the organizational life of the Church. That is what this book is about.

Although the Church of England and the church situation in England since 1945 serves as my major illustration, there are principles and general ideas in the following chapters which I trust will appeal to other Churches. It is not my intention either to advance the Church of England as an exemplar nor to denigrate it as a laggard. But this is the right time for the Churches to share their experience with each other, and to check their bearings for the future. Therefore I hope that much of what I write about can be divorced from its context and speak to all Churches in any part of the world.

1

Looking at the Christian Church

The Church is such a familiar concept, especially to those who believe and belong, that it becomes difficult to think about it in realistic or creative ways. This chapter begins with an explanation of the related meanings we give to the word, ranging from the highly concrete to the abstract and intangible. Then I describe the perspectives through which we can study the Church. By themselves they give us a partial view of its reality; taken together, they allow more light to enter the mind, but the image will still remain in motion. It is important to broaden vision in this way, however, because seeing leads to understanding, and understanding determines the rightness of action.

The metaphor of looking contains the corresponding assumption that the Church is a phenomenon, an object existing in space and time. Theologians would counter immediately that the Church is not a phenomenon which can be so discerned through the physical senses, represented by the king of them, the eyes. Looking at the Church, they would say, gives you only a scientific account of externals; to know the Church as the thing-in-itself—the essential reality—you will need prayer, thought and intuition to grasp what is in effect a divine revelation. Such an unveiling or disclosure of the hidden truth is unlikely to be vouchsafed to outsiders.

Even if we accept the distinction between sensory and revelatory knowledge we should be careful not to allow it to crack open into a false dichotomy. There is a relation between attention (the direction of our total gaze) and the seeing of insight or vision. Nor should we accept a hard-and-fast division between knowledge of phenomena and knowledge of things-in-themselves. Although to draw that conclusion is to beg the question in the whole debate between phenomenology and ontology, I do so here with confidence because the exploration of the question of how do we know that we know—the central issue for epistemology—lies outside my present concern in this book.

Nor should we be willing to accept the other common dichotomy between those who look at the Church from 'outside' and those who view it from the 'inside'. In the first place, that notion implies a clear

5

frontier between the Church and the Non-Church, a definite barrier like a medieval city wall or a river. There is a frontier, but it is not marked on the ground; it runs somewhere through the hills, and a traveller like Simone Weil can be unsure in which territory she walks. Secondly, it is easy to underestimate our capacity to transcend our categories. By creative imagination working in the form of empathy it is possible for the 'insider' to see things from the 'outside' and vice versa. If we wish to understand, it is at least worth making the attempt, despite the pain that may be involved.

Looking is the prelude to doing. Or, to stand the statement on its head, decision and action always involve a prior activity of looking. The man who looks upon a woman with lust has already committed adultery; the act of adultery reveals that he has looked upon her in a certain way. It is the quality of our vision, and in particular our ability to see what really is the case, that determines the nature of our action—or inaction. (The fact that the word 'real' can be understood as a value judgement of a peculiar kind does not invalidate that general point.) I shall assume that there is such a thing as reality, and that religious and moral thinking are as much concerned with it as what we now call science. Moreover I shall take it as axiomatic that it is our perception of the realities of a situation, including in it our real selves, which largely makes our decisions as to what we should do.

In a sense we are taught to see. The flowers outside my window I see as flowers because long ago I have learnt the name 'flower', the fact and the idea operate together. Language helps our general work of seeing, but at the price of conditioning our minds. It helps because it makes available to us the perceptions of other people: vision becomes in part a social activity. But we can develop habits of looking determined by our language. This has been demonstrated many times in experimental psychology, and it should come as no surprise to most readers.

In higher education we learn to know and use special vocabularies associated with the act of looking. Again this new 'language' both helps us in the work of looking and also forms our minds, so that we tend to look exclusively and habitually in that way. A botanist will see far more than you or I in a sunflower. But his specialized language may restrict him to conversations with other botanists. They in turn will tend to strengthen his botanical way of thinking about flowers. Moreover, a botanist will find it difficult to 'switch off'; take him on a country walk and he will instinctively botanize. The same is true of other groups of people with an interest in flowers, such as horticulturalists, herbalists, and artists. Their specialized knowledge both stems from and reinforces habitual actions in relation to flowers: the botanist collects, dissects, and classifies; the horticulturalist grows and sells; and the artist draws or paints. Yet the flower is a single reality.

On this analogy the Church is also a reality, like the flower. Everybody sees it. We all learn an elemental language, of which the 'church' itself is the chief term. For the vast majority of people that word and a few other related terms prove sufficient for their purposes. Thus 'church' does the donkey work covering a range of common uses, some employed or known to everyone and some reserved for those who have learnt at least a smattering of a more specialized language.

Rather than arrange these usages on a scale of commonly used to rarely used, I chose to place them in an order with the most concrete and local first, ranging up to the most abstract and universal. In fact the two scales of concrete-abstract and local-universal are virtually identical. Most people tend to think or see in concrete, substantial, or material terms and are correspondingly disinterested or even hostile to the general and abstract, the intangible and invisible. The reverse may also be true, in so far as the abstract thinkers tend to dismiss the more concrete-minded majority as crude or literal. The suggested distinction between the two cultures—arts and science—pales to insignificance beside the contrast between abstract and concrete kinds of thinking. Yet human thinking oscillates between the concrete and abstract, resting in neither, and the range of meanings can give a richness to general words like 'church' or 'love'. Therefore it would be wrong to try to define them too narrowly, cutting away this wealth of associations. The context must fix the meaning. But the reader may like to keep in mind the five senses of the word given below. They are not to be taken as watertight definitions but as five stations or halts on a continuous railway line of meaning. The engine of the mind has to shunt up and down this line all the time; there is no easier way of doing it.

THE CHURCH CONCEPT

Ranging from the concrete and local to the abstract and universal, 'church' is used to describe:

1. *A building for public Christian worship*
The word 'church' comes from an old German derivative of the Greek *kyriakon*, 'the Lord's House'. A Northern European variant 'kirk' also

entered this language from the Old Norse and Scottish. Originally the
'Lord' in question meant God rather than Jesus, although of course early
Christians would not press that distinction. The archetypal church in
this sense was the Temple in Jerusalem. In time the word has come to be
applied to places of worship in any religion, such as a Muslim mosque.

2. *The clergy*

As the common phrase 'going into the Church' reveals, many people
think of the clergy as being in some sense the Church. This meaning is
closely related to (1) above, for the clergyman is visually associated
with the Lord's house; he is seen to lead worship in it and to be largely
responsible for maintaining the building. Moreover, the clergy are tangible in the sense that they can be seen and touched as visibly the Church;
they wear distinctive clothes both in and out of the Lord's house, which
makes such recognition possible.

3. *A congregation of Christians locally organized*

A congregation is literally a body of persons assembled for religious
worship. In this context 'church' is translating a different Greek word
from *kyriakon,* namely *ecclesia.* An *ecclesia* was an assembly; it
derived from the Greek verb for calling out or summoning people
together. Behind its use in the Christian context lies the Old Testament
image of the assembly of the Israelite tribes in the wilderness. On occasion *ecclesia* is used in the Greek Septuagint to describe the collective
body of Israel, which relates it to (4) below.

4. *A religious organization uniting a number of local congregations*

This definition is flexible enough to include sects, denominations, and
communions, all of which are known as churches. In the larger
churches there is an infrastructure of groupings of congregations, such
as deaneries, dioceses, and provinces.

5. *The body of the Lord's faithful people*

This more abstract and general meaning rests upon a holistic sense that
the whole equals more than the sum of the parts. The whole is one: 'One
Lord, one faith, one baptism'. But who belongs to this body—what in
fact constitutes a Christian—is in dispute. While not nearly as
acrimonious as it used to be, the disagreement between the churches

about the nature of the Church is still real and fundamental. In other words, the relation between the Church in its present organizational forms and the Church as 'the body of the Lord's faithful people' is problematic. Moreover, from the theological point of view this concept of the Church as a whole, spanning space and time, has to be related to the still more general and abstract notion of the Kingdom of God as a coming reality which is in some sense present already.

In summary, these five definitions are not separate watertight compartments. They are more like screens in a large room which are adjustable. On some occasions it may be necessary to define the term, but more often than not the reader will have to judge the sense in which it is being used. The concept of the Church acquires overtones and shades of meaning which should not be constantly shorn off by the academic shears.

The Church in all forms can be seen through different perspectives, and understood within them to various degrees of depth. For example, we have all seen a church in the shape of a church building. The majority of the population actually enter a church building at some point in their lives. But there are minorities who look at church buildings with an educated or trained vision: they are looking in a distinctive way. If we really wanted to understand parish churches we should turn to such disciplines as architecture, history, and theology. These ways of looking have implicit in them different prescriptions for action. If it came to building a new church, for example, the architect, social historian, and liturgical theologian would come up with distinctive ideas on what should be done or not done.

In this book I do not intend to say much about churches as buildings, important topic though that is. My focus is much more upon the other ranges of the Church concept. Here there are five major ways of looking, each with a distinctive perspective or viewpoint: theology, history, sociology, politics, and creative thinking. It is tempting to plunge ahead as most books about the Church do, adopting one or more of these perspectives. But if we look upon them as optical instruments or languages, it is surely wise to pause and check how reliable they are. What are their strengths and imperfections or limits?

One obvious fact is that the five approaches have different but overlapping interests, which are displayed in the dominant ideas or concepts they habitually speak or write about. Listen to or read anyone on the subject of the Church and you may be able to identify their particular viewpoint from the following table:

Perspectives	Concepts
Theological	God, Kingdom of God, Body of Christ, Ordained Ministry, Sacraments, Mission, Eternity, Biblical Images, Revelation
Historical	Past, Stories, Changes in Time and Space, Growth and Decay, Temporal, Relative, Human, Past, Tradition
Sociological	Society, Statistics, Typologies of Organizations, Ideology, Institutions, Bureaucracy, Roles, Culture
Political	Polity, Organization, Structure, Constitution, Purpose, Policies, Party Politics, Decision-Making, Communication, Leadership, Goals
Creative	Innovation, Future, Hypotheses, the Unknown, Imagination, Prophecy, Inspiration, Change Agents, Evolution, Natural Images

Each of these perspectives can be used to observe and study one or more facets of the Church phenomenon. There are difficulties in combining them, however, because there are tensions between them which are not always evident to outsiders. In the past these tensions have erupted into a series of conflicts—skirmishes or even pitched battles on the disputed frontiers of knowledge. Therefore it is necessary to draw up some sort of sketch map of knowledge about the Church, delineating the boundaries between the different perspectives and dispelling once and for all their imperial claims—however lately unasserted—to own the whole territory.

THE THEOLOGICAL PERSPECTIVE

Theology is defined in the Oxford Dictionary as the study or science which treats of God, his nature and attributes, and his relations with man and the universe. The sixteenth century Anglican theologian Richard Hooker called it 'the science of things divine', and in Cambridge the old name 'Divinity' has still survived the centuries. But God is not an object of science in the more modern sense of that word; he is not a phenomenon who can be seen or studied through the senses however aided by technological inventions. Therefore it is now best to drop the word science as misleading, and regard theology as an advanced study which seeks to be objective.

What is the relation of theology to religion? All religion implies the recognition on the part of man of some higher unseen power as having control over his destiny and as being entitled to obedience, reverence, and worship. This belief results in certain mental and moral attitudes, whether in an individual or a community. Religion is therefore basically a feeling which can develop into a more formed spiritual and practical life, but does not always do so. Feeling is a better word than emotion; it suggests the possibility of intuition and is less associated with the notion of subjectivity.

From that description it is obvious that many people can be religious with little or no exercise of their mental capacities for analysing, synthesizing, or valuing. The presence of intelligent people within a particular religion makes it more likely that reflection will happen, at least in the shape of what Albert Schweitzer called 'fundamental thinking'. What is divinity like? That basic question is the starting point. A theology is the answer given to it within a religion. Theology as a discipline is the study of those answers. Therefore theology turns out —perhaps rather disappointingly—not to be about God directly, for even the monotheistic concept of 'God' is but one answer held in a particular family of religions.

Within the Christian religion the answer to the basic theological question, 'What is divinity like?' can be stated in simple terms: Jesus Christ. God revealed his nature and attributes in the life, death, and resurrection of a special person called Jesus at a given point in time and space. But this supreme revelation, it must be added, was preceded by a revelation of God to the People of Israel, the sons of Abraham, and it was followed by a further revealing activity of God among those who associated with Jesus and maintained their sense of communion with him. Consequently, Christian theology has three related focuses: upon the life and meaning of Jesus, the sacred history of Israel up to his day, and the nature of being of the early Church in and near New Testament times.

In combination during the first centuries of Christian history, this trinity gave a powerful answer to the question 'What is divinity like?', not least because it could be interpreted in the language of Greek philosophy and expounded in it according to the methods of the academies. Yet through the debates, definitions, and compromises of the early centuries, Christian theology began to harden like concrete into creeds and formulas, culminating perhaps in the great 'Summa' of St Thomas Aquinas. Within this general system the Church, identified with the Catholic Church of medieval Christendom, was still seen as the continuing and tangible place of divine revelation and action: the Holy Church.

By the later Middle Ages, however, the gap between theory and practice yawned ever wider. When the Faith became the state religion of the Roman Empire the Church had found itself involved in a series of compromises with the world, some of them manifest at the time and some more latent, awaiting future situations. Worldliness invaded Christianity at the same time as the Church overcame all opposition to its religious authority. The wealth and luxury of the Church became a scandal. St Bernard condemned it in the form of ornate church buildings and elaborate ritual; St Francis implicitly reproved it in the clergy by choosing to become a poor lay brother; while Erasmus poured scorn on the pomp and ceremony of Rome.

Luther also began by attacking the same enemy in the shape of the sale of indulgences. He was primarily a theologian who found that the theology of the day did not answer his own question, critical for his personal confidence, 'What is God like?'. The unanswered question drove him back to a deeper study of the Bible. His own illumination came reading an early piece of theology about Jesus within the New Testament, the Epistle to the Romans. Confidence flowed into him, that very assurance which all the practices prescribed by the Church had failed to produce. Further study of the Old and New Testaments and the early Church Fathers convinced him that the Church had deviated from the Christian religion.

The sermons of Luther struck a mighty chord in the hearts of his German hearers. His personal problem—that sense of chronic lack of faith—proved to be a general one. Many who shared his question were ready to accept the answer he propounded as a theologian and preacher. The invention of the printing press gave him an enormous congregation, and the same means brought to countless homes a Bible in the vernacular language, containing the three related answers to the basic question of divinity: Israel, Jesus, and the early Church. Preachers became students and expositors of the Bible to audiences already acquainted with the rudiments of Christian theology.

As the Catholic Church would not accept Luther's diagnosis of its sickness he parted company with it. He saw his new and emerging Church as essentially the congregation of God's faithful people, made and kept so by the reading and preaching of the Word with prayer. It was a theologian's church. For political and social reasons, with nationalism falling under both headings, Luther's views established a firm foothold in large tracts of Western Europe. Calvin, a French lawyer by background, imposed an order upon Reformation theology and developed it in certain respects. Above all, he produced some solutions to the organizational problems of running a Protestant church, and the institutional relations it should seek to establish with the civic authorities. Some saw the Church in Calvin's Geneva as proof that once again God was present and revealing himself in a body of truly religious people gathered together. Thus the nature and form of the Church became again a matter of theological concern. Common to all the reformers was this belief that the Church ought to be part of the divine answer to man's question about God, or, putting it another way, that it should become like the early Church of the New Testament.

In this context the role of the priest was turned into that of a theologian in the pulpit. Pastoral work in the congregation, associated with the office of preacher, could also be seen almost as a form of theological study and prayer with individuals. Protestant theologians in universities developed themselves into advanced students of the Bible, delving behind the Vulgate to the Hebrew and Greek versions. Their main task was to equip future Protestant ministers with the necessary theological knowledge for their preaching and pastoral work. Modifications in this basic position of theology have taken place as the result of the growing secularity of society over the last four hundred years, but they have not altered it out of all recognition in those universities influenced by the Protestant tradition, such as Oxford and Cambridge.

The Catholic theological reply to Luther declared that the Church, personified in the episcopate and especially the Pope, possessed the authority to interpret the revelations of God to Israel, in Jesus Christ and through the early Church. An important part of that case hinged on the doctrine of the apostolic succession, that the Pope and the Catholic bishops stood in a direct line formed by ordinations and consecrations to St Peter and St Paul. In other words, despite all appearances, the Catholic Church was the only real continuation of the early Church, and therefore the place where any new revelations about divinity could occur. The Council of Trent and the Counter-Reformation in the second half of the sixteenth century attempted to make the appearances correspond more closely with this concept of theological reality. Within Catholic countries the study of theology reflected this emphasis. It was carried out by members of the Church, almost always priests and often members of the more intellectual preaching orders, the Dominicans and Jesuits. They spent their time less in Bible study and more in the revision and exposition of systematic theology, largely Thomist, and the teaching of dogmatic theology, as doctrines authoritatively held and taught by the Church were known. A tradition of moral theology was also developed. This science of casuistry embraced the application of the corpus of theology to cases of conscience, actual or theoretical.

The location of the study of theology firmly in the Catholic Church rather than the universities, and the relative immunity from secularization possessed by Catholic countries into the late nineteenth century, helped to fossilize Catholic theological thought until its liberation in the post Second World War period. Since then a major theological upheaval has centred upon the nature of the Church. Setting aside the questions posed by the ecumenical movement as relevant but literally peripheral, the main ones concern the way in which God reveals himself and his will in the Catholic Church: through the Pope alone, the bishops in council, or some wider body, or some combination of all? These questions have social as well as theological roots. The appeal to history plays a large part in the discussion of them. Lastly, political changes are already involved in the present lines of answering them. All these factors will be considered later.

In England the basically Protestant role of theology in the universities survived after the restoration of the Church of England in 1660. The Church of England took shape as a compromise between the existing Catholic faith of the land and Protestant theology, and it continued to try to keep the mean between two extremes. The history of Anglican theology reflects that compromise and its inherent tensions. To some extent it was polarized between the two universities. As one wit said, Cambridge produced the reformers and Oxford burnt them. But theology even at Oxford always remained an essentially Protestant enterprise.

During the nineteenth and twentieth centuries secularization affected Protestant theology as an advanced study in a variety of ways. Many intelligent people could no longer accept the orthodox view that the question 'What is God like?' received a sufficient answer in Christian theology. Theologians continued to work the system but the mainstream of intellectual life had moved on. At a hundred points the idea that God had revealed himself uniquely in Jesus Christ, with a preliminary revelation to the Jews and a further self-disclosure within the Church, came under critical fire. The Judaeo-Christian concept of

'God' seemed untenable to many as science progressed, and therefore the question 'What is God like?' had to be rephrased. The ready-made answers of Christian theology suffered a corresponding loss of relevance and meaning.

Theology survived in British universities, despite erosions in the size and status of departments, by presenting itself in secular terms as a good intellectual discipline and as a piece of cultural transmission. 'One of the problems with the subject is that there is always the element of commitment involved in it, but doing academic theology you have to be reasonably detached. Your colleagues, especially in Science, think you are biased, and that therefore you can't be really academic', said Dr Morna Hooker, a Methodist woman appointed Lady Margaret's Professor of Divinity at Cambridge from 1976, during an interview. 'On the question of whether theology has a place in university, I defend it as an academic subject and in terms of our culture as knowledge essential to understanding one's heritage. It's a very good intellectual discipline because it takes in so many languages and ideas.'

The role of academic theology in the Protestant churches as a training ground for preachers has naturally been influenced by these changes. Theological colleges are supplements or substitutes for studying theology in the universities, so that university theologians contribute only part of the teaching (but still write most of the books) to the work of training clergymen. Students intending to teach Christian theology in schools, mostly women, form the other main group, with only a tiny minority studying theology for the general reasons Dr Hooker gives. In 1975 there were more places vacant in British university theological departments than there were qualified applicants.

These changes have deepened the traditional ambivalence with which many church members, clerical and lay, now view theologians. Simple people tend to fear and distrust intellectuals anyway. Christianity is primarily a religion, not a theology. It is a matter of feeling and faith, expressed in prayer and a way of life. Reason and analysis, critical discussion and questioning, can seem to be deadly enemies of any religion. On the other hand, the same simple people tend to look for an authority outside themselves, someone to tell them what to do, whom to believe and where to go. Hence the ambivalence with which theologians are regarded or treated.

In retrospect, the Protestant Reformation paved the way for this marked ambivalence. For in the Church the authority of knowledge replaced the authority of rank or position. The theologian stood at the top of the hierarchy of knowledge, and so his authority reigned supreme. He ruled in the name of the Bible, and the Puritan clergy and laity looked to him as an oracle. But when theologians failed to agree on the meaning of Scripture, Protestantism fragmented further into denominations and sects each claiming to possess the true interpretation. In England the failure of Puritan divines to agree upon an alternative church order to episcopacy paved the way for a restoration of bishops in 1660. Nor could theologians settle relatively minor questions of church order within the churches or between them. By the end of the seventeenth century the authority of the theologian had taken a dive from which it has never quite recovered.

In the secular age the authority of knowledge remained but shifted towards the professors of science, with the exception of Germany, where all professors were regarded as authorities. In the Protestant churches the ecclesiastical leaders still look to theologians for utterance, although sometimes such consultations appear to be more in the nature of rituals. For the distance between academic theology and the popular theology of the pulpit, let alone the religion of the pew, is matched by a widening chasm between it and the concerns of the contemporary Church. Thus the theologian has become a professional, operating highly competently within a closed system of knowledge, which can be shaken about like a kaleidoscope, and communicating mainly with other professional theologians. There is an analogy here with what has happened in the related disciplines of philosophy and classics. Thus there is a paradox within all the churches that while theology is accorded first place of honour in any discussion about the Church, the expectation of what theologians can really contribute to the solution of contemporary problems is small.

How did this state of affairs arise? The importance of advanced theological study in the context of the Christian religion (as contrasted for the moment with the Church) should be self-evident. For it is the study of the Christian answer to the basic theological question which arises in any religion, 'What is divinity like?' All theologians agree that part of that answer included a continuing revelation of the divine nature and will through the Holy Spirit within the community or fellowship of the early Church and its inspired writings. But application of the theological language written about the early Christian fellowship to the contemporary Church (however conceived) is quite another matter. To apply that language is to move beyond the safe encircling arms of the harbour wall of academic theology and into the open sea—an ocean of storms, rocks, and wrecks.

Most theologians are members of particular churches and so they have confessional theological beliefs of various strengths on the relation of the early Church to the present ecclesiastical scene. Obviously subjective factors such as their own religious beliefs and church membership will partly determine how they apply these early concepts in the present day. But when a university professor or lecturer in theology applies biblical (or theological) terms to the contemporary Church or churches, specifically or by implication, he is not speaking as an academic theologian *ex cathedra,* but as a Christian intellectual, a wise man or woman who happens to be a theologian. Whether or not you agree with what he says depends upon the intrinsic merits of the content, and the extent to which you agree with his general standpoint. There can be no appeal to something called Theology—viewed as an independent authority with its oracles—to settle arguments or issues in the contemporary world.

Therefore theology has made progress as an academic discipline at the cost of largely secularizing itself. Compared with the medieval 'queen of the sciences' it has become a much more humble and modest subject. Of course those Christians who study academic theology will make transferences in one form or another to the present day. For Christianity is all about these slow or sudden connections of meaning, the bridgings of the span of relevance. The oscillating process of thought necessary for it may include the application of general ideas or concepts, such as 'the body of Christ', to one or more of the contemporary senses of the Church. But it is important to remember that such reasoning is more in the nature of theological speculation. There is a gap between theology and the Christian religion which must not be disguised by the fact that most theologians are Christians. It explains why theology can easily associate itself with other theologies in what is now called Religious Studies in some of the newer universities.

Thus the theological perspective as a unity slowly evaporates under the light of examination, and we are left with academic theology, denominational theologies, and the general view of the Christian religion. The latter certainly identifies the contemporary Church, in the sense of 'the body of the Lord's faithful people', as a present reality. But it does not go beyond asserting belief in it—'I believe in the holy Catholic (i.e. Universal) Church, the Communion of Saints . . .' Thus the Christian religion does hold that the images and metaphors of the New Testament apply to the contemporary Church; it recognizes no gap between past and present in that respect. Yet there is a 'No Man's Land' fixed between this very general tenet of the Christian religion and the various explanations of how and where they apply. Therefore the theological perspective in this context is little more than an intellectual Christian's assertion of a central Christian belief, namely that the Church is the 'body of Christ'. It bears also the corollary that any attempt to understand the Church without taking that idea seriously would fall short of a reality known to the Christian, if only by faith, although it might still satisfy others.

THE HISTORICAL PERSPECTIVE

History is the study of the past. A historian is concerned with two basic questions: What happened? Why did it happen that way?

A historian, however, is part of the society in which he lives and for whom he writes. Only with difficulty can he escape even partially from the wider influences of its prevailing religion or philosophy; he remains largely a prisoner to its interests. It is true that great historians rise above their generation, but they can never completely transcend it. For the given society largely determines what field of the past the historian chooses to work—where he will direct his metal-detector for the significant past. And the dominant social frameworks of ideas, especially those entertained in the community of historians, will influence his method of explanation. Hence, for example, the wide division between Marxist and non-Marxist historians.

In the West the modern historian stands at the temporary end of a long tradition of historiography, stretching back via the Renaissance and Reformation to roots in both the Graeco-Roman and Judaeo-Christian worlds. Secularization and the rise of science wrought their slow changes on the study of history throughout the nineteenth and twentieth centuries. History as a subject emancipated itself from the thrall of Christianity and theistic religion in general as society became less associated with either. The study of secular history flowered. Moreover, history came to be seen essentially as a phenomenon, with natural causes or explanations or reasons for what happens—political, social, economic, and intellectual.

The secular and scientific approach to history clashed with Christian religion on the common ground of the Bible and the history of the Church. The Bible came under general attack as a reliable collection of sources for what actually happened. History triumphed in so far as Christian scholarship adopted the historical approach itself, treating the

Scriptures critically as historical sources and restricting their explanations in terms of theology in a way already described.

Under the impact of secularization and the establishment of history departments in universities, the history of the Church became just one topic among many in the late Roman, medieval, and early modern European periods. The study of church history, especially of doctrine, took place in the new theology departments, as part of the preparation of men for the ordained ministry. But this church history came to be taught by historians trained themselves in the contemporary secular schools; some of them being lay men and women. Historical writing on the Reformation and the Post-Reformation history of the churches in the early modern period showed signs of more objective standards from about the turn of the century onwards, a development which played a significant part in the changing relations between the churches today.

What use is a historical perspective on the Church today? The first and obvious answer is that no one without some historical knowledge would understand the phenomena of the churches today. The past is a dimension in every decision. For this reason it is natural for anyone joining a group to be initiated—formally or informally—into its history. If we are going to marry someone we find out about their history: it is part of the process of understanding. (The word 'history' itself comes from the Greek word for inquiry.) The alternative is not between history or no history, but between good and bad history. The academically-trained historian can contribute by critically examining what passes for history in a given society or community, and by distinguishing it from popular myth. To do so, however, he has to stand apart far enough to see but near enough to be heard.

Secularization in another of its forms—the growing division between study and action—has affected history as much as theology. History in action is politics, the making of history. Many eminent politicians have been historians, well-versed in it and sometimes writers of histories as well. Few successful politicians have had no sense of history. The historical perspective therefore influences the politics of any community or organization. Sometimes historical studies preface a political career; sometimes politicians or statesmen write history books about their times.

It is not really possible to link the study of history or a sense of history with any particular attitudes in given decision-makers. Such factors as nationality and age and temperament probably play a far larger part in determining why some men are more conservative than others.

A conservative wishes to maintain existing institutions, keeping them intact and unchanged. Historically in England this disposition to preserve what is established has embraced a package of political and ecclesiastical institutions, notably the Crown and the Church of England conceived as dependent upon each other. It is a frame of mind conditioned by history rather than determined by it. The erosions of secularization have influenced the traditional Anglican-Tory alliance, and produced some remarkable natural shapes in the limestone in this century, such as a Communist Dean of Canterbury.

History is often deployed in the defence of a conservative position. The answers to the questions 'Why do you wish to preserve this or keep on doing that?' can be given as a temporal cause—'Because it has been here for a very long time', or 'Because it has always been done that way'. But history is the study of the past, not the present. Moreover, the only constant factor in the past is change. Therefore the historian is unlikely to support a thoroughgoing conservatism, just as he would not underwrite the view that the past, present, and future can be severed from each other, despite the sudden dislocations of revolutions. The decision to change or not to change rests upon other considerations, a mixture of practical factors and value-thinking. The study of history, however, may develop and educate the sense of history: the way things are going and what might be the appropriate next steps within an unfolding general situation. As Francis Bacon wrote, 'Histories make men wise'.

THE SOCIOLOGICAL PERSPECTIVE
Sociology is defined as the study of society, social institutions and social relationships. In the guise of the sociology of religion, it provides another perspective upon the churches.

In order to understand sociology it is essential to know its genesis. In the secularization process, when the pattern or relationship of Christian values slowly fell apart, some values rose to challenge for the empty throne of 'God' or the supreme moral value. Chief among them was the value of society. Thus Society came to be seen as the true God, the ultimate human concern. The Abraham of this new branch of religion of Man, Auguste Comte, saw the need for a theology to explain the movement of society towards perfection, and he invented a word for it—sociology. Utilitarianism would serve as the ethical system of the religion, while altruism—a word also coined by Comte—would replace the Christian feeling of love as the moral motive. The word 'unsocial' replaced the older words 'bad' or 'wicked'. Original sin could be explained by social factors, and changed by social legislation and—above all—education. As for the Church, some sociologists led by Elton Mayo in the 1930s thought that they had discovered a natural equivalent in natural communities and working groups in organizations. Thus sociology developed a missionary outreach into industry, seeking to make such organizations serve Society as its supreme-value, not Mammon. Education became the road to human perfection.

The new religion developed its theology by marrying the value of Society with the dominant ethos and methodology of Science. To theories generated in the minds of the founding fathers it joined the compilation and use of statistics. The potential of this method of collecting and using facts and figures for bringing about social change had been already demonstrated by social reformers of all persuasions in the nineteenth century, especially Florence Nightingale. The offspring, christened Social Science, advocated its use as a research tool rather than as a campaigning device. The infant discipline established bridgeheads in the universities, not without opposition from the historians, who saw their status as the oracles of society challenged by it. But this 'legitimation' was balanced by a crisis of identity as father Science came to disown the child.

For events and time revealed that here was a secular religion and secular theology rather than a science proper. The worship of Society in the form of a nation turned demonic in the case of Germany. The Nazi religion, complete with messiah, religious rituals and persecutions, exposed the dark face of the new god hungry for human sacrifice. One main trunk of the religion of Society survived as Communism, with Marxism as its theology; but in the Western democracies the young discipline of sociology, alienated from its religious parent and disowned by science, had to make its own way. Fortunately the heightened value of society in British and American society attracted students to the new subject, and it grew rapidly between 1960 and 1975, the great expansion period in higher education in both countries.

If we set aside the dominant idea of sociology that Society is the ultimate reality, the chief cause and main end of human behaviour, what is left? In theory, very little. For the sociologist looks upon religion, in the sense of denominational or sectarian activity, as an expression of society and as a functioning part of society. The various theories of Emile Durkheim, Max Weber and other founding fathers, which the empirical research was supposed to verify or falsify, were abstract articulations of that central core of value assumptions. Thus the sociologist collects and interprets data according to a peculiar value-system and a related set of internal theories.

In becoming academic it was in danger of developing an intellectually closed system, like theology. Yet the present generation of sociologists adopts a less theoretical and a more general social interest in religion. As Professor David Martin, a specialist in the sociology of religion, writes: 'Science is not invalidated by its failures or by the existence of hypotheses which are wholly or partially false or which can only make sense in a wider context which has been omitted. What is essential is the idea that religious belief acquires different colourings, undergoes mutations and developments, retreats and advances in response to man's social experience.'

Another branch of sociology which needs to be noted for the purpose of this book is the sociology of organizations. This includes the academic exercise of trying to categorize organizations into different types. Typologies of functions, technology, regulation, and structure have all been suggested. In the religious sphere, sociology attempts to place churches in a typology, distinguishing for example sects from denominations. Some useful work has been done also on the concept of organizational culture. Above all, the sociologists have drawn attention to the not uncommon discrepancies between the stated goals of an organization and those which it actually pursues. The goals of groups or individuals within the organization may well be at variance with both the official 'purpose' and also the policies pushed through by the dominant political section. Under the sociological microscope, organizations look less like the rational creations of enlightened man, and more like multi-interest groupings beset by tensions and conflicts about goals, roles, and rewards.

THE POLITICAL PERSPECTIVE

This perspective follows naturally from the last one. 'Policy' comes from the Greek word *politeia*, citizenship, government. Thus policy or polity meant first, the form, constitution, or government of an organized body or society. Richard Hooker used the word in this sense in his *Laws of Ecclesiastical Polity*: 'Nor is it possible that any form of polity, much less polity ecclesiastical should be good, unless God himself be author of it.'

Politics (in the plural) is defined by the Oxford Dictionary as 'the science and art of government; the science dealing with the form,

organization and administration of a state or part of one, and with the
regulation of its relations with other states'. As such, it has roots in a
branch of medieval moral philosophy dealing with the state or social
organism as a whole, which in turn reaches back to Aristotle's treatise
on political science, *The Politics*.

A policy—in the singular—is 'a course of action adopted and pursued by a government, party, ruler, statesman . . . adopted as advan-
tageous or expedient'. It is a definite course or method of action selected
(consciously or unconsciously) from among alternatives and in the light
of given conditions to guide and determine present and future decisions.
Clearly policy in this meaning is bound up with polity (as I shall continue to call it, for the sake of clarity, although the word may seem
somewhat archaic). For the making and execution of policies requires a
polity with the necessary levels of authority. Conversely, a particular
polity may tend to produce certain kinds of policy.

A fourth sense of politics, related to the others, signifies the competition between competing interest groups for power in a government or
other group. When people say that they hate politics, or 'there is too
much politics in this university', they are usually referring to the
struggle between parties or individuals for power or influence in a particular organization or society. Over the years artful and dishonest
practices, self-interest and personal ambition have become associated
with politics in this sense. Coupled with the frequent failures of
politicians to bring about what people desire, they are sufficient to
explain the bad odour of the word in many conversations.

In the light of the evident importance of the political perspective it
may be a matter for surprise that no related academic study called
Church Politics has developed in the way that Politics or Government
has emerged as a distinct subject in universities. Yet Politics and
Government as discrete disciplines in universities have only established
their independence from philosophy and history in recent times. Why
has the same process not happened in the ecclesiastical field? Certainly
neither theology nor church history have shown signs of innovation in
this area, and their own situation within secularized universities may
prohibit it. As we have seen, theology as an academic discipline has
been steadily withdrawing from concern with the contemporary
churches for a hundred years or more, and church historians in this
country have only tunnelled forwards as far as the nineteenth century.
For their part university departments of Politics and Government are
probably now too secular in their interests and sources of finance to ex-

pand in order to embrace such a contemporary study of the Church. The churches themselves, singly or in combination, cannot alone provide the necessary basis for a detached and objective viewpoint even if they had the money to do so in a period of inflation.

Could sociology form the necessary base? Clearly it has a contribution to make to the study of polity, but it is a limited one. As I have said, sociology is really the theology of another religion, akin to Christianity but also different. In its unreligious form its focus is still essentially social and not political. The political perspective draws as much upon philosophical or theological values and history as it does upon sociology, but it is still more than an assembly of parts. Politics is about people, organization, ideas, and society in a kaleidoscope of combinations; it is about how people think things ought to happen as well as what really is the case. Thus it embraces Moses and Machiavelli as well as Marx.

Another possible base—management studies—must also be dismissed. Management studies emerged in the past century out of a practical activity, training or vocational education of businessmen. By extension, and the growing use of the more general word 'manager', these graduate or adult students came to include a small percentage of those who were not directly intending for or employed in industry or commerce. Management studies assembles segments of established disciplines—economics, law, social sciences, and sometimes ethics—which are judged to be relevant for the training of a manager.

The spread of the management ethos during the 1960s into such areas as government, the civil service, the armed forces, and the public services (helped by a sudden spurt in that decade towards a social capitalist society throughout the Western world) brought in its train a proliferation of management training courses in these spheres. For the churches it raised the question, In what sense is the minister or priest like a manager? At one extreme, some Americans equated their churches with businesses and saw their ministers as business executives; at the other, some Englishmen declared that ministry and management were totally distinct roles and the Church was not even an organization, let alone comparable to a business one. In fact there are some concerns common to minister and manager, notably administration. Churches are organizations even if the Church is not, and they are certainly in business in the sense that they are employing essential resources—people and money—to a purposeful end.

Yet the differences between ministry and management are equally marked. For example, a minister may have an apprentice or colleague working with him, but he does not have a paid team under his leadership. Moreover, the business perspective on organizations, which sees them essentially as producers of phenomenological results, does not illuminate more than a small part of church life any more than it does that of a school, library, or hospital. For these reasons, church politics can never become a branch of the new subject of business policy (although the *Journal of Business Policy* has published several pioneer articles on the subject). On the other hand the advanced student of the Church, using and developing the political perspective, needs to study business policy as much as civil politics as a source of fruitful analogies. The political problems of a multi-national corporation, for instance, resemble those of a large denomination, just as there are parallels between the constitution, evolution, and political life of the Commonwealth and the Anglican Communion, which is possibly its ecclesiastical counterpart. Certainly this important political perspective should be placed upon a more secure intellectual footing, possibly in a university in association with a department of theology.

THE CREATIVE PERSPECTIVE

The creative perspective defies close definition. Here I take it to be essentially the ability to see and make things new. Associated with this idea of the new are such concepts as imagination, innovation, renewal, invention, discovery, exploration, and pioneering. In action the highly creative person may reveal himself as an artist, as an inventor, or as an entrepreneur—developing new forms to meet new needs or opportunities.

Implicit in the creative perspective and its complementary patterns of action is the idea of change. But it is a purposeful kind of change. For the new that is seen and made is not mere novelty; it is a statement of value. The truly creative new is better than the old. The creative person has the problem of seeking to communicate that his vision of the as yet unreal new is *better* than the present form of the ancient or recently old. As people like the familiar, and also progressively fear change as they grow older, he has a difficult task on his hands. Like Moses, he has to persuade people to keep on to the promised land which lies ahead, when they wish to remain with the familiar and known imperfections of their past.

Thus it is the marriage of seen values with the uncreated future which produces the truly new or original, rather than gimmicks, novelties, or reproduction. All creative people work by and develop within their own fields a sense of perfection. 'An understanding of any art involves a recognition of hierarchy and authority', writes Iris Murdoch, herself a philosopher and novelist. 'There are very evident degrees of merit, there are heights and distances; even Shakespeare is not perfect.' The creative perspective therefore involves—perhaps paradoxically—an extremely dispassionate and realistic gaze: the capacity to see things both as they really are and as they might be. Thus artists are able to criticize their own work, possibly discarding an inferior piece which looks good to a casual onlooker who has no educated idea of perfection incorporated in his vision. 'Attention is rewarded by a knowledge of reality', concludes Miss Murdoch.

Unlike the other four perspectives, this one has no academic community behind it as far as the Church is concerned. Therefore there has been no sustained and corporate thinking, tested and supported by research, about the future of the Church. It still has to be done by individual thinkers. The basic questions here are, What will the Church be like in ten years time? What ought the Church to become by then? An attempt to answer the first question can be made by extrapolating from the observable trends of the present—the method of the futurologists in the 'think-tanks' of this decade.

Futurology is too new a word to have found its way into many dictionaries, but the perspective behind it is an ancient one. In essence it views the present from a stance taken up in the future. We are able to do this to some extent because of a range of natural abilities which Christians believe can be transformed into spiritual gifts. At their centre lies imagination, the ability to think in pictures. In purely natural terms this ranges on a continuum from being able to see some familiar object not present to the eyes, to being able to visualize things which nobody has ever seen because they do not exist. In the hands of a creative person such phantasies or visions can become powerful works of art in all its forms—literature, drama, painting, sculpture, and architecture.

Closely allied to imagination, but not necessarily associated with phantasy or creative work in general, is the natural ability for foresight. To foresee is to know beforehand what is going to happen. It implies nothing about how the knowledge is derived and may apply to ordinary reasoning and experience. Within the context of religion, however, the art or practice of divination arose whereby people sought to foresee or foretell future events or discover hidden knowledge by means of auguries or by the aid of supernatural powers.

Both forms of thinking about the future—creative imagination and foresight—are present in both Old and New Testaments. The books of Daniel and Ezekiel illustrate the phantastic imagination in the former, while the Revelation of St John the Divine does so in the latter. These early pieces of futurology concerned the Church, whether it was conceived as the people of Israel or as the Christian churches listed by St John. In the shape of apocalyptic vision or eschatological expectation it has continued within the Christian tradition, but not as a part of theology. For theology, like sociology and politics (though not history to the same extent), has become an analysing and synthesizing activity, not one requiring a truly creative imagination.

Perhaps the more a mind is trained to be critical and analytical, the less it is likely to become constructive and creative, even on simple levels. G. M. Trevelyan, writing about a decision he made in 1903, tells us in his *Autobiography*: 'I had also a feeling that if I wanted to write literary history I should do so in more spiritual freedom away from the critical atmosphere of Cambridge scholarship. . . . I feared the impalpable restrictions of the Cambridge ethos, to which, as I have already shown, I was not insensible. The wise Henry Sidgwick said to me that if I wanted to write books as my chief work in life I had better not stay too long in academic circles.'

The prophets in the Old Testament claimed to foreknow events because they had received insight into God's purpose. But some of them felt called to practise 'prophetic symbolism', the doing of a symbolic act (and there was no distinction between a word and a deed in this respect) in order both to express what was coming and also to make it happen. There is the shadow of a secular parallel in the current concept of 'a self-fulfilling prophecy'. If, for example, you predict to Sally that she will not do well at school, your prophecy may help to create such an attitude in her and those about her, that it can be said to have fulfilled itself. Therefore prophecies about the future may be often interpreted as attempts at influencing the present. Hence the classic association of futurology with social theory and politics in the Marxist ideology.

Within the Christian religion futurology is usually mixed up with a theology or a particular version of history, and it has become associated with sectarian belief. The sects may have arisen, however, because the main churches became past-centred and present-centred, dominated by uncreative theology, history, and politics. It is often overlooked that the early Church contained its prophets and seers, who were certainly more than merely teachers as has been recently suggested. The most significant impact of the futurological perspective on the Christian churches in recent times has been the ecumenical movement, with its vision of 'the coming great Church', but the discussion of that idea must be left to a later chapter.

There are other uses for futurological thinking. The immediate future tends to be highly predictable. You do not have to be an inspired prophet, for example, to predict the amount of church-going in the Church of England next year. But uncertainty increases if you extend the time scale. Moreover, the character and shape of the Church itself becomes problematic as the time span lengthens to long-term. Beyond an optimum point, say between five and ten years, we realize that the future is no longer largely fixed by the past and the present, that there is an area of choice and freedom. In this long-term view, politics becomes more about what we are becoming than what we are doing, more about polity than policies.

The seeds of the future lie in the present. The modern futurologist seeks to escape the gravitational pull of both past and present into an orbit which allows him to see what is both probable or also possible. His work requires observation, foresight, and a disciplined creative imagination. For example, Thomas More, Christian humanist and man of the world as Lord Chancellor of England, could include in his *Utopia* the first suggestion of an eight-hour working day and street-lighting. He is the patron saint of futurologists.

The creative perspective can enter into every discussion or study of the Church in its changing social environment. Often it works in combination with other perspectives: theological, historical, sociological, and political. All can be creative in their spheres, though most of them are not or have no call to be so. Yet the creative perspective needs to stand on its own feet, to exist in its own right. With an uncommon way of thinking, which demands its own disciplined life beside considerable analytical and critical abilities—albeit kept firmly in their place—the creative person does have a major contribution to make in any walk of life. The Church should be a great believer in things linking up and providing a new direction. It was Pasteur who said 'Chance favours the prepared mind', and the minds of Christians—individually or corporately—need to be always prepared.

A MATRIX OF CHURCH STUDIES

It is possible to draw up a matrix or grid arrangement of possible church studies as follows:

Church as → Perspective ↓	Building A	Clergy B	Congrega-tion C	Denomina-tion D	Body E
Theological 1					
Historical 2					
Sociological 3					
Political 4					
Creative 5					

A Matrix of Church Studies

This framework is useful for placing single-perspective utterances on the Church. Most statements about the Church can be given a code number, according to the dominant vantage-point of the speaker or writer and his focus at that time. A sociologist writing an article about the clergy, for example, falls into box B3. You can expect a certain range of interests and assumptions, a particular kind of knowledge and even a certain sort of conclusion. A theologian writing about the Church in its more general sense (E1) is equally predictable. Hence my conclusion that with a bit of practice the majority of statements about the Church—ranging from academic books and articles to single sentences at committee meetings—can be placed on this scale.

The matrix, however, has another use. The word itself means a womb—the place or medium in which something is bred, produced, or developed, the point of origin or growth. Thus, in spite of its prevailing use in mathematics, the matrix is a holistic or natural metaphor related to birth. Contemplate the matrix for a few minutes. Fill in with pencil the squares which are already familiar to you, or which you feel are already occupied by learned and compelling studies. See how many squares remain blank? These represent the major gaps in our understanding of the Church.

For me another result of contemplating and living with this matrix for some years is a growing dissatisfaction with mono-perspective studies or approaches to the Church. The cliché word 'inter-disciplinary' leaps to mind, but it does not quite fit because it leaves out the creative dimension which cannot be classified as a discipline. Therefore I shall call the necessary approach a multi-perspective one.

The most common method for pursuing it is to assemble together in a university department, church committee, or working party, advanced teachers of the discrete disciplines—theology, sociology, history and so on. In principle this arrangement offers a neat solution to the problem without interfering with individual career structures. The difficulty, however, lies in making it work. Despite two decades of talk, the latest research evidence suggests that truly inter-disciplinary study is a rarity in British universities. The ideal is a fine one, but more often than not the practice turns out to be a ragbag of miscellaneous contributions loosely linked to a common theme or subject. Academic standards tend to be much more problematical when the student is allowed to stray from the confines of a single discipline. Nor have inter-disciplinary studies attracted the best scholars, with some notable exceptions.

To use a chemical analogy, inter-disciplinary studies represent the compound in contrast to the mixture method. The mixture in this case happens when two or more disciplines mingle in a single mind. The resulting chemical solution depends upon the qualities of the original disciplines. We should perhaps set aside a specialist who is playing with another perspective like a child with a toy—for example, the theologian who is historizing or the church politician who is theologizing. The mixture only becomes significant if there is a high concentration of two or more perspectives at levels which would stand up to scrutiny in the discrete fields. To jump back to the language analogy: the test is whether or not you are sufficiently inside to be able to *think* in Arabic or French. The ability to stammer out a few tourist sentences does not count! The multi-perspective thinker should have some identity problems in the sense that he no longer belongs fully to any one discipline, and he may become an object for multi-disciplinary suspicion. The case of Teilhard de Chardin illustrates that general point.

Where the constituent standards are high, the results are impressive. The best account of the Puritans in England before the Revolution comes from the pen of the historian Christopher Hill, the Master of Balliol College, Oxford. In a review of his *Society and Puritanism in Pre-Revolutionary England,* Gerald Aylmer could write with justice, 'As a study in the sociology of religion this book will be of lasting interest and importance, and it will be indispensable for understanding the century from the Reformation to the Civil War'. The conjunction of historical scholarship and sociological insight in Dr Hill's mind, guided by an interest in the history of ideas, produced a much fuller understanding of the Puritans than conventional church historians or sociologists have achieved.

History and sociology—social history—is but one example of a synthesis of approaches and the problems they raise. Intellectual integrity is needed when historical realities clash with sociological theories, notably the Marxist socio-economic theory of the class struggle. Sociological concepts such as 'class struggle' certainly provide some insights into the phenomenon of England Puritanism, but the dispassionate historian can discern the stronger influence of theological ideas upon Puritan attitudes.

Turning to the study of the contemporary Church there are very few mixed-perspective writings of any quality. The historical and sociological perspectives emerge again in Dr Kenneth Thompson's thesis on the General Assembly of the Church of England, published under the title of *Bureaucracy and Church Reform: The Organizational Response of the Church of England to Social Change 1800–1965* (1970). But sociological interest and language predominate, and the historical aspect is ancillary. Moreover, the lack of the theological and political perspectives robs the book of much of its significance for the serious contemporary student of the Church.

An Australian Anglican clergyman Dr Peter Rudge wrote a book called *Ministry and Management* (1970), which was based upon his doctoral thesis at Leeds University. It was a pioneer attempt to relate theories about religious organizations and leadership, drawn essentially from sociology, to the contemporary polity of the Church. Since then, as Director of Research of the Christian Organizations Research and Advisory Trust, Dr Rudge has sought to apply his conclusions to a number of religious organizations. His work certainly confirms the unsatisfactory nature of the old divorce between the theological and the political (or organizational) perspectives, but it highlights also the problems first of relating disparate concepts and then applying them in such a way that creative change occurs in religious organizations. Dr Rudge's original university thesis also contained some interesting historical case-studies of Anglican church leaders in this century.

Another major book on the Church, Dr Leslie Paul's *A Church by Daylight* (1973), is written from a sociological stance by a Christian author, who prefaces his social description and analysis of the contemporary Church of England with a potted history of it. Here again there is an attempt at bringing together historical and sociological perspectives. The book is written from the standpoint of Christian concern, but the author does not think through for himself a theology of the ordained ministry and the laity. Therefore his edifice of church reform rests upon traditional assumptions about their roles. Dr Paul reiterates in the book some of his earlier creative ideas upon the future of the Church, notably his suggestion for a major redeployment of many clergy from the countryside to the towns on purely demographic grounds. Only the political perspective is completely missing. Yet if we were to ask why Dr Paul's remedy for the obvious unfairness of clergy distribution was not accepted until it had been watered down almost beyond recognition, and then not for some years after he proposed it, the answer lies as much in church politics as in the imperfections of theological, sociological, and political thinking behind the original idea. Where existing powers, patterns and the established polity are challenged by new ideas, it is usually the latter which retire hurt from the encounter.

These brief notes on four books which combine two or more of the perspectives reveal both the possibilities and the difficulties of this general approach. The perspectives themselves have behind them their own ideology, history, sociology of knowledge, political life, and characteristic attitudes to the new and the future. They are living communities or ways of life rather than lifeless optical instruments. The magnetic attractions and repulsions vary between them in intensity at different times. Theology and history, for example, have a record of association, but there is also a story of tensions between them which are far from resolved. The same is true of history and sociology. Theology and sociology are now bedfellows in secularized universities, each occupying its separate compartment. Both have distanced themselves sufficiently far from their religious bases to secure academic survival, a process which paradoxically makes difficult any genuine interdisciplinary work between them. Yet both inside and outside the universities it has been demonstrated that the advanced studies of theology and society can at least be prosecuted in a single human mind. In this book I shall seek to draw upon all five perspectives in order to achieve a better understanding of the Church as a contemporary phenomenon.

2

Church in Decline

A striking contemporary phenomenon of the Church is its steady decline in membership. Although the individual sets of statistics may be questionable, and the picture varies considerably in different countries and churches, the general trend is perfectly clear. If any reliable statistics for the denominations are contemplated, the falling away of membership becomes obvious. It is partially disguised from those who are not interested in social statistics by the fact that the decline is very slow, like the shrinking of an iceberg upon its ponderous journey southwards.

In this chapter the view of the social scientist must come first. For the present answers to the question 'What is really happening?' are as confused as reports from distant war correspondents. The Church of England's membership is a good starting point because a professional statistical unit was established by that Church some years ago, to its enduring credit. This small research unit may be compared to the 'black box' carried in air-liners, except that its findings can be digested in advance of any institutional crash.

THE CHURCH OF ENGLAND
What is happening to the membership of the Church of England?

1. *Easter Communions*
Easter communicants were once taken to be the standard guide to the size of the Church of England's membership. Such factors as changes in holiday habits and the marked drop in the age at which children are confirmed may confuse that unreliable guide still further. Yet the returns for the country as a whole over a period of years cannot be meaningless, for most Anglicans know that it is one of the few rules of their Church that they should make their communion at Easter. In 1956 the attendance at Easter Communion was 2,348,000. In 1970 there were 1,631,506 communicants on Easter Day in Anglican churches out of a population aged 15 years and above of 35,450,100 that year. This can be expressed in another way by saying that roughly an average of 51 people in every

1,000 over 15 years were Anglican communicants on 4 April 1970. As there were 98 people in every 1,000 at Easter Communion in 1908 the real decline between 1900 and 1970 must be put at about 50 per cent. The trend between 1956 and 1970 showed a steady but slow fall of 2 or 3 people per 1,000 each year. By 1973 the figure had fallen to 1,510,204, a drop of 121,302 in just three years. If it continued at that pace there would be about 250,000 Easter communicants in Anglican churches at the end of the century out of a total population in excess of 60 millions. On the other hand, Christmas Day communicants slightly increased—from 1,689,236 in 1970 to 1,719,992 in 1973.

2. Regular Churchgoers
This yardstick is rendered imperfect by the presence of those who still go to church twice on Sunday on the one hand, and the decline in the habit of attending more than one service on the other. In 1970, however, the figure of 'usual Sunday attendance at all services' stood at 1,541,828, or 33 people per 1,000 total population. The Church of England only began to publish these figures in 1968, and the 1970 report revealed a fall of 63,742—about four per cent in two years. By 1973 that figure had dropped again to 1,410,398—a loss of 131,430 churchgoers in three years.

3. Electoral Roll Names
In 1919–20 a new system of parochial government was established, based electorally upon the roll which had to be prepared in each parish. The present franchise rules provide that a person may be put on the roll or apply for entry if he (a) is baptized; (b) is a member of the Church of England or another Church of the Anglican Communion (or an overseas Church in communion with the Church of England); (c) is seventeen or over; and (d) is resident in the parish or if not so resident has habitually attended public worship in the parish during the six months prior to enrolment.

The annual revisions of the roll were not always thorough. Yet they confirm the general picture of declining numbers. In 1924, when the first roll was compiled, there were about 3,500,000 people qualified and enrolled as electors of Anglican parochial church councils. In 1970 the electoral rolls contained 2,558,966 names, and the lists had fallen by 1973 to 2,021,137.

4. *Young Members*

In the 1920s about 700 babies in every 1,000 live births received baptism at the fonts of the Church of England, 347,167 in 1920. By 1970 that figure had fallen by gradual steps to 466 per 1,000, the lowest average yet recorded. Adult baptisms have also come down from an average of 11,000 a year in 1956–62 to 7,933 in 1970. In 1973 baptisms had dropped to 297,580, or 465 per 1,000, and adult baptisms fell to 7,130.

Confirmations show a drop from 34 in every 1,000 of English young people between twelve and twenty years in 1956 to 20 in 1970, that is from 167,000 to 113,000 youngsters. In 1974 that total had tumbled down to 96,379. Falling confirmation figures imply a continuing trend of falling communicant numbers in later years.

Lastly, Sunday School attendance has dropped from 303 in every 1,000 children aged three to fourteen years old in 1897 to 149 in 1958.

THE CATHOLIC CHURCH IN ENGLAND

The Catholic Church is the second largest denomination in England. In April 1975 Mr A. E. C. W. Spencer, who until 1964 ran the Newman Demographical Survey, the official statistical service of the English Roman Catholic Church, published some estimates of its changing size. In 1958, he calculated the Roman Catholic population at 5,569,000, which included an estimated 249,000 former members who were 'alienated' in so far as they did not even use their church for the 'rites of passage' at birth, marriage, and death. By the end of 1971, Mr Spencer concluded, there were about 2,600,000 such alienated members out of 7,074,000 baptized Roman Catholics, which caused him to comment: 'What emerges is that drop-out (as distinct from religious practice levels below canonical norms) was marginal in the late 1950s, but had assumed massive proportions by the early 1970s. The Catholic folklore that "once a Catholic, always a Catholic", that Catholics seldom totally abandoned their religious identity even if they ceased going to Mass and did not carry out their Easter duties, was substantially true of England and Wales in the late 1950s; it had altogether ceased to be true by the early 1970s.'

Mr Spencer arrived at these figures by considering statistics for conversions, immigration from the Republic of Ireland and fertility among Roman Catholics. He discerned a high rate of drop-outs among children: about three out of ten baptized infants do not proceed to their first Communion, usually at the age of seven or eight, while a further one out of ten are not confirmed at the normal age of about nine or ten. Drop-outs before marriage could not be so easily ascertained owing to lack of figures, although it could be said that whatever the proportion of Roman Catholics married in their own church in 1958, it had fallen by 43 per cent between that year and 1972. Conversions also showed some decline. The 1976 figure of 5,253, a slight fall on the previous year's figure of 5,352, compares with nearly 14,000 in 1959, the peak year when they amounted to about a tenth of the total of Roman Catholic live births. By 1972 they were no longer such a large source of new membership.

The Bishop of Hexham and Newcastle, Chairman of the Catholic Information Office, wrote to *The Times* disputing the estimate of seven million baptized Roman Catholics. 'But no one knows exactly how many there are. The projections of opinion poll researches indicate that there are about six million people who claim to be Roman Catholics. All told, about 4,100,000 Roman Catholics are known to the clergy. This makes one wonder whether Mr Spencer's estimate is too high and, consequently, whether his "drop-out" rate is too bad to be true.'

The count of those attending Mass on the first Sunday in May gives the following figures:

	Sunday Mass Attendance
1962	2,092,667
1966	2,114,219
1970	1,934,552
1971	1,899,803
1972	1,885,960
1973	1,831,550

Whether one sets these figures in the context of the 4,173,773 Catholics 'known to the clergy' in 1975 (a fall of 4,000 from the previous year) or Mr Spencer's estimate of 7,974,000 baptized Roman Catholics in England and Wales in 1971 is relatively unimportant. The Roman Catholic population has increased in size but the trend of church membership is very gradually downwards. Baptisms in 1975 numbered 80,537 compared with 137,000 ten years ago, evidence in part of the effect of birth control in Catholic families.

The numbers of those entering training seminaries for the priesthood serves as another indicator. In England it reached its peak forty years ago. The Roman Catholic Bishop of Portsmouth comments: 'Nationally, the priesthood is top-heavy with older men. The number of those entering the training colleges reached its peak 40 years ago. In the past three years ordinations to the diocesan clergy numbered 101, 108 and 103. It is undeniable that some priests in this country leave the ministry. From 1963 to 1967 the figure for diocesan clergy applying for laicization was 81. More recent statistics suggest an annual figure for Great Britain of 25 priests returning to the lay state. Each case has its element of personal tragedy. But the annual figure for England and Wales represents less than 0·5 per cent of the nearly 5,000 diocesan priests in this country.' The supply of priests is being well maintained, with a fall of only three from 1974, and the total of 7,453 priests only 57 fewer than the previous year.

OTHER BRITISH CHURCHES

The Methodist Church in 1975 produced a report drawing attention to the continuing decline in membership. About three-quarters of the local Methodist churches in 1974 failed to attract a new member. In 1964 there were 750,000 Methodists; a decade later that figure had shrunk to 601,000. In the three years prior to 1975 there was a 44,000 drop in full membership of the church, and an increase of 46,000 in the membership of the 'community roll', i.e. those who are not fully committed church members.

In 1974 the Baptist Union of Great Britain and Ireland reported a fall of 3,421 in a total membership of 187,144. Yet the Baptists lay great emphasis upon the number of adult baptisms in their chapels, and these increased by 28 to 5,323. In 1975 the membership was down by a further 78 adults. The United Reformed Church (Congregational and Presbyterian) announced a slightly increased membership at 192,136.

THE WORLD PICTURE

With regard to Roman Catholicism the situation in the British Isles forms a microcosm of the world picture. The number of Roman Catholics by birth and baptism increases rapidly, especially in the Third World, but the recruitment to the priesthood presages a decline. Somwhere in between come estimates of the state of church life based upon statistics such as Sunday Mass attendance, which show a gradual falling off. The number of Roman Catholics in the world, as estimated by the Vatican, increased from 526,500,000 in 1969 to 534 million in

1971. In the same period, however, the number of Roman Catholic priests decreased from 351,000 to 347,000.

An analysis of church membership in the United States and Canada, carried out in 1973, reveals that the Roman Catholic and most of the major Protestant churches either lost members in 1971 or failed to keep pace with the population increase. The 1973 edition of the *Year Book of American and Canadian Churches* disclosed that 223 Christian churches in America reported a total membership of 131,389,642, or 62 per cent of the population. The Roman Catholic Church reported 48,390,990 members, a gain of 0·3 per cent over 1970. Some denominations showed continued substantial gains. The Jehovah's Witnesses reported a gain of 7·2 per cent, the Seventh-Day Adventists an increase of 4·9 per cent and the Mormons one of 2·9 per cent.

The figures for declining church membership in America are supported by surveys of church-going habits. The 1971 Gallup Opinion Index report *Religion in America* stated that 49 per cent of all religious faiths attended church or synagogue in 1955, and that it had fallen steadily to 42 per cent in 1970. For comparison purposes, the report gave the following figures:

Church Attendance
% of Population

Canada	44
Netherlands	36
Greece	26
Australia	25
United Kingdom	20
Uruguay	18

There are exceptions to this general picture. A survey published in Dublin during 1975 established the Irish as the most church-going nation on earth. The research and development unit of the Irish Bishops' Conference confined the survey to Roman Catholics, who form 96 per cent of the population of the Republic of Ireland. The representative sample of 2,500 people reveals that nine out of ten attended church at least weekly, and nearly a quarter go more than once a week. Half the population goes to confession at least monthly. Unskilled manual workers have the lowest rate of weekly attendance at Mass—86 per cent. Younger age groups are less inclined to church-going; only 67·9 per cent of men between 20 and 24 years old attend every week. But there is no significant difference between attendance in the various age-groups of women. In all, 93·3 per cent of women attend church, in comparison to 88·4 per cent of men. Only 29 of the 2,500 gave lack of interest as their reason for never attending Mass. But the Republic of Ireland is exceptional in this respect.

CHURCH REACTIONS

Facts are barren unless they are correctly interpreted. Church leaders have rightly protested against a sensational interpretation of such statistics. In some cases, as already noted, they have queried the actual figures. Whatever the arguments about a particular set of figures, however, there is no doubt about the general decline in church membership as measured in ways other than infant baptism. It proceeds at different rates: faster in industrialized and secularized countries, slower in agricultural and traditionally religious areas. The main exception is the growth of sects such as the Jehovah's Witnesses.

Many writers have interpreted these facts as the symptoms of a crisis for the Church. A crisis is a turning-point in the progress of anything; also, a state of affairs in which a decisive change for better or worse is imminent. It implies an unstable or crucial time, such as the period of strain following the culmination of a period of business prosperity when forced liquidation occurs. By this analogy the Church is said to be experiencing a crisis because it has moved from a long period of growth and prosperity into organic decline and poverty.

Among churchmen who do not seek to evade the evidence by suppressing pieces of data, playing it down, or simply ignoring it, there are those who question whether or not the general trend will continue. Will there be a revival or renewal of church membership? Will the figures swing upwards? Sometimes church leaders seize upon one set of figures, say an upturn in ordinations or confirmations, as a sign of such hope. It is certainly true that other general social trends, such as inflation and population rises or falls, have been reversed. Why not church membership?

In dealing with the future we can only talk in terms of probabilities or possibilities. To try to assess the chances of church membership continuing to fall or beginning to rise we have to consider what is happening in the twin contexts of the churches—the Christian religion and the given societies of the world. The temptation to optimism or pessimism, to wishful thinking or doom-watching should be kept in check until that necessary exercise has been carried out.

THE SURVIVAL OF RELIGION

The sociological evidence, such as it is, supports the conclusion that religion is not declining at the same rate as the church membership, but it is changing in content and shape. In 1970 the Harris Poll conducted a survey into British religion, taking a representative cross-section of 2,472 people aged 16 years and over. Forty-eight per cent believed in the existence of a personal God, 32 per cent did not, and 20 per cent just did not know. The highest believing element is the over-55 age group—56 per cent. More of the sample believed in God than believe in life after death. Women are more religious than men: 55 per cent believe in God and 50 per cent in life after death.

Question: Do you or do you not believe in a personal God who can respond to individual human beings?

	All Aged 16+ %	Sex		Age			
		Men %	Women %	16–24 %	25–34 %	35–54 %	55+ %
Yes, believe	48	40	55	41	43	46	56
No, don't believe	32	40	26	38	39	35	24
Don't know	20	20	19	21	18	19	20

Question: Do you believe in life after death?

	All Aged 16+ %	Sex		Age			
		Men %	Women %	16–24 %	25–34 %	35–54 %	55+ %
Yes	41	32	50	36	37	43	45
No	38	47	30	42	45	37	33
Don't know	21	21	20	22	18	20	22

Harris Poll, 1970 (Britain)

Three out of ten never darken the church door; nearly half go occasionally. More than half of the Roman Catholics said they were once-a-weekers. Only seven per cent of the Anglicans attended church once a week. The latter were asked about the causes of this state of affairs; some 29 per cent blamed 'too many distractions, such as TV, cars, bingo', and 13 per cent thought the Church had become too old fashioned, boring and drab. The representative sample favoured the retention of the Church-State link. Not only did seven out of ten Anglicans opt for this, but also four out of ten Catholics.

In 1973 a special Gallup Poll tackled the same subject with a nationally representative cross-section of 892 adults. The church attendance figures showed a predictable drop since the Gallup survey in 1957, from 28 per cent who went once a month or more then to 21 per cent. Twenty-seven per cent expressed their intention of going to church that Easter, compared to a normal Sunday church attendance, which Gallup calculated at 14 per cent of the population. There are, however, substantial audiences for religious programmes on radio and television: on an average Sunday, church services and religious programmes are viewed by 24 per cent on T.V. and heard by 20 per cent over the radio. Thus the churches reach considerably more through television and radio than they do through their own establishments.

Women outnumber men in church by nearly two to one, and they tend to hold more religious beliefs than men, as the following analysis shows:

Religious Beliefs	Men	1973 Women	All	1968 All
	%	%	%	%
God	65	83	74	77
Heaven	41	60	51	54
Life after death	30	43	37	38
Reincarnation	19	25	22	18
Hell	18	21	20	23
The Devil	16	20	18	21

Gallup Poll, 1973 (Britain)

Gallup confirmed that the older a person is, the more likely he is to believe in God, Heaven, reincarnation, and Hell. There were two exceptions to this generalization. Young people in the 16–24 age group are more likely to believe in life after death and the Devil, 35 per cent and 24 per cent respectively, than are persons in the 25–34 age group (28 per cent and 13 per cent).

A cross-analysis of the answers to the belief question—for example, how many people who believe in God believe also in the Devil—produces some interesting findings. Almost everyone who believes in Hell believes also in Heaven, but only 37 per cent of those who think Heaven exists feel the same about Hell.

Believe in

Also believe in:	God	Heaven	Life after death	Reincar- nation	Hell	The Devil
God	—	98	95	93	96	98
Heaven	67	—	78	74	95	93
Life after death	47	57	—	70	75	76
Reincarnation	28	32	42	—	36	33
Hell	25	37	40	32	—	79
The Devil	24	33	37	27	72	—

A Cross-Analysis of Beliefs

Between three and five people in every hundred attend the state churches in Protestant Europe on every Sunday. Yet a vague christian religiosity still affects the majority. They make use of religious rites at birth, marriage, and death; in Scandinavia most of them are confirmed. They pray to the Deity, accept the establishment of the church, watch or listen to religious broadcasts and go to church on occasions such as harvest festival. In Finland, with a three or four per cent church attendance, nine our of ten parents teach their children prayers, while about half say that they have felt a strong wish to thank God at times. Some 50 per cent also believe in life after death, and a third of those who do not do so still favour Christian burial.

Professor Martin has summed up these and other studies in this conclusion: 'The religion of modern Britain is a deistic, moralistic religion-in-general, which combines a fairly high practice of personal prayer with a considerable degree of superstition'. (*Theology,* February, 1973).

Consequently we must distinguish between this religion transmitted by the family and culture on the one hand, and Christianity and the institutional church on the other. Professor Martin again: 'The crisis of institutional Christianity is not on all fours with a break up in the kinds of belief and semi-belief I've just outlined. The latter is passive, resistant, and crosses barriers of milieu and status more readily than does association with the institutional church. Thus religious belief alters relatively little from middle class to working class: in Britain indeed it alters hardly at all. What alters and is altering is active association with the on-going life of the church. And this is an aspect of a general crisis of communal, active participation in voluntary associations as such. . . .

The church has been reduced to one form of the organization of leisure and that is also the sphere in which the privatized individual of contemporary society has his habitat.'

PERSPECTIVES ON DECLINE

The decline in Church membership is a phenomenon. It is one symptom of the decline of popularity of Christianity as a religion or way of life. In Europe and America fringe religions, such as the occult, have also increased. It looks as if sects and religious movements of various kinds will occupy some of the vacant space created by the decline of Christianity, especially for the less educated people, while the residual Christian religion of the more advanced will steadily lose touch with Christian theology and the Church. What have the disciplines to say about this striking phenomenon of decline in the postwar period?

THE THEOLOGICAL PERSPECTIVE

Academic theology as such had nothing to say, but there has been a considerable number of theological speculations about secularization. These thoughts as to where God is now, what he is doing or saying and how he is doing it or saying it, possess one common theme. They posit a shift of interest in God's mind from the sacred to the secular. God now values the world as much if not more than the ecclesiastical sphere. The temporal order matters to him as well as the spiritual order. Thus the fading of the eternal into the clouded background is a divine way of concentrating man's attention on this world, and not on heaven or the life after death. God has deliberately withdrawn himself from the temple sanctuary, and gone out into the market-place of the city. Mankind has come of age (in Dietrich Bonhoeffer's famous phrase); God is boldly leaving him alone to get on with the management of a part of the universe.

There is of course a long theological tradition behind this general theme, and it has had a major influence on the churches in modern times, turning them more towards social reform and political action. There is the corollary that the churches as such are of less interest to God; that church membership and attendance now matter less in the scheme of things. Correspondingly the differences between churches seem less important.

The idea of God changing his mind is clearly an anthropomorphic one, and we must at least substitute for it the idea that the Church—or part of it—has become more aware of the mind of God. Those Christian theologians converted to this theology of 'holy worldliness' have grown rapidly, as have the clergy and laity who also embrace what can be called a secular-centred Christianity. The old sacred image of the church, with its emphasis on membership, correct belief, attendance, and observance, survives best in Roman Catholicism, the quasi-Protestant sects and the Orthodox churches, whereas a preoccupation with the secular and non-church activity of God affects most the Protestant churches of the West.

In an article entitled 'Secularization in the New Testament and the Early Church' (*Theology*, 1968), Dr G. W. H. Lampe, the Ely Professor of Divinity at Cambridge, usefully summarized this new attitude in Christian theological thought:

> The secularization of religious thought, practice and devotion does not imply a denial of God, nor is it to be identified with materialism. For this it is better to use the term 'secularism'. Secularization means, rather, a reorientation of religion; its transposition into a different key, not its replacement by an atheistic view of life. The laicization of the Church is part of the process of secularization, but it is by no means the whole of it; for secularization means the setting of faith in God within a this-worldly frame of reference. It involves a general emphasis on the immanence rather than the transcendence of God. Transcendence is not denied, but it is conceived of in a way different from that of much traditional thought. It is transcendence within the world rather than beyond it. . . .
>
> This present world is therefore of ultimate value. It is God's world, and man is called to claim it and vindicate it as such. Man is nearest to God when, instead of detaching himself from the concerns of the world and society, he involves himself in them most deeply. The world is the place where God is served, and God is served through concern for his world and ministry to its needs. It follows that the ancient dichotomy of two realms, sacred and secular, is totally rejected. The world is one and indivisible. It is sacred in so far as it is recognized and treated as God's world, and it is secular in so far as it is apprehended and exploited without reference to God and without moral responsibility towards the grace, love, and demand with which the world confronts man. Church and world are therefore not to be set over against each other as separate entities. The Church is not a community saved out of the world. God's will is not to destroy the world and save the Church but to save the world. The Church is that

part of the world which acknowledges its responsibility towards God, recognizing that the world is created. As such, the Church is that part of the world which is called to be God's instrument in the restoration of creation and the renewal of the world which is his ultimate purpose. The things of God with which the Church ought to be concerned are not the ecclesiastical institution itself or its own peculiar interests and affairs, but the things of the world. There is no reason to hold that ecclesiastical persons, institutions and objects are holy or pleasing to God in a sense which is not also true of the world which is traditionally called 'secular'.

Professor Lampe continues his article by exploring the roots of the secularization of Christian thought in the New Testament and Early Church, illustrating the fact that it is a theological outlook which has a long development behind it.

It is tempting for sociologists to dismiss this kind of theological thinking as a form of rationalization. There is some substance in that charge, but on the whole, it is too simplistic. The roots of such a theology of the secular lie deep in Christian soil, breaking surface visibly in the Puritan intellectual revolution in the first half of the seventeenth century. Even sociology itself can be understood as an off-shoot from one or more of those roots. We have to resist a tendency by sociologists to use the social and cultural phenomenon of secularization to explain away everything that is happening in the Church.

THE SOCIOLOGICAL PERSPECTIVE
Those who view the scene through the sociological perspective interpret the decline of the churches more in the context of a general breakdown of community. Thus they see a purely organizational (or 'bureaucratic') response to falling membership and fading religion as ineffectual. In reviewing Canon David Edwards' book *Religion and Change* (1969), for *The Observer* Dr Bryan Wilson, Reader in Sociology at Oxford University, could write:

Theology is pre-eminently a non-cumulative discipline. Its warrants are derived from revelation, primitive practice and foundation charters, and even in the forms of words it employs there is no ready response to the impact of social change.
This quality of theology marks it off sharply from the natural and social sciences, and reassures the faithful that it deals with abiding

truths, things deeper than the findings of the sciences. For its exponents it provides an interminable discourse, in which no particular development need too much disturb those who oppose it, since, in the course of the shifting fashions of a discipline but lightly in touch with the real world, the dance will sooner or later lead again in their direction. For theology feeds, not on social experience, but on itself. . . .

Although he takes up social issues, Mr Edwards is unversed in sociological analysis. Thus, high church attendances suffice for him to call Americans 'a profoundly religious people': low attendance in Sweden leads to the assertion that religion there 'is ruined'. But the difference in the cultural meaning of 'going to church' in different societies remains unnoticed. Bland acceptance of the institutional aspects of religion as the crucial aspects is again found in the author's approval of existing church structure—there are even kind words about bishops.

Religion 'is experienced as a community', Mr Edwards tells us, but since he never faces the implications of the eclipse of community, he fails to see the real religious dilemma of modern times. Religion grows and thrives in stable communities of 'known' people, and there, rather than in its inherited, centralized political structure, lay the strength of past Christianity. But today, men interact much more as mobile, anonymous persons, and to compete with other organizations that are also seeking to persuade men about this or that, the modern church finds need to imitate their structures and procedures. The *communal* ideals of religion and the *bureaucratic* means of promoting them present a sharp contradiction.

Modern denominations become bureaucratic organizations, even though, marginally, at local level, some still manage to preserve some spirit of community. What Mr Edwards fails to see in discussing ecumenism is that because churches are large-scale bureaucratic institutions, organizational goals are always likely to usurp distinctive religious values. The competition that he recognizes as a useful stimulus to American denominations is not competition in religious values, but only in organizational techniques. The high rate of transfer of American clergy from one denomination to another (in the interests not of truth but of career prospects, better conditions of work, and better pensions) makes this apparent.

But if he does not analyse social data adequately, at least Mr Edwards faces the gross social facts that might discourage faith. His

procedure is like that of a scrupulous accountant whose examination
of each discrete account shows them all in debit. But when he does
the final sums, he somehow produces a cautiously healthy over-all
credit balance. The affairs of Christianity, despite the 'severe shock
to theology' at the 'decline and fall of Christian dogmatism', are committed hopefully into the hands of the Lord, even though, as the
evidence was marshalled, the hands of the official receiver were also
ready.

Dr Wilson's words serve to remind us of the tensions between
sociology and theology which I have already described in the opening
chapter. The heirs to the nineteenth century movements to create a more
perfect society (or community) on earth, such as socialism, Marxism, and
the social sciences—economics and sociology—can now contemplate a
situation of international divisions and hatreds, financial disorder and the
steady disintegration of community. But their faith in Society, and man's
ability to reach that *receding* shore, remains constant. The sociological
diagnosis of the decline of religion as a symptom of the general weakening
of community life, carries with it a sociological prescription—namely,
political action for a more communal society at national and international levels, and community development at the grass roots. But these
also require organization and bureaucracy. Nor are there signs of any
real effectiveness in community development as yet.
yet.

There is no reason to doubt the sociological conclusion that church
membership and the sense of local community are in decline together.
One does not cause the other; they are connected essentially in a
process of interacting changes. Equally Christians would now admit the
historical conclusion that social factors were connected in the rapid
spread of Christianity in the first three centuries of its existence. Indeed
the work of historians has encouraged many Christians to look with
equanimity on the decline of the Church, on the dubious grounds that
between about A.D. 300 and 1945 the Church merely filled up with a lot
of social conformists and fringers, whose present-day counterparts are
now flocking out—thank heavens and good riddance! Church leaders,
clerical and lay, who have adopted a historico-sociological interpretation of church membership and attendance, may find that it inoculates
them against one virus of despair, but it leaves open the question why
the Church has failed to met the religious needs of man in Western
society.

THE HISTORICAL PERSPECTIVE

Professional historians are characteristically suspicious of the generalizations common in popular history, especially those which seem to contrast one age with another in terms of white and black. Historical research shows that earlier centuries were in some senses more secular than our own and in others less so. For example, church buildings and yards were once used for secular purposes—such as keeping the town's armour and mustering the militia—which would appear sacrilegious to us now. The historical evidence for church membership, attendance, and Christian belief in any given period is relatively scanty, and the historian is wary of drawing conclusions from it, let alone comparisons with other ages. If anything historical research will tend to lengthen the time-scale of secularization, discovering roots beneath roots.

But a historian has to have the courage to generalize, otherwise his heap of facts adds up to nothing. The difficulties and status of such primary conclusions about the past must be left to the historiographer and the philosopher of history to explore. But there is a general consensus among historians that a shift of values did occur and is still happening in the West which can be called secularization. It affected the position of the Church in society. For secularization means also withdrawal of areas of thought and life from church and finally from religious control, and the attempt to understand and live in these areas in the terms which they alone offer. It does not mean necessarily a decline in religious belief as such.

Church historians are reluctant converts to the concept of secularization, not least because their knowledge of the past warns them against assuming a dramatic modern decline in Christianity compared with an Age of Faith which was in fact probably more myth than reality. 'Some things were secular, others less', concluded Owen Chadwick, Professor of Ecclesiastical History at Cambridge, in his magisterial *The Victorian Church*, II (1970), p. 473. In his Bampton Lectures, entitled *The Secularization of the European Mind in the 19th Century* (1976), Owen Chadwick speaks more strongly of some 'elusive shift in the European mind' which had taken place in the second half of that century, for which he reluctantly chooses the umbrella-word 'Secularization'. That term is regarded by him as a retrospective label, like 'Renaissance' and 'Enlightenment' (the latter not used with our meaning until a hundred years after the fall of the Bastille). It is to be used on condition 'that the word is used, neither as lament of nostalgia for past years, nor as propaganda to induce history to move in one direction rather than another, but simply as a description of something that happened to European society in the last two hundred years. . . .' A description of something that happened . . . and, of course, continues to happen. Secularization is therefore a phenomenon open to historical description and analysis. But the insufficiency of evidence about the past in this more intangible area of popular values, attitudes, and beliefs will always drive us back to the theological and sociological perspectives in order tentatively to pencil in some primary conclusions about the nature and extent of the process.

THE POLITICAL PERSPECTIVE

These theological and sociological reflections upon the process of secularization have produced changes in thinking about the policies and polity of the Church. By about 1955, for example, the clergy of the Church of England had largely abandoned their traditional parochial strategy of spending most of their time visiting all the homes in their parishes, reminding people explicitly or implicitly to come to church—'a home-going parson makes a church-going people', as the old adage put it. Henceforth visiting tended to focus around the sacraments and services of the church. Those who partook of neither were unlikely to see their vicar, sometimes much to their chagrin.

This tendency formed part of a much larger pattern, to be discussed later, whereby the Church of England is slowly drawing apart and asserting its Christian character as in distinction from secular English society. In sociological language, the Church of England progresses further along the road from a national church, where church and state are two sides of the same coin, to the status and self-consciousness of a denomination. This development is accompanied by a marked increase of consciousness in being Anglican (a word invented some time after 1660).

In terms of church polity or organization, one change concurrent with secularization has been the introduction of synodical government, which in effect means a greater degree of self-government. This movement began in the nineteenth century, parallel to the growth in democracy in the State. In this century it became more urgent as the House of Commons—ostensibly the elected representatives of the laity of the Church of England—became a virtually secular institution. The movement also picked up some impetus from the rising value of the laity in post-Second World War theology. In a later chapter the significance of the synodical system in the religious *milieu* of the next thirty years will be discussed.

Turning to the wider aspects of church politics and polity, much the same can be said for the ecumenical movement—'the great new fact of our time', as Archbishop William Temple called it. It is no accident that it has arisen in this age of the relative decline of Christianity and church membership. Again, a wise historian would avoid the language of cause-and-effect, but the connection between the two phenomena is not in serious question. The difficulty of making converts in the mission field during the early part of the century caused Protestant missionaries to blame their denominational differences (rather than Christianity itself), and they gave a powerful launch to the modern ecumenical movement. Again, an assessment of the position and prospects of the ecumenical movement in this new and complex environment must wait until a later stage in this book. Certainly the optimism of the 1955–65 period, which saw the ecumenical movement as the spearhead of a resurgence of Christianity, is now departed.

SUMMARY

Most students of contemporary society agree about the fact of secularization, although there is an understandable tendency in the churches to play it down or minimize it or theologize about it as a substitute for real thought. The fact that the process of decline in both church membership or allegiance and Christian belief is so gradual makes it hardly noticeable and quite comfortable once you are used to the general idea, like you or I growing old. Each of us has about ten thousand million brain cells in our heads and we are losing several thousand cells every day, but it takes time to notice the difference. Moreover, there are always false prophets who hold out specious hopes. They watch the straws moving on the face of the water, announcing the ebb and flow of tides in muddy inlets, but it is the sea itself which is diminishing step by step each year.

A most interesting fact about secularization is that it does not mean a decline in religion as such. Man seems to have religious needs (although that phrase is metaphorical). In a commercial analogy, the Christian churches are slowly losing their dominant share of the religious market, gradually in the industrial societies and much less evidently in converted societies at an early stage of 'westernization' in the Third World, notably Africa and South America. The Roman Catholic Church is better insulated against the process than the Protestant churches, but is no longer immune from it in plural industrialized and urbanized societies.

Interpretations and attitudes go hand in hand. Setting aside those clergymen who dispute the phenomenon of church decline, usually on the grounds that church-going has increased in their suburb, there are those who accept that attendance and membership is falling but dispute whether or not the solid amount of true Christianity in the world is diminishing. There are others, however, who accept that both church membership and Christian belief to a lesser extent are in decline.

The attitudes are as various as the interpretations. In the 1950s and early 1960s, the most important division to appear—cutting right across the churches and party lines within them, affecting all age groups—opened up between radicals and conservatives. The radicals advocated accepting—and even accelerating—the decline of the denominations. In its place they envisaged or advocated some sort of cell system for the remaining Christians. The conservatives initially resisted the idea of any change. By about 1965 it had become clear that the 'dismantling of the structures' advocated by the radicals was not going to happen. Much of this kind of talk can be dismissed as a theological fashion, for the talkers if pressed intended no action where it affected themselves. But it had an influence on the new generation of church leaders in the late sixties and early seventies. It gave church politics their present conservative-radical temper, a varied mixture according to denomination and geography.

Whether or not these interpretations and attitudes, and the policies which stem from them, represent the true ones is quite another matter. The historian and sociologist can record the phenomenon or chart the process of secularization, but they cannot tell Christians, individually or as a corporate body, what to think or do about it—or even whether or not to think or do anything about it at all. Alas, I am growing older, but I do not think much about it or do special things: no transplants, hormones or special diets, just faith and hope.

Thus the facts of decline should not drive us to instant thought about how either the Church or Christianity can survive. We ought to shut a door temporarily between the alarming signals flashing in from the environment, now perceived as hostile, and the instinct to preserve or conserve self at all costs. The self-preservation instinct, powerful though it is in individuals, groups and organizations, is not the key to enlightened action. The prevalent philosophy—a kind of social Darwinism—can easily lead us into the trap of seeing the churches as a breed of extant dinosaurs, who are either frenetically rushing around trying to survive, or else sitting forlorn and still in the shade conserving their dwindling mountains of fat. Rather, we should ask the corporate questions: what is our life about, why are we here, what is the purpose of it all?

3

Like a Mighty Army: the Laity

Between the idea
And the reality,
Between the motion
And the act,
Falls the shadow.

T. S. ELIOT

The years between 1950 and 1960 saw a 'discovery' of the laity by many theologians. Their theologizing about the laity, which seemed revolutionary at the time, had in fact been foreshadowed in all the main traditions. What had changed, however, was the cultural climate, and this made possible the 'theological revolution' about the laity.

The slow change of values known as secularization, working like leaven in the corporate depth mind of Western man, issued in a general emphasis upon the worth of the secular, of 'this age' rather than 'the age to come'. In Christianity, starting at the time of the Reformation, this development was mirrored as the secular or temporal part of the Church—the laity—began to climb in value. The theologies of the laity written in the 1950s and 1960s did not cause that basic shift in value towards those Christians rooted by occupation and interest in this world; rather, it gave an intellectual expression to it. Practical factors such as church decline, and the diminishing number of clergymen, converted many waverers to the doctrine that the Church had now moved into the Age of the Laity.

A THEOLOGY OF THE LAITY
Theologizing about the laity seems to have emerged first in the Protestant churches during the 1950s. It was preceded by a diffuse but marked feeling about the importance of the laity. Speaking for myself, at the age of 20 years, living on the Mount of Olives as a National Serviceman in 1954, I had felt by intuition the significance of this world and the laity in theological terms. At Cambridge University the following year I found some who shared that view. Sermons, lectures, and discussions at that university during the next four years—a flourishing period for

Christianity, with full college chapels—certainly developed that general feeling about the positive nature of lay Christianity.

Following in the steps of Martin Bucer, a Dutch theologian came to give the Hulsean Lectures to us in the Cambridge Divinity School in February 1958. Professor Hendrik Kraemer, a former missionary and late Director of the Ecumenical Institute at Bossey, expounded the thesis that the laity had been consistently undervalued since the Reformation in theology. Doubtless deterred by his monotonous delivery, his mainly clerical audience dwindled as the lectures progressed. As the published version *A Theology of the Laity* (1958) reveals, Dr Kraemer certainly expounded his case well, and spelt out its implications for clergy and laity alike with deep feeling. He concluded the lectures with a ringing challenge to the remaining audience of four or five people, which included myself:

> Will you take seriously the essential place of the laity (as essential as that of the clergy) in your work of rethinking the doctrine of the Church or not? If so, this means an important change in the ecclesiological quest. If not, then all talk about a theology of the laity is an interesting intermezzo in the Church's realm of discourse, but in essence it is vain.

By this time some individual Roman Catholic thinkers had begun to explore the same territory. In France Father Yves M. J. Congar published a book entitled *Jalons pour une théologie du laïcat* in 1953, and this voluminous work of scholarly erudition appeared in English translation four years later as *Lay People in the Church*. The Fathers and the scholars of medieval times had a total view of the Church, but then Roman Catholic theology went on the defensive against the heretics of the later Middle Ages. Thus the ecclesiology of the Church developed in a one-sided way as a doctrine of a clerical hierarchy. 'Therefore', Congar wrote, 'the rediscovery of the laity will force Catholic theologians to correct this one-sidedness and to see that the Church is not just the hierarchy.'

In 1960 an ecumenical bibliography on the theology of the laity contained a list of no less than 1,300 books and articles on the subject, and still they poured from the printing presses. By that year it had become plain that something of a theological revolution had taken place, one which would have profound implications for both Church and world if it was taken seriously. As the 1960s unfolded there were some popular paperbacks which carried the message further afield, such as the two

1963 books *We the People,* by Dr Kathleen Bliss, and *God's Frozen People,* a title suggested to authors Mark Gibbs and T. Ralph Morton by a phrase in Kraemer's lectures. But this theological revolution stemmed not from any particular book or teacher, but a general consensus of theological or intelligent Christian reflection which reached a musical crescendo about 1960. In church terms, it can be compared to the Industrial Revolution, and its real impact has yet to be felt. Like that earlier upheaval, the theological or intellectual aspect of it was but one facet of a complicated train of political, social, and economic changes associated together in interactive ways.

THE CHURCH OF ENGLAND 1960–1970
A HISTORICAL CASE STUDY

The theological rise of the laity in value at first seemed to have little effect upon the Church of England as an institution. Like all revolutions it had small beginnings. Most theologians did indeed regard the subject as a talking-point, the fashion of the day; a few speculated upon the changes that might be required in the Church, but even this was pipe-dreaming. If this theology had been taken seriously, one sign would have been a devotion of far more of the Church's resources of men and money to the training of the laity. In other words, one test of the sensitivity of the Church of England to theological truth would be whether or not it adopted a new policy for Christian adult education or training. For lay people as a whole, so long accustomed to a passive role, simply did not possess the awareness, confidence, and training to assume the strategic role which theologians had discerned for them.

Before 1960, relative to the size and influence of the Church of England, little or nothing had happened in this sphere. Historically, the first green shoots of the theological reappraisal of the laity appeared during and after the First World War. The Church of England Men's Society, founded in 1899, swelled to 60,000 members by 1925 (compared to 10,000 in 1975), but it was seen more as a fraternity than as a training or educational organization. The Church Tutorial Classes Association was the most significant experiment in this latter direction. Modelled on the Workers' Educational Association this body came into being in 1915 and lasted until 1951. At its high point in the winter of 1929–30, some 3,482 people were enrolled in its classes. The history of the C.T.C.A., which has been traced and discussed in an unpublished university thesis (Nottingham University, May 1968) by the Reverend Alun Virgun, provides many interesting parallels with the history of lay training in the Church of England during the 1958 to 1970 period. Indeed almost all the factors which limited the success of laity training in the 1960s, such as disagreement over aims, shortage of money, and lack of teachers, were already foreshadowed in the earlier history of the Church Tutorial Classes Association.

Another development in lay training before 1960, the establishment of lay training centres, may be traced back to the conferences held at various centres by chaplains to the Armed Services during the Second World War. Canon R. E. Parsons produced two pamphlets in 1942 and 1945 advocating the setting up of People's Colleges. Archbishop William Temple wrote in a foreword to the first of them:

> I have read this memorandum with very great interest and very keen agreement. I think that in the stage upon which we are entering the equipment of the clergy for adult education will be much more important than the training of them in the teaching of children. Of course the latter will always be important, but I hope we may be getting an increasing number of qualified teachers from the teaching profession and to some extent from outside it. Whereas for a good long while to come there will be very few able to take adult classes in religious knowledge.

In a similar vein he expressed in a preface to the second pamphlet his hope 'that it may be widely read and become a stimulus to great developments in this field, which is, I am sure, of quite primary importance'. Alas, those 'great developments' died a few days later with the Archbishop.

It is true that 1949 did see the opening of one such college, appropriately named after William Temple, but there were no other foundations. Many dioceses did acquire conference houses during the period before 1958, yet they tended to be used more for devotional retreats, clergy meetings, and youth club gatherings than for anything which could be called laity training on a significant scale. There were experiments overseas, such as the evangelical academies in Europe and one or two centres in America, for example Parishfield in Michigan which I visited in 1962, yet the People's College idea never took root in English Church soil. Indeed in 1972 the William Temple College ended its days as a residential college at Rugby, but continued to serve its purpose as a trust with a small staff based upon Manchester Business School. By that time Parishfield had also closed its doors.

At least one reason for the relative failure of the Church Tutorial

Classes Association had been its adherence to the model of the university extra-mural class. This model dictated that the *content* would consist of the same subjects taught in university theological departments or theological colleges, often by their staffs, and it relied exclusively on the *method* of the lecture. Already before the demise of the C.T.C.A. doubts had arisen about the appropriateness of this university model of education for the majority of adult Christians. Fortunately at about the time of Kraemer's lectures an alternative approach to lay training had been discovered.

The development of the parish life conference in the United States owed much to some pioneer work native to that country in the field of social psychology, which was known in the 1950s as Group Dynamics and associated with the name of Kurt Lewin. The model of the parish life conference came to Britain in the late 1950s in the train of a Group Dynamics course, and two participants in the latter proved to be instrumental in spreading the message.

Before ordination the Reverend Harold Wilson had served in the war as a senior non-commissioned officer in the Royal Army Medical Corps, and afterwards he worked in advertising on the 'creative' side. After ordination in 1951 he had served as youth chaplain in Sheffield Diocese, during the episcopate of one of the few diocesan bishops in the 1950s who had grasped the message of the theological revolution—Bishop Leslie Hunter. In 1959 he became Secretary of the Adult Education Committee of the Church of England Board of Education, and thus the staff officer at the centre responsible for laity training. The second of the two leading figures, Canon Richard Herrick, had followed a more traditional clerical path. In 1957 he became the Director of Religious Education in Chelmsford Diocese.

These British clergymen took over the Parish Life Conference 'package' of tutor's manual and materials, but they adapted it in certain respects. But the resultant laity training weekends possessed some essential characteristics which taken together justify the claim that here indeed was a new approach. They can be listed as follows:

Impact	the sessions were grouped together in a weekend programme lasting from Friday evening until Sunday.
Participation	the use of small group discussions, with report-backs in plenary sessions, guaranteed

maximum participation. Written-up findings
gave it a visual dimension.

Simplicity   the theology of the laity was 'discovered'
by members in group study in such simple
biblical images as 'salt' and 'light'.

Practical   the weekend concentrated upon what the
Church was doing in the parish and what it
should be doing. By means of role play
situations and case studies members were
invited to apply what they had learnt to
concrete situations.

Action-orientated   members evaluated each session and the
course as a whole. In the final session
they reported on what they had learnt, what
they still needed to know, and—above all—
what they intended to do as a result of the
weekend.

Having witnessed two or three of these weekends in 1960 and 1961
being led by the Reverend Harold Wilson I became convinced of their
value. Therefore, I attended a small conference on lay training in May
1961, chaired by Bishop Cockin, lately Bishop of Bristol, with considerable interest. It began with a survey of the present situation concerning the participation of the laity in the life of the Church. Some 36 out
of 43 dioceses had appointed stewardship advisers, and over 20,000 lay
people had become involved in stewardship visits. But only Canon
Herrick could report progress in laity training: about 340 laity from 40
parishes had taken part in 12 parish life conferences in Chelmsford
Diocese. He pointed out the shortage of leaders for these conferences,
and the need for changes in attitude among the clergy in some of these
parishes. These conclusions were endorsed by the dozen or so people at
the consultation.

My views on the worth of parish life conferences were amply confirmed in the next two years when I led some six or seven of them
myself. What impressed me most was the universality of the
programme. University lecturers and industrial managers, citizens of
the great cities, inhabitants in market towns, parishioners of suburban
churches and country villages—all responded to laity training offered in
this way on the weekends in which I was involved. Moreover, the three

or four other voluntary staff working with Harold Wilson amply confirmed this positive evaluation of the parish life conference method.

By 1967 the numbers of lay people in Chelmsford Diocese who had attended parish life conferences passed the 4,000 mark. But no other diocese out of the remaining 42 came anywhere near that total: indeed in that year all but one or two had yet to achieve a figure of 400 participants in this programme. Consequently, about ten years after Dr Hendrik Kraemer had articulated the theology of the laity with its implications for the Church, and an appropriate method of laity training had been developed, the Church of England as a whole had failed to exploit the breakthrough. Laity training certainly continued in the dioceses, but the numbers involved remained minute in proportion to the number of the laity. Towards the end of the 1960s it seemed to be accepted as a minor feature of Church life. By this time the theologians of the laity were mostly silent or dead and its prophets, great and small, had grown frustrated. The theology and the means for making it effective had been there, but somehow it had not all happened. There is a cluster of factors which may help to explain why this failure occurred.

1. *The Clergy as Lay Trainers*
'The main part of the ministry of the clergy should be to enable the laity to fulfil their peculiar, inalienable, ministry', wrote Dr Kraemer in 1958. 'Only, if conceived and understood in this way, a "theology of the laity" is a serious business, and not merely a more or less captivating diversion of thought.' By 1961, however, it had become clear that there were few clergy with both the inclination and competence to lead parish life conferences. Through their weekly sermons the clergy did contribute greatly to the reservoir of background knowledge which received clarification in the experience of a lay training weekend. But many clergy had remained in ignorance of the rediscovered theology of the laity, and most of those who had been touched by its fire felt themselves to be inadequately equipped for the educational leadership of lay training programmes.

Of course the staffs of theological colleges in the 1950s were certainly talking about the theology of the laity, but more or less as 'a captivating diversion of thought' in the preparation for an essentially old-style parochial ministry. It is true that the curriculum sometimes included a few days on education in general, and some talks on adult education in particular, but there was no searching re-appraisal of the role of the ordained ministry nor any thorough initiation into the nature and skills of communication. Indeed, as the next chapter describes, the theological colleges in the early 1960s were only on the threshold of the debate about the role of the ministry which the rising theological value of the laity was bound to precipitate.

As soon as the extreme shortage of leaders became apparent, some clergy training programmes were mounted as first-aid attempts to remedy the situation. In 1962 some 200 clergy and laymen attended the two consecutive one-week courses in Sussex in Group Dynamics, organized by the Church of England Board of Education and led by their Adult Committee staff (including myself) and a team of 'opposite numbers' from the American Episcopal Church. But this programme produced no more than one or two leaders for the parish life conferences. On the other hand, as a result, the full-time Adult Committee staff became increasingly diverted after 1964 into running Group Dynamics courses for the staffs of Church of England colleges of education; others among the participants were already professionally involved in the Group Dynamics movements as members of such organizations as the Grubb Institute of Behavioural Science, which later worked in conjunction with other purveyors of this approach in the 1960s, notably the University of Leicester and the Tavistock Institute. Thus part of the effort turned into secular social or group psychology, linking up in some cases with group psychotherapy.

The tendency to drift away from lay training may also be discerned in the increasing number of 'clergy training institutes', usually three sessions of 'stages' of four or five days' duration each, mounted by the Adult Committee staff of the Church of England, which was never more than two clergymen and some volunteer associates during the decade. For example, there were 26 of the first, second, or third stages of such clergy training institutes in 1968. Although in theory these could be justified as an activity of the Church of England's lay training professional staff on the grounds again that they would develop leaders for parish life conferences, in practice they did not do so. The Group Dynamics orientation of the staff and the lack of virtually any further education for the clergy combined to shift these institutes towards a clergy-centred rather than a lay-centred axis of advance. Individual clergymen reported great personal and professional benefit, but the starvation of inspired and equipped leaders for lay training activities grew worse.

As another and more specific consequence of this state of affairs there were very few clergymen or laymen capable of acting as staff specialists in lay training on the staffs of diocesan bishops, even if there had been a wide determination to appoint such men in the 1960s. Clearly some provision would have to be made for such diocesan appointments, and for selecting and training these specialists, if the potential resources of the laity were ever to be actualized. The need for some sort of staff course of training remained even towards the end of the 1960s when—ten years too late—many dioceses were appointing lay training specialists and finding good applicants coming forward.

2. *Financial Resources*

'Where your treasure is, there is your heart also.' In order to measure the effects of the rediscovered theology of the laity upon the Church of England it is instructive to see how much money it was willing to devote to lay education employing the most effective methods of the day. The reader may bear in mind that the assets of the Church of England were then judged at somewhere around £600 million, and that sums in the order of £9 million a year were being spent on church colleges of education for training teachers who might or might not teach in church schools. Yet in 1969 the budget of the central lay training committee, a sub-committee of the Board of Education, amounted to £2,295, and it faced a reduction that year by £50. Clearly something serious had gone amiss with the allocation of the Church of England's financial resources.

This impression is confirmed by an unpublished survey of adult education in the Church of England produced in 1968 by Professor Andrew Gottschalk, then a lecturer in the department of adult education at the University of Nottingham. Only 18 out of the 36 dioceses approached returned his questionnaire. The budget for lay training in the 18 dioceses varied considerably. The committee to which one adult educator reported had been given a nil budget by the diocese concerned. Others ranged from £60 to £700. Only two of the diocesan committees concerned reported overspending; the majority had a surplus of £50–£150. The average budget of the 36 dioceses during 1967 was £366. The conclusions of Professor Gottschalk (cited in Alun Virgun's thesis), written by one who declared himself to be 'outside the Church of England', make a striking commentary:

> The survey which had been carried out has shown that the adult education work which is at present undertaken is both limited in terms of its scope and scale. . . . The future of adult education

within the Church of England is dependent upon the consideration of two problems. The financial resources devoted to this work are ludicrous. An average annual budget of £366 hardly seems worth describing as such. This weak financial position is not helped by the lack of a systematic training programme which should be based on diocesan needs. Such a programme would need to concern itself with the training of organizers and tutors, as well as larger use of laity training. . . .

The other consideration must be the role perceived for adult education within the whole field of Christian Education. Outside the Church there is a growing awareness of the links that exist between the various sectors of our educational system. Such thinking has not yet affected the Anglican Church. If a balanced view is to be obtained, then adult education needs to be integrated into a broad policy which considers it along with all other fields of Christian Education. At present no more than lip service is paid.

3. Senior Leadership and Decision-Making

The responsibility for the allocation of a significant annual budget lay with the Church Assembly at Westminster, a body that aroused considerable criticism in the 1960s and was due to be reconstituted as the General Synod in 1970. Certainly the Church Assembly gave no spiritual leadership to the Church of England in respect to laity education or training in the 1960s. Yet for a combination of historical, legal, sociological, and ecclesiastical politics reasons it is unlikely that the Church Assembly could have re-aligned the Church of England to a lay-centred strategy of change, even if the corporate will had been there.

What of the bishops? Individuals, such as the Archbishop of York with his 'Opportunity Unlimited' campaign of 1968–9, had indeed given a lead in their dioceses and others devoted a part of their time to participating in weekends. As a body the bishops provided no leadership to counteract the organizational inertia of the Church as an ancient institution. The diocesan bishop who above all had taken to heart the implications of the changing theology of the Church—Bishop Leslie Hunter of Sheffield—suggested in a 1966 article that some underlying value priorities or assumptions might explain their omissions:

> As things are diocesan bishops are under great pressure to substitute short-term tactics and little bits of salesmanship for a thought-out strategy of engagement with society as it is and is likely to be tomorrow. In my time I have taken part, I should guess, in more than

a hundred meetings of diocesan bishops, formal and informal. It is a happy memory of friendly association in which differing opinions could be discussed with good humour and fair debate. Some of the subjects discussed were of urgent passing importance; others of recurring importance. But I cannot recall many occasions when we really faced the revolution in English society since the Book of Common Prayer was promulged in 1662, or the radical change in thought and belief and in the pattern of life since the industrial and scientific revolutions; and in the light of these changes, the need for a new policy of engagement and penetration. Linked with this demand to lead the Church in a missionary initiative there is also the responsibility to encourage the new thinking that science is requiring of theologians and the changes in the liturgy of the Church that must ensue. A national Church and its leaders have a special responsibility; for they still have unique opportunities and points of personal contact at the parish, diocesan and national level with the life of the people.

The disillusionment with episcopacy which was so marked a feature in the Church of England in the 1960s (and even infected the editor of *Crockford's Clerical Directory*) may have been a reflection of Bishop Hunter's analysis. Institutional remedies were advocated, such as reforming the methods of selecting bishops. Others hailed synodical government as the panacea. Still others proposed that bishops should operate as small groups or 'colleges', rather than as individuals. But by the end of the 1960s a significant part of the longer-term solution had made its appearance: an adequate staff college programme supported by special courses for newly-appointed bishops.

4. *The Attitudes of the Laity*

So far it may appear that the relatively dismal story of laity education in the Church during the 1960s must be attributed to the bishops and clergy, theologians and staff specialists. But this picture is a false one. A Church needs not only good leaders but also good members. In many dioceses, deaneries, and parishes it was the laity who dragged their feet, not the clergy. They saw the clergyman as the expert, and had no desire to increase their own knowledge. Willing to assume such duties as sidesmen or treasurers, these churchmen nevertheless maintained a distinction between these activities and the spiritual work of the Church, which was the parson's job.

Still others of the laity mustered on the parochial electoral rolls were secularized church-goers rather than churchmen. Church-going formed a slowly diminishing part of the routine of their family and neighbourhood life, but they were only 'fringers' as far as Christian belief was concerned. Just as they were church attenders partly as a result of the kind of factors which the sociologists of religion began to identify by the end of the decade, so they were often drawn initially to parish life conferences in order to become more part of the community. For the parish life conference fulfilled a social function as well as a theological or religious one.

These question-marks against the quality of 'the man in the pew' stretched up to include the lay members of diocesan conferences and the Church Assembly itself. To many clergymen the laity seemed on the whole to be a rather uninspired lot. Meanwhile the majority of the laity fed this impression by continuing to imitate the actions of a sheep: docile, stolid, unimaginative and undemanding. The few 'active' laity on joint councils with the clergy sometimes caused them irritation, not only because they talked too much or else had some axe to grind, but because they belonged more to the church-centred variety rather than those more silent legions of laity living in the world whom many of the clergy now felt called to serve. Beneath the facade of outward politeness an indignation at the spiritual sloth of the laity in the face of a rapidly deteriorating religious situation began to develop among the more *avant garde* clergy.

In fact it was a common misinterpretation of the theological revolution that it could be translated into practice if the laity could be cajoled into becoming more active. As Dr Kraemer had declared:

> The issue is not that if the laity were only given the opportunity and the right to do so, they would come to the rescue of the Church. The issue is that both laity and ministry stand in need of a new vision of the nature and calling of the Church and their distinctive places in it, which means conversion and reformation of the whole Church, laity as well as ministry.

Despite these question-marks about the early willingness of the laity to fulfil their part it is worth recording the response to the Lent 'package course' of five evening sessions supplied to over 15,000 Anglican parishes in 1965. Some 6,194 parishes did the course, which was entitled *No Small Change*. Over the 1,763 parishes which returned evaluation cards some 78 per cent found the course useful, and many commented warmly about the parish life conference training methods involved. (The Reverend Harold Wilson had acted as an adviser on the package materials and approach.) About 1,600 lay people in 3,580 of the parishes had attended leadership training sessions before the course, some 204,000 Anglicans took part in the course, and about one-fifth of a small sample of the participating parishes reported plans for further study. But the factors already explored above probably made unlikely any follow-up to *No Small Change*. For example, the lack of diocesan staff specialists of a high calibre in lay training meant that the right materials necessary for the further study requested by a large number of parishes just were not available. Without the time or specialist skills to prepare their own programmes the parochial clergy were like soldiers without ammunition. Although *No Small Change* was a bold attempt, the motto for developing the full resources of the laity should have read *No Short Cut*. Significantly, the attempt to repeat the course the following year with a programme called *The People Next Door* was far less successful.

Yet by the early 1970s the clergy had begun to remark upon the emergence of a new quality of lay people. A variety of factors contributed to this phenomenon, not least the parochial labours of many clergy who became incumbents for the first time during the 1960s. Other agencies, such as university and school chaplains, radio and television programmes, and pioneer bodies like William Temple College and William Temple Association, augmented these slow changes in the atmosphere and activities of the Church of England. Thus the theological revolution centred upon the laity had at last begun to bear fruit. Yet did they emerge in too small numbers and too late?

The Church of England certainly reacted slowly to the interrelated process of theological, social, and cultural change in the period between 1955 and 1970. For one reason, its leaders and constituent organizations remained partly insulated against them. Yet it could be said that all British institutions reacted equally slowly, a national pattern that continues to this day. A critic might say, echoing a famous jibe about the British Army, that in 1977 the Church of England was about ready to face the situation of 1957.

SUMMARY

The theology of the laity, that universal consensus which developed roughly between 1955 and 1965, can be interpreted as an expression of secularization surfacing in the hitherto sacred pool of Christian intellectual thought. In that sense it was one more symptom of the underlying shift of values in society and in the churches seen as microcosms of society. Those who expected this theological revolution to cause an upheaval in the churches mistook this point and also possessed too high an expectation of the influence of theology on contemporary life.

Those who did try to actualize the theology of laity by introducing or developing schemes for lay training soon discovered that the churches as institutions were not structured or manned with that sort of thing in mind. If we study budget decisions in the Church of England between 1960 and 1970 at diocesan and national levels it can be shown that theological talk about the laity, while a fashionable topic of conversation, made relatively little impact upon the direction of the parish system.

If a new quality of Christian lay men and women emerged in the 1960s it was largely in spite of the Church of England rather than because of it. That judgement has to be qualified, however, to take into account the generation of clergy who were becoming incumbents for the first time during that decade. Many certainly believed in and preached the theology of the laity. Some church leaders felt that by providing such men in the parishes the Church of England had done all that it could. But education or training is not to be gained by listening to sermons alone or even attending parish discussion groups. New forms of developing the great if diminishing asset of the laity were needed. Some were found, but the opportunities they created were missed by inappropriate forms of leadership and indifferent organization. Consequently the structural reforms at the end of that decade, which strengthened the element of lay participation at deanery, diocesan, and national levels, while easy to introduce and enthusiastically welcomed, rested upon a faulty foundation. By the early 1970s it began to look as if it was all merely a face-lifting operation. The real tasks implicit in the theological revolution still remained to be done, and there were sufficient pioneer experiments to show that they could be undertaken successfully by the churches providing they were willing to change themselves in the same way that they were exhorting other social institutions to change themselves.

4

The Corps of Ordained Clergy

The ordained ministry is a visible phenomenon. Sometimes, in popular language and even in theology, the clergy have been equated with the Church, as the phrase 'going into the Church' still reveals. As a phenomenon, therefore, the clergy have attracted much attention in theological, historical, and sociological studies, especially since the end of the Second World War. But it is not always easy to see in them the wood for the trees. There are some important broad changes affecting the ordained ministry which can be identified. Some are invisible, and are to do with how the clergy think or are thought about, and even how they feel. Others are more visible, such as the decline in clerical numbers proportionate to the population. In this chapter I shall discuss some of these general developments.

A REVISED THEOLOGY OF ORDAINED MINISTRY

The new sense of the theological value of the laity in the 1950s raised some acute questions for the theology of the ordained ministry. If the laity shared fully in the life, mission, and ministry of Jesus Christ, in what sense were the clergy different? What in fact was a priest? The Reformed churches and the more Evangelical wing of the Church of England did not feel the force of that question, because they had accepted long ago that the difference between clergy and lay was one of *function* and not of *kind*. The Protestant minister resembled his Catholic counterparts because he was a full-time pastor of a congregation, but he would not hold himself to be priest in any sense other than 'the priesthood of all believers'.

Indeed, these questions could be pushed further into a radical challenging of the assumption that there should be a separate 'spiritual' order of priests in the Church, 'set apart' by a mystical ordination from the laity. Were they even there in the beginning? Professor Lampe, writing in *Theology* in 1968 about the valuing of the secular order in the New Testament and early Church, noted:

> Another aspect of secularization is seen in the fact that the Church had no priests. The separation of the Church at Jerusalem from the

68

Temple cultus was only gradual, and according to Acts 6.7 there were at one stage many Jewish priests in the Christian community (it is not said that they abandoned their priesthood). The puzzling description of John as a priest, given by Polycrates of Ephesus, suggests that there was a tradition that the link between the priesthood and Christianity continued for some time. But the main thrust of the Church's expansion was in a different direction and the Jewish priesthood, as such, played no part in it. The Church instituted no priesthood of its own, partly, perhaps, because its roots lay to a large extent in the Diaspora synagogues, which, so far as their everyday life was concerned, represented another priestless religion, but chiefly for the theological reason that Christ was the sole true priest, the antitype and fulfilment of that which the levitical priesthood had foreshadowed, the one in whom both priesthood and sacrifice had been finally consummated.

There were many ministries in the Church, charismata of all kinds; and Paul lists these in a way which indicates a certain order and precedence. . . . It remains true, however, that there is no real distinction in the primitive Church between laymen and a *cleros*.

Thus, if you took seriously the theology of the laity, a major theoretical problem was posed about the nature and work of the ordained ministry. Nor did theological study bring answers. There seemed to be no act or function which a priest or clergyman performed which could not be done by a lay man. Pastoral care and preaching were obviously not exclusive to the clergy. The laity could baptize, thus administering one of the two great biblical sacraments. The captain of a ship could marry people. Lay men and women gave the chalice in Holy Communion. From the theological point of view, there appeared to be no reason apart from considerations of good order why they could not conduct the entire service of Holy Communion. What then was the essence of the job? To what was one called? On the assumption that all Christians were called to the work of ministry in the world, what then was the special avocation of the priesthood?

In 1958, when I was a student at Westcott House in Cambridge, there were no satisfactory answers to this conundrum. Most of the books about the ordained ministry had been written before the theological revolution concerning the laity, and therefore before the problem had been properly formulated. Those written during the 1950s and 1960s were unconvincing. There is no doubt that the failure to find a satisfactory intellectual answer contributed to those doubts about the ordained ministry which helped to cause such a sharp decline in the numbers of men coming forward to ordination after the peak year of 1959. Certainly I was among those who failed to find a satisfactory solution or to solve it myself by dint of hard thinking. The key to the solution which ultimately has put the question to rest in my mind came to me ten years later in 1968 after reading and reflecting upon a book by the celebrated geneticist Professor Theodore Dobzhansky, entitled *The Biology of Ultimate Concern* (The New American Library, 1967). In discussing the difference between man and animals in evolutionary nature Professor Dobzhansky observed: 'Now, the point which the believers in unbridgeable gaps miss is that the qualitative novelty of the human estate is the novelty of a pattern, not of its components.' Moreover, 'no component of the *humanum* can any longer be denied to animals, although the human constellation of these components certainly can.'

Suddenly I saw an analogy here between man/animals and priest/laymen. A layman could exercise one or more of the 'components' in a clergyman's work, but it was the pattern or constellation which made the nature of the ordained ministry different from a layman's calling. Although this 'whole' formed around a cluster of functions such as leadership in worship, preaching the Word and administering the sacraments and the pastoral care of church members, it included also the sociological factors and expectations which still attended the role of an Anglican vicar, though the latter might change according to the changing social situation.

As a corollary, laicity might also be understood as a constellation of components whose uniqueness lay in the pattern or whole rather than in any single part. Luther had partly laicized the priesthood by enjoining marriage upon his ministers, but that is only one element in the bundle of the lay Christian's vocation. Thus each of the components of the two vocations could move freely from one camp to the other, but the patterns remained distinctive, positive, and complementary. In 1958 and afterwards, I had failed to solve the problem because I had adopted a *linear* approach, placing the functions or activities of the clergy and laity alongside each other, and scoring out those common to both, a process which left me with virtually nothing. In a sense I had been looking for an 'unbridgeable gap'. The more *holistic* approach of Dobzhansky, however, the creative parallel with nature, presented the functions of the clergyman or priest as a package, a composite role which could be altered in part without losing its overall pattern.

Thus, having tended to question the image of the priest as a pastor or shepherd because it implied that a layman was a sheep, I began to see that there was a sense in which the analogy of man and animal did point to the distinction between a priest and layman. I suppose another analogy would have been the difference between man and woman, whereby there can be a certain fluidity of male or female characteristics within patterns that are indisputably man and woman, so that we are faced with a continuum with the main clusters at the polar ends.

A theological answer along these lines was broadly accepted by a theological commission set up by the Church of England to find an answer to the problem, upon which I served as a member. A version of it appeared in our report *Ordained Ministry Today* (Church Information Office, 1969). In a sense, however, it was a very minor theoretical or theological problem, and its solution justifiably passed unnoticed. I mention it here, almost in parenthesis, to illustrate that theological questions are sometimes soluble by creative sparks of relevance jumping across the man-made gaps between disciplines.

The much larger work of reinterpreting the work of the ordained ministry in terms of a proper theology of the whole Church had of course been proceeding apace both before and after 1969. Most theologians had come to see by the late 1960s that the ordained ministry did not make theological sense unless understood within the context of the laity. In particular many writers saw the ordained ministry as occupying a leadership role in the Church.

The report *Ordained Ministry Today* had much to say about leadership, and so also did *Ministry and Ordination* (1973), the agreed statement of a joint commission of Anglican and Catholic theologians. The commission declared that they had adopted two policies which were new for the two Churches after all those arid debates over the validity of Anglican orders. First, the commission went straight back to the New Testament and early Christian sources. Secondly, they looked at the contemporary practice of both churches and asked the question: 'What in fact do our ministers do?'.

The commission placed the role of the ordained ministry within the context of a high doctrine of the ministry and priesthood of all Christians. At the heart of the role lay the idea of leadership:

The goal of the ordained ministry is to serve this priesthood of all the faithful. Like any human community the church requires a focus of leadership and unity, which the Holy Spirit provides in the ordained ministry. This ministry assumes various patterns to meet the varying needs of those whom the Church is seeking to serve, and it is the role of the minister to co-ordinate the activities of the Church's fellowship and to promote what is necessary and useful for the Church's life and mission. He is to discern what is of the Spirit in the diversity of the Church's life and promote its unity.

Reflecting the general fear in all the churches of an introspective church-centred ministry which secularization seemed to be imposing upon them, the theologians called for a secular orientation: 'Because God's concern is not only for the welfare of the church but also for the whole of creation, they must also lead their communities in the service of humanity.'

In other respects the combined waters flow less strongly. For example, a distinction between the laity and the ordained ministry is handled uncertainly. Christian ministers 'share through baptism in the priesthood of the people of God', and they are 'representative' of it—particularly in presiding at the Eucharist. 'Nevertheless, their ministry is not an extension of the common Christian priesthood but belongs to another realm of the gifts of the Spirit.' The holistic image of the pattern or constellation might have helped the theologians to express this other 'realm' in a more intelligible way.

The same holistic approach allied to the historical perspective on the two ordained ministries underlines the difficulties in securing agreement between the two Churches. Starting from the same indeterminate beginnings and sharing a common history the two ministries took different evolutionary paths after the Reformation. We can compare them much as we might a horse and a zebra. We can identify the common ancestry and the functional similarities. But each possesses some distinct characteristics which it has acquired and learnt to value during its years of separate development. Thus the Anglican ministry, for example, is made up of *general* material (i.e. shared with other churches, such as leadership and preaching), and *special* material, such as the particular social role of the Church of England vicar. Further explorations of common ground may result, so to speak, in more friendship without necessarily leading to a marriage between the two Churches.

Moreover, the idea of leadership as the key to the role of the ordained ministry may be part of the answer, but it also poses another set of problems. 'All officers ought to be leaders', it has been concluded, 'but not all military leaders are necessarily officers. There is more to the concept of being an "officer and a gentlemen" than effective leadership. For one thing, you have to hold the Queen's Commission.' Are the ordained clergy analogous to the officer corps in the army?

All organizations and communities do have those who can be identified as their leaders. One problem is that those who occupy such positions of leadership do not always possess the natural gift for leadership. This fact is true also in the churches. The gift of spiritual leadership, which is not unconnected with natural leadership, may be present outside the ranks of the ordained ministry and also absent within it. But it could be argued that the development of leadership, natural or spiritual, is a slow process, and there is plenty of evidence that clergymen learn it from the example of others, further training, and above all experience.

A second question about the ordained ministry as leadership, however, is perhaps more searching. Is the ordained ministry in the forms we have it the most appropriate form of Christian leadership for the laity today? If the laity are called to live and love in the secular world, with the constraint of having to earn their living, would not their leaders be wise to live as they lived? The problem here was not the theological 'setting apart' of ordination, but the sociological differentiation of a full-time and paid ordained ministry from the laity.

Again in his *Theology* article, Professor Lampe comments upon this sociological factor as a phenomenon rooted in the history of the early Church:

> There is, perhaps, one feature in the apostolic age which points towards the later separation of clergy from laity. This is the right of the apostle to be maintained, with his wife, by the Church instead of earning his living in the world like all other Christians. This exception, however, was necessitated by the peculiar circumstances of the pioneer missionary which made even Paul, who took such pride in not exercising this right, accept contributions from the Philippian church. The ministers of the early Church were not withdrawn from the world, and did not constitute a clerical caste. Hierarchy began to establish itself when the Church's ministry began to be equated with the Old Testament system, as by Clement of Rome, who also likened Church order to the hierarchy of ranks in the Roman army. But the division of the Church into two almost separate worlds of clergy and laity did not become complete until the clergy came to be wholly

maintained by the Church's funds (a salaried clergy was first instituted by Montanus); and this may have been a sign, not as Apollonius thought of worldly greed, but of other-worldliness, associated with the negative attitude of Montanists to marriage and all other aspects of the present order. The final stage in the severance of clergy from laity came later with the adoption of clerical celibacy.

A major recent development, although still in its early stages, which challenges this sociological and historical (rather than theological) differentiation, is the emergence in the early 1970s of an auxiliary pastoral ministry in the Church of England and many other churches. These unsalaried priests pursuing their own secular jobs are already beginning to find that all kinds of pastoral opportunities are opening for them in their places of work. It is demanding both to become a priest and also to contribute to the parochial ministry as well as earning a living and bringing up a family: in their very example of costing service these men are exercising leadership among the laity.

A third objection to the full-time ordained ministry, one felt more by the clergy themselves than by the laity, may also be partly met by the development of the auxiliary parochial ministry. According to this objection, the very presence of a full-time priest gives the laity the impression that the spiritual or pastoral work of the Church in that locality is being done for them: it has all been delegated to a paid professional. Hence the full-time ministry acts as a disincentive to the emergence of the laity. The potential of lay people is never actualized by responding to the challenge of leadership.

Certainly there is something in this objection. As a lay reader working in the suburban parish of Stoke Poges—the church of Gray's Elegy—during a long interregnum I saw some of my fellow laity in the choir and congregation 'coming alive' and assuming far more responsibility than under the former much-loved vicar, who had done it all for us. For this reason I cannot look upon the decline in the number of clergy as an unmitigated disaster. Rather, it is full of creative possibilities. There is a need for courage to leave creative gaps in the pattern of the parochial system, confident that lay men and women will be moved to respond to the needs of ministry, mission, worship, and management according to their several interests and abilities.

That, however, is not an argument against a full-time ordained ministry. But it does suggest that for the changed theological, social, educational, and financial climate of the 1980s the ordained ministry is relatively overmanned. The assumption that there should be one full-time man in every 'living', already questioned by the introduction of team ministries, no longer holds water. The natural but very slow decline in the number of full-time ministers—what industry so badly calls 'natural wastage'—may bring the establishment down to a more realistic level for the 1980s, but it may have to be assisted by a programme along the lines of that operating in the Episcopalian Church for helping clergymen who want to train for full-time secular jobs, so as to become auxiliary and non-stipendiary ministers. A non-stipendiary minister in charge of a small church would be in a much better position to challenge the laity to participate fully in the spiritual, pastoral, and administrative work of the parish. Then both bishops and clergy would be able to modify that approach to the laity which equates 'sacrificial giving' to supplying ever more money for supporting a full-time or-dained ministry which does much of the work the whole body of the Church should be doing. The real sacrifice is our time, those measures of our short and precious lives here on earth. Of course a full-time ministry is still needed, but in much smaller numbers and much better trained.

A DECLINE IN NUMBERS

This judgement is strengthened when we consider what is happening to the full-time ordained ministry of the Church. All the major churches reported in the early 1970s a decline in the numbers of their corps of or-dained ministers, coupled with a fall in the numbers of those being accepted for ordination and a rising average age of men in holy orders. The figures for the Church of England illustrate these general trends:

Year	Ordained Clergy in Parochial Work	Population of England & Wales (in millions)
1851	16,194	16·9
1901	23,670	30·6
1951	18,196	41·3
1971	15,223	46·4
1976	12,056	49·0

Anglican Parochial Clergy Numbers

The 1971 figure was taken to be a sign of crisis by those unversed in statistics. But the *total* number of Anglican clergymen at work on 31 December 1972 who had been ordained in Canterbury and York Provinces, including chaplains in the armed services (288), clergy working overseas (1,576) and extra-parochially employed clergy (2,552), came to the sizeable figure of 19,725. To these might be added 3,700 retired clergymen with permission or licence to officiate at services, whom I shall call semi-retired. The Church in Wales, independent only since 1920, contains about another thousand clergymen. Thus considerable caution has to be exercised in comparing the figures of 1971 with those of, say, 1851.

Although we can estimate the number of Anglican clergymen in the active or semi-active ministry in England and Wales at about 20,000, the general trend had been of course for a fall in the number of Anglican clergy in ratio to the population, and a more marked decline (due to the modern introduction of specialized ministries and more staff jobs) in the ministry deployed in the parishes. Owing to a confused and alarmist use of statistics it was feared in the 1960s that the ordained ministry would collapse, but the annual decline in the *total* number of Anglican clergymen has been very gradual, so as to be at times almost imperceptible. The same can be said of the Roman Catholic Church. The Catholic Directory of 1973 revealed that the number of priests in England and Wales had fallen only slightly in the past year—from 7,658 to 7,535—while the number of churches and chapels open to the public had actually increased from 3,599 to 3,668.

On the other hand, there are signs that the decline in the numbers of the ordained ministry will continue into the 1980s. On 1 August 1976 the average age of the Anglican clergymen (excluding curates) was 53 years, and the average age of curates was 36 years, giving an overall average age of 50 years. But there are balancing factors, such as the number of men returning from overseas work. All that the analysis of clergymen's ages shows is that the average of the ordained ministry has risen, but not as much as many people imagine. In 1851 and 1971 the average ages of the clergy were respectively 44 and 49 years, the latter year's figure being based on those 15,511 men actually deployed in the parishes. Because of the peak period of ordinations in the 1930s, however, there is still a surplus of clergy seeking livings. But 40 per cent of the clergy are now aged over 55 and, partly because of the new pension arrangements, it is estimated that as many as 6,000 will have retired by 1980.

The other relevant statistic here is the rate of ordinations. In order to maintain a corps of clergy at around the 20,000 mark an average of about 600 ordinations a year seems to have been required. In the 1890s the yearly figures for ordinations to the diaconate were between 600 and 700 men. There were some troughs during the two world wars and also in the 1948–52 period (a yearly average of 427), as well as some peak years, such as 1959 with 757 ordinations. But from 1962 onwards the numbers of ordinations declined steadily from 633 in that year to the very low figures of 393 in 1971 and 362 in 1972. There was a slight up-turn in 1974 with 393 ordinations. In addition to the last figure of or-dinations to the full-time ministry there were 45 men ordained as auxiliary parochial ministers. The Church of England's figures from its selection conferences of those recommended or conditionally recommended for training suggests that this upward trend is likely to continue. Some 348 men were recommended in 1975, compared with 277 in 1973. Possibly, however, these figures reflect the difficulties in the employment market during this period: recruiting for the armed ser-vices showed a similar increase. Thus there may be a temporary en-vironmental factor at work, which may be influencing some men at a less than conscious level. The figure for the auxiliary parochial ministry has risen steadily from 17 in 1970 to 90 in 1975. My own expectation is that the figure will level out at about 500 ordinations a year to both the full-time and non-stipendiary ministries in the 1980s, with the latter becoming the larger proportion. In the light of financial constraints and in the context of a revised overall ministry policy, the Church of England should be ordaining between 250 and 300 men to the full-time ministry in the 1980–5 period, and encouraging the other ordinands to contribute as auxiliary parochial ministers.

Contrary to popular belief in the 1960s, secularization has not produced a widespread exodus from the ordained ministry. The numbers who withdraw from any form of ministry is probably less than eight per cent in the Church of England. This low figure was found as the result of recent research by Professor Alec Rodger (then of Birkbeck College in the University of London) upon a sample of 1,823 men who were ordained between 1951 and 1975. Of these 1,769 or 97 per cent appeared in the 1971–2 *Crockford's Clerical Directory*. Of the missing three per cent, some had died, some had resigned their orders and some had transferred to other denominations. Of those whose names appear in *Crockford*, 89 men (or five per cent) were discovered to be not exercising their ministry. Of all those ordained and active 70 per cent (1,278) were still working in the parochial ministry.

THE ORDINATION OF WOMEN

One possible source of recruits to the full-time ordained ministry is the womanpower of the Church. The reasons against the ordination of women to the priesthood are historical, sociological, and church political rather than theological. The debates about the issue since 1970 have graphically illustrated that point. Equally the impetus towards the priesting of women comes not from the theologians nor from some creative impulse in the Church but from the shift in values of which secularization is but a part. Among the values in the ascendant is the value of nature (or the environment, to give it a more contemporary name). Elsewhere, in my book *Management and Morality* (1974), I have discussed this phenomenon fully and related it to the history of Christianity.

In particular I suggested that possibly man's attitude to woman has been deeply influenced by his view of the goodness or evil of nature. Both in biblical and Hellenic civilizations there is evidence that man regarded himself as less close to nature than women and more as a consciously rational and distinctive being. Thus, when he looked upon nature he had woman in his field of vision as well. She had only half-emerged from nature compared to himself. We may speculate on how this view arose, but prudence forbids me to do so. Consequently man's assumptions about the moral worth of women follows his conviction about nature. Where he has despised nature as anti-moral or immoral he has tended to react in the same way against women.

We may note the persistence of the idea in the monotonous and sub-human toil done by women in industry. The old agrarian belief that the hard labour of the fields is fit work for beasts, women, and tamed savages or slaves has its counterpart in contemporary life. Some women feel that they are the last of the trilogy to attain to emancipation. Certainly many more feel that their values as members of human society and as persons in their own right are not really appreciated by men. Such a conviction has already influenced British industry and commerce in this decade by the movement towards equal pay for women, albeit under the stimulus of government legislation. From the law against discrimination in employment on grounds of sex the Church of England has gained an inglorious exemption. After much pressure from the women's lobby, the General Synod of the Church of England posed the 43 diocesan synods two questions. The first was whether or not they considered there were any fundamental objections to the ordination of women. Thirty-one replied that there were none. The second question was whether or not the General Synod should proceed to remove the legal and other barriers to the ordination of women. Here only fifteen dioceses out of 43 (34 per cent) voted in favour. In four dioceses the motion was lost because of the bishop's vote and in a further three because the bishop abstained. If this had not occurred 22 dioceses would have voted in favour—51 per cent.

In July 1975 the General Synod debated the issue of the ordination of women to the priesthood. Voting on the motion that there are not fundamental objections to women priests was: Bishops 28–10; Clergy 110–96, two abstentions; Laity 117–74, three abstentions.

The motion sponsored by the Synod's Standing Committee that in view of the significant division of opinion in the dioceses, it would not be right at present to remove the barriers to the ordination of women, was defeated as a result of an adverse vote in the House of Laity. The figures were: Bishops 19–14, one abstention; Clergy 127–74; Laity 80–96. Then the Bishops split equally and the Clergy voted against a counter-proposal that the Church *should* now proceed to remove the barriers. The General Synod then carried on a show of hands a compromise motion inviting the House of Bishops to bring before the Synod a proposal to admit women to the priesthood when they judged the time to be right, in the light of developments in the Anglican Communion generally as well as in this country. Certainly there are changes in the Anglican Communion afoot. For example, by the end of 1975 the number of women priests in the Episcopal Church of the United States, which has a nominal membership of about two millions, stood at fifteen. Four were ordained in 1975 in defiance of a ruling that the question should wait until the Church's general convention. In 1976 Canadian Anglican bishops voted to proceed with ordaining women.

After considering these factors it is probable that the barriers to the ordination of women will be removed at some time between about 1977 and 1980 in the Church of England and the Anglican Communion generally. The Roman Catholic Church, while also conceding that no substantial argument can be shown to *prove* that women should be debarred from ordination to the priesthood on theological grounds, will probably hold out for at least another decade.

Only some very tentative guesswork is possible. But what will the ordination of women priests mean in terms of numbers? If the proposal was accepted in say 1980, there may be two or three hundred candidates, of whom perhaps half would be accepted. By 1985 women might be supplying about one third of the annual intake of the Church of England's ministry, about 80 or 90 ordinations a year. The first woman suffragan bishop might be consecrated by the end of the 1980s, and we should expect then a woman diocesan bishop by the end of the following decade.

TRAINING THE ORDINANDS

Until about 1960 training of the clergy was limited to pre-ordination courses, followed by some post-ordination training during the diaconate under diocesan arrangements. The work of providing those pre-ordination courses of two or three years' duration was undertaken on a private enterprise basis by a score or so colleges, many of which had been established by church political interests—Anglo-Catholics and Evangelicals—in the nineteenth and early twentieth centries. Largely through the power of the purse, these came more under the control of the bishops as a corporate body in the 1960s, and underwent with varying degrees of unwillingness a programme of rationalization during the closing years of that decade, designed to cut down expensive unfilled places in unsuitably placed colleges.

Looking to the future, when a new structure of area dioceses associated together on a regional basis under a senior bishop (see pp. 114–6) may begin to emerge in the mid-1980s, it would be right to establish one training college in each region. This college would then form a centre for all training to the parochial ministry in that region: full-time, auxiliary, lay readers, short-service, religious education teachers in the parishes, stewardship street visitors and church social workers. It would also be linked with a university, and pursue an adequate programme of post-graduate and doctoral research upon the contemporary life and work of the Church, basing itself upon the intellectual disciplines listed in Chapter One. This would give it a basis for engaging also in the further training of the clergy, running courses for clergymen before they take up their first incumbency, for team and group ministers, for rural deans and clergy in mid-service. Men ordained in the region would train at the college, and so it will be possible to marry up what happens in the initial course and post-ordination training much more effectively than at present.

The content and methods of training also need a searching review. At present every college goes its own way, subject to the guidance of the General Ordination Examination. There is little comparing of notes between those who teach the same subject—say Christian Ethics—in the different colleges. For no one at the centre has the responsibility to make this valuable sharing of ideas and experiences happen. It is true that the staffs of the colleges do have an annual conference together, but this falls far short of the necessary level of co-operation over content and methods. The day will come when a teacher in a regional theological college will be appointed to both that college and to a national course team in his subject area.

The subjects or contents of the syllabus will also need revision. For example, Christian Ethics has yet to include a serious study of Business Ethics, although far more members of a priest's congregation will be managers or otherwise involved in organizational life than, for example, doctors or nurses. The amateur dabblings in social studies and group work need to be supplemented by a more comprehensive syllabus in sociology, social psychology and psychology on the one hand, and a more practical programme of leadership development within its context, using exercises, films, and case studies. By the mid-1980s there will possibly be Open University-type television courses available to the regional colleges in many aspects of the work and worship of the Church. In all these suggestions, I am of course, assuming a continuation of worship and deepening of Christian spirituality in theological college training.

Writing in *The Church Times* in 1976 about her visits to colleges, Margaret Duggan has spotted another major area of weakness—communication studies:

> But whatever way a man is trained, whatever balance is struck between theology and pastoral practice, if he is to have any ministry at all among lay people he still needs to be able to communicate the faith so that people will hear. One could hazard the guess that the most resilient enemy to the Word of God today is not so much hardness of heart as sheer, muddled misunderstanding—culminating in prejudice—of what the gospel is actually about. . . . And there is the garbled residue of all those over-scholarly, jargon-ridden sermons preached from parish church pulpits: sermons which entirely overestimate the theological education and interest of the congregation; sermons which first saw the light of day when they were preached to fellow theological students, and have never been rewritten since. It will still take years to undo the damage which has been done by a century of inexpert communication.

Will the coming generation of clergy manage any better? 'Communication' appears in the syllabus of several colleges, but it means very different things. Most often it is a generic term for a whole range of skills: one-to-one counselling, group dynamics, and preaching.

But most of it is still aimed at the captive audience.

The usual objection to adding new subjects to a syllabus is that something valuable must be left out or else the course lengthened. But if the principle is accepted that a man must go on learning—with assistance—throughout his ministry, it becomes more a question of establishing a pattern of priorities at different stages of his career. Some subjects are best tackled after some practical experience, while others will justifiably have to come in that initial period before ordination.

SUMMARY

The most obvious phenomenon about the ordained ministry is its decline in numbers, slight in absolute terms but marked in relation to the growth of population. At the same time a theology of the ordained ministry has developed which emphasizes a role in relation to the laity. The fewer clergy, it is felt, can only be more fruitful if they come to see their role as locating, leading, and inspiring the laity to fulfil *their* vocation as prophets, priests, and pastors.

Much lip-service was paid to this changed theology of the ordained ministry by the senior clergy in the period between 1945 and 1965, but it was theological talk unrelated to any visible change in action. The theological colleges of 1965 looked much the same as those in 1945, although their quite modest changes in syllabus or methods were sometimes advanced as major revolutions. But perhaps every revolution needs a period of twenty years or so of talk, and those who merely talk are serving the cause of change. (Otherwise, I suppose, there would be no justification for a book such as this one.) The reason for this apparent discrepancy, however, lies in the fact that any church is conditioned by its history, by the sociology of professions, and by a political bias in favour of maintaining the existing state of affairs. Theology usually has to wait for the change of generations before its influence is felt.

The ordained ministry as a corps has yet to respond fully to the light reflected upon it through the theological perspective. In particular the structure of training, exemplified by theological colleges, still partly embodies the assumptions of a bygone age. To some extent, in the general conservative tradition of the older churches, these structures can be adapted to train men for ministry in a changing ecclesiastical situation. But in other respects—notably because the lack of more searching changes in training the ordained ministry helps to account for the relatively low participation of the laity in pastoral work—it ought to be altering much more rapidly if the Church is to be loyal to its calling.

No responsible practical theologian now advocates the dismantling of the full-time ordained ministry. That kind of radical talk belonged to the period in the early and middle 1960s when disillusion with the parish system was at its height. Adopting the creative perspective, however, it is possible to see the decline in numbers of the ordained ministry as an opportunity. It enables us to challenge the false constraints we have imposed upon the ministry, to the end that it may better fulfil its function of creative leadership in the Church.

5

The Parish System

So far the churches have been considered essentially as people. Traditionally those people have been divided up into priests or ministers on the one hand, and the laity on the other. As a whole this body of people is declining steadily in numbers, although this fact can be sugared by theological theories about the 'remnant' and by pseudo-sociological reflections to the effect that those who have dropped out of active membership or ceased to attend church or chapel regularly were not really Christians anyway. These fruits of secularization have been accompanied by alterations in Christian intellectual thinking about the laity and the clergy. The laity have risen in theological value, while the clergy have come to see their own function more in relation to the laity and—by implication—the secular order.

But both clergy and laity are joined together or related to each other in the context of a particular kind of organization; or—to use a biblical metaphor—they are yoked together in the parish system. Indeed the yoke is a good image because, as we shall see, the parish system has its roots in the predominantly agricultural past. Having contemplated the comparative failure of the English parish system to respond to the training needs of the laity in the period between 1955 and 1975, the reader may well have been tempted to adopt a radical position and add his voice to the chorus which has called for the scrapping of this form of organization. But stay! Let us consider the parish system as a phenomenon, including in our vista the significant changes within it and—more important—its creative possibilities for the future. In order to understand the parish system we must adopt first the historical perspective.

HISTORICAL DEVELOPMENT
The acceptance of Christianity by the official head of the Roman Empire greatly facilitated its expansion as a religion. Paradoxically the Church had commended itself as a means of preserving the social order, and it guaranteed the powerful aid of its deity to safeguard the frontiers. The Church became a system within the Roman Empire respon-

sible for what could be called the religious function. This function included worship and prayer for the safety of the state. Thus the Church acknowledged that the whole social system, made up of all the peoples and functions of the Empire, was itself but a part of a wider system where God was King. As such it was dependent upon God's protection and aid, which the Church (in return for appropriate concessions and privileges) could alone draw down upon it. In addition, as we have seen, the Church provided individuals with the means of salvation, and with some earthly welfare benefits into the bargain.

This alliance between Church and State led to other consequences. The rather haphazard collection of Christian communities or churches began to conform to the civil and administrative divisions of the Roman Empire. The origins of the parish system lie here, for the word parish ('neighbourhood' in Greek) originally stood in medieval Latin for both a diocese and a parish; in other words it meant an ecclesiastical division of any size. Townships which had their own church and priest became known as parishes, and were subdivided as they grew larger into new parishes. The bishop had a governor's jurisdiction over his diocese or province; he was the supervisor of the parishes within his boundaries.

Thus the parish was developed as provinces were also divided into new dioceses. Meanwhile the Bishop of Rome emerged as the ecclesiastical counterpart of the Roman Emperor, eventually acquiring the imperial high-priestly title of *Pontifex*. When the Emperor transferred his capital to Byzantium it might be thought that the Patriarch of Constantinople would become the new Pontiff, but the Roman location of the papacy had been buttressed by the commission and martyrdom of St Peter, and it survived the change. The conversion of the north European tribes soon saw the papcy in league with the new masters of the Western Roman Empire, thereby paving the way for the development of medieval Christendom.

In England Theodore of Tarsus, Archbishop of Canterbury between 669 and 690, described by G. M. Trevelyan as 'perhaps the greatest Prince of the Church in all English history', laid the foundations for the parish system by creating a sufficient number of bishoprics with defined and mutually exclusive sees all subject to Canterbury, in contrast to the roving missionary type of bishop in the Celtic Church. Before the Norman Conquest in 1066 most of the island was served by parish churches and parish priests. The monasteries were also integrated into the system, losing something of their former independence. The parish network developed as a result of co-operation between the diocesan bishops and the local thegn or lord of the manor. The latter gave the land or endowment. Often in the early days the priest was the private chaplain attached to the thegn's hall, but in course of time he or his successor became the parish parson. To this day many parish churches stand next to manor houses, sometimes remote from the village. The heirs of the original lay benefactor continued to exercise the right to patronage, that is nominating a man when the benefice fell vacant, but the bishop had jurisdiction over the priest. Gradually the parish church and graveyard became the centre of the village, for purposes secular as well as spiritual. Ecclesiastical taxes, enforced by severe penalties, based upon a tithe or tenth of the total produce of the soil in the parishes, were levied to support the clergy. Anglo-Saxon kings and nobles, not without encouragement from the clergy and with an eye to their salvation, endowed bishoprics and monasteries with manors and lands for their support. The feudal system and the parish system grew up together, both based upon territorialism, the sharp distinction of social functions and classes and the increasingly unequal distribution of wealth, land, and freedom. For, as F. W. Maitland wrote, 'richly endowed churches meant a subjected peasantry'. Shortly after the Conquest, for example, the four minsters of Worcester, Evesham, Pershore, and Westminster owned more than half of Worcestershire.

In many ways it became virtually impossible to distinguish between Church and State. The English people, baptized soon after birth, grew up in a parish which was both a civil and an ecclesiastical area. For military defence and tax collection parishes were grouped into hundreds and shires; for ecclesiastical purposes into deaneries and dioceses. The counties were formerly under control of feudal lords, but the fragmentations caused by the law of primogeniture and the evolution of royal administration and parliament considerably modified that picture as time went on. The king, duly anointed and crowned by the Archbishop of Canterbury, took counsel with his lords spiritual and temporal, and in due course of time with knights and burgesses elected in the shires. Yet the English Church remained very much a part of the larger Catholic Church system. The Pope appointed bishops and acted as the supreme court in ecclesiastical causes. The two provinces of Canterbury and York also maintained their Convocations, with the right to pass canon laws and to set their own taxes, and also their own courts for trying cases concerning religion and morals.

Thus the parish system was evolved, elaborated, and finally adorned with those glorious parish churches and cathedrals. The monastic system (or rather systems, for there were many orders) grew up alongside it. Worship became still more grand, and the methodology of salvation more prominent. Reformers such as St Bernard challenged the growth in ritual and church ornaments, but it was Martin Luther who called into question the Church's claim to guarantee individual salvation through its precepts and practices.

During the Reformation King Henry VIII abolished the monasteries, leaving the cathedral churches with small chapters of canons. He virtually nationalized the parish systems. Henceforth, for example, the monarch possessed the right to appoint bishops. But he intended to maintain the pattern of worship in the parish system more-or-less unaltered, as well as the theological system that had developed around it. The Puritan movement brought pressure to bear on this conservative *via media* in Elizabeth's reign on one side, while on the other front the country narrowly survived the counter-attack of the Catholic system, or such of it as remained intact, in its deliverance from the Spanish Armada in 1588. The Puritan gentry who captured political power in the 1640s initially wanted to purify the Church of England's doctrine and worship, not to abolish the parish system. True, the Puritans did eventually abolish bishops, ostensibly in favour of some undefined form of presbyterian government, but their failure to agree upon an alternative way of administering the Church paved the way for a return of episcopacy with the monarchy in 1660.

Alongside the parish system of the established Church after 1688 there developed the non-conformist churches based upon minister, chapel, and congregation. In course of time these non-conformist churches or Free Churches evolved their own equivalents to the parish system, for example the Methodist circuit and district system. The restoration of the Roman Catholic hierarchy in the nineteenth century saw the imposition of yet another parish system on the already complicated ecclesiastical map of Britain. Throughout that century and during the first half of the twentieth, Parliament in conjunction with the bishops employed the traditional method of subdividing dioceses and parishes to form new ones in order to cope with the rapid expansion of population and the exodus from the countryside to the sprawling industrial cities and towns. For example, the following twenty new dioceses were created during those 150 years: Birmingham (1905), Blackburn (1926), Bradford (1919), Chelmsford (1914), Coventry (refounded in 1918), Derby (1927), Guildford (1927), Leicester (restored 1926), Liverpool (1880), Manchester (1847), Newcastle (1882),

Portsmouth (1927), Ripon (reconstituted 1836), St Albans (1877), St Edmundsbury and Ipswich (1914), Sheffield (1914), Southwark (1905), Southwell (1884), Truro (1877) and Wakefield (1888).

Since the Second World War there have been a number of attempts, some of them creative, to develop or adapt further the parish system, such as team and group ministries, the introduction of synodical government with its emphasis upon the deanery, the attempt to evolve a better diocesan structure, and the reform of the general means for holding together the system as a whole. Many of these changes or attempts at change are of course still in process, and call for interim evaluation. But first it is necessary to consider a recurrent theme in church history which erupted with particular force in the late 1950s and early 1960s, and still rumbles in the depth mind of the Church, namely the radical questioning of the whole system as no longer the appropriate predominant form for the Christian Church.

SOME OBJECTIONS TO THE PARISH SYSTEM

This brief sketch of the history of the parish system at least underlines its antiquity. It has survived a thousand years of political, social and theological changes, and is now moulded into the English mental and physical landscape. It has survived because it is basically simple: one man and one building in one territorial area. It is also highly adaptable. Who the man is, how he is trained, what he does and says and wears in church, the furnishings and periodically the shape of the building, and the bounds of his territory, are all subject to alteration. Church politics have been very largely about what changes if any should be made in these areas of discretion. Sometimes, as we all know, these politics have been acrimonious to say the least of it. In the 1630s, for example, there were fights in church not unlike those on the terraces at football matches today between those who wanted the altar in the middle of the building and those who insisted that it should be behind the rails in the chancel. But besides being simple and very adaptable, the parish system (like the railway system) has certain fixed characteristics which have exposed it to some critical objections.

In the first instance, it has been pointed out that the parish system costs a lot of money to run. Most of the money predictably goes on paying the stipend and the expenses of the man and maintaining the building. It comes from land and endowments (now largely managed centrally by the Church Commissioners), contributions by those who use the building, and special appeals. In times of inflation the finding of sufficient money to keep the system going proves difficult but not impossible so far. The Church Commissioners have invested and managed the Church's wealth with success; the churchgoing laity have increased their financial giving after such stimuli as stewardship campaigns; and appeals for church causes, especially the preservation of cathedrals and churches, have still won national and local support. By a combination of cutting costs through various forms of rationalization—reducing buildings and paid men—and by raising more money, there is no doubt that this financial objection can be successfully parried, although it may take more sweeping and more timely changes to do so than many ecclesiastical conservatives realize.

Another fixed characteristic of the parish system is that it takes a great deal of time to administer it, a factor which causes considerable disquiet among the clergy. All of us in any walk of life have to spend more time on administration in order to maintain our place in contemporary society, and the parish system is no exception. The clergy, from archbishops downwards, have frequently groaned since the Second World War at this increased burden. For example, old buildings get older and inevitably demand more attention as time goes by. With the growth of the government bureaucracy we have become a nation of form-fillers. The churches have also greatly developed their own administrative systems: synods, boards, councils, committees, and meetings consume time, and many of them in practice turn out to be concerned with maintaining the parish system as a going concern. It is not surprising that such research as has been conducted upon how clergy spend their time reveals an exceptionally large slice on administration, a labour for which many clergy feel that they were not ordained.

This objection can be countered in several ways. First, the Church of England is employing a large body of lay people in administrative and secretarial posts to undertake much of the administration. Although this practice has added to the real cost of running the system it does at least relieve the clergy of a great deal of administration, especially at diocesan and national levels. For example, a parson does not have to worry about arranging for a regular inspection of the fabric of his church building or parsonage—it is done for him. This extended use of lay people in professional capacities, beginning many years ago with ecclesiastical lawyers, has been one response of the Church of England to the mounting complexity of maintaining a corporate presence in a modern state.

Secondly, much has been done—and could be done—to make the administrative burden sit easier on the shoulders of the clergy. Several dioceses, deaneries, and parishes have called in management consultants to advise them on how they can operate more efficiently in organizational terms. But at diocesan level there are limits to what can be done, for most dioceses seem comparatively well organized for the administrative side of their work. At deanery and parish level, the cost of employing specialist administrators, or purchasing and operating the necessary hardware, may rule out the proposed remedies. Consequently, at these levels, the clergy will still find themselves lumbered with most of the administration. It must be a modest target to provide them with the secretarial assistance appropriate for their situation.

A certain amount of administration, however, is inseparable from the work of a parish priest. It can be expressed in theological terms by saying that when a man becomes a priest he does not cease to be a deacon. The diaconate appears to have been essentially an administrative office. Moreover, it is fitting in the Church that leaders should also be servants, that the man who leads the congregation as a Christian community should also stoke the boiler, cut the churchyard grass and stick down the envelopes. Administrative ability is a natural gift, resting upon clear thinking, a love of good order and a capacity for regular and systematic work. Clergymen, in company with artists and authors, are not always blessed with this talent. Therefore theological colleges and seminaries should emulate the pioneer example of Salisbury Theological College in the 1960s and include Parish Administration in its syllabus.

Thus the objections to the parish system on account of its costs in terms of money and administrative time can to some extent be countered by a combination of changes, including changes in attitudes. Those who argue for the retention of the system would readily accept such realistic alterations to meet the straightened economic circumstances of our time. For implicitly or explicitly they would value the parish system far above these costs. In other words, what the clergyman does in the rest of his time and the functions of building in the double context of the local church congregation and the territorial parish, are judged to be worth—or more than worth—the money and effort needed to keep it all going. Is this true? It could be argued that this much more fundamental issue has been insufficiently debated, partly for the obvious reason that most practical theologians are ordained, and have thus felt called to serve God—at least initially—in and through the parish system or its off-shoots in university chaplaincies. Moreover, the structure we call the parish system has evolved over centuries. To some extent that makes it difficult to understand, because we take it so much for granted. Among other things, baptizing babies in the font of the parish church is a very good way of ensuring that the parish system will continue on its way down the Christian centuries relatively un-questioned, not unlike an early inoculation against criticism which works as we come to know and love our parish church through Sunday School, Confirmation, and Communion.

In order to consider the more vague and fundamental feeling that the parish system may have outlived its usefulness we must go further or deeper into the nature of the Church. For ultimately the parish system must stand or fall on how far it both expresses already—and enables us to actualize what is as yet unrealized—the truth of the Church.

FAMILY OR ORGANIZATION?

There are at least two kinds of primary group which we can trace in the dawn of human history: the family and the hunting party. In the former the human relationships are essentially ontological; that is, they spring out of a common fund of *being*, symbolized by the image of blood. By contrast, the bonds in hunting-type groups are basically functional in character, and centre upon *doing* together in order to achieve common tasks. Thus the relationships in the hunting-party type of group are less permanent and more a means than an end in themselves, compared to those which constitute family life.

There is also an important contrast in the realm of leadership. The natural head of the family is the father, who is usually the oldest member of it. Hunting parties or their equivalents, such as war groups, probably acclaimed or elected their own leader. This leader would be the man most fitted to lead in the dangerous environment of the hunt, and he would not necessarily be the oldest man in the group. He would be chosen for his qualities as a huntsman, his technical knowledge and his powers of leadership; he could not survive as leader for long if he did not enable the group to catch or kill their prey often enough.

If pressed too far, however, this distinction between the two kinds of human group can become a false one. Families, and the clusters of families we call tribes or clans, did hunt, fight, or build together as units. Our word 'team', for example, derives from teams of oxen who were often made up from a family of beasts. Moreover, to blur the distinction at the other end of the continuum, work groups which stay together for some time do seem to take on some of the attributes of the family. Indeed the fellowship or unity which comes from living, working, and possibly facing death together can sometimes feel more real than the given relationships of the natural family.

Beyond the tribe or clan the extensions of the family are to be found in the particular nation, then the distinct race and finally in humanity as a whole. On the other hand, the development of the hunting party type of group takes us first to the formation of armies and then in later times to the emergence of other organizations in all shapes and sizes, set up to achieve a variety of industrial, commercial, and public service tasks.

Society and community are two words much more vague in their content. They mean simply people living together in time and space. Of course the people thus living together, say in a small town, are in-dividually participating in both family and work groups. Thus societies and communities are made up of both kinds of relationships in a rich profusion of different shades and blends.

These considerations should warn us against the trap of identifying the Church as *either* a family *or* a work group in its fundamental character. Any study of the New Testament images or word pictures of the Church, and the subsequent discussions of them by theologians in the Christian centuries, should serve to bear out that warning. Indeed the story of the Church exhibits an ancient tension between the family, tribe, and people set of assumptions (with accompanying attitudes) on the one hand, and those which reflect the natural hunting party, transformed by grace, seeking to complete the tasks entrusted to it by its young leader.

The emphasis upon the family aspect, both in the Church's un-derstanding of itself as a spiritual family and its alignment with the natural family, community, and nation, have brought about great benefits. For empire, state, neighbourhood, and family have all gained new dimensions of value from Christianity, a legacy which continues and grows even when overt religious belief has fallen away. And the worship or celebration of the family, in all its concentric rings of size and influence, may be a major factor in explaining why the Church in-itially won acceptance in our ancestral tribes and then has retained such a large membership well into the present century, despite the prevalent intellectual doubts and moral difficulties which have since gathered around Christianity as a religion.

Yet in recent times a sense of an unfolding and unfinished task for the Church in the wider tapestry of God's purpose for all creation has emerged into the contemporary Christian consciousness. Thus it is impossible today to understand the Church merely as a spiritual family, still less as merely a useful buttress to the natural family and its social frameworks of government, education, and community welfare. To some extent it is an organization with a purpose to accomplish.

WHAT IS AN ORGANIZATION?

During this century there has been a marked value shift in theological discourse about the Church from seeing it mainly as a community, a spiritual family, towards seeing it as an organization in Pauline terms, composed of interdependent members working together to fulfil a corporate purpose. The word 'mission' came into prominence during the 1950s to cover the area of purpose. Like the word 'gospel' in Christianity or 'revolution' in Marxism it was not too clearly defined but it represented a real gain in understanding about the Church.

Now there is—or ought to be—a relation between the purpose or task of an organization and its structure. Putting it in wider terms, organizations are not just people. For an organization to exist at all, for example, there must be a purpose or *task* to be accomplished. Having said that, there are a number of other things which are parts of all organizations.

To accomplish a task an organization needs raw materials, new people, knowledge, and skills. These come from outside the organization, the area beyond its boundaries which we can call the *environment*. The environment does not just contain suppliers of course, it also includes other realities which prevent the organization from doing whatever it likes. For example, government legislation, competitors, customers, trades unions, and public opinion can act as constraints on action. No organization is like a sealed box. All the time various forces or factors in the environment are putting pressures on the organization to behave in certain ways. Organizations therefore react to their own special environment, and those organizations which work well tend to be those which can recognize and respond appropriately to changes in their environment.

The environment of any organization can be very large and also very varied according to the nature of its task. The task of an industrial organization, for example, is not just what it does or makes or how it makes it. It is a description of the product, the particular market it is going to sell it in, the kind of customer it is going to sell to, and what the product is intended to achieve. An example is British Rail whose task is moving goods and passengers around the British Isles and to Europe—not running a railway.

Whatever the task, some process is usually involved in its completion. All organizations, whether a hospital, school, or factory, bring in raw materials, do something to the raw materials (i.e. convert them into something) and then send them out somewhere or to somebody else. The process looks like this:

$$INPUT \rightarrow CONVERSION \rightarrow OUTPUT$$

In industrial contexts this conversion process is called the *technology* of the organization. In a general sense it could be argued that all organizations have a technology of some sort, depending for its character upon the environment and the task.

In order to achieve its task and operate the constituent technologies the people setting up an organization must decide which jobs need doing, who can do what, who reports to whom, and who communicates what and to whom, and so on. These relationships within an organization we can properly call its *structure*. If the organization is going to operate well, then the structure must fit the task, the environment, and the technology.

The last essential ingredient in all organizations is, of course, the *people,* and they must have the knowledge and skills necessary to work in the organization. If they do not have them, they should be educated and trained to get that knowledge and skills. Getting the right people and helping them to work effectively in the organization to achieve the common task is the job of management and supervision. Managers and supervisors—or their equivalents—must clearly understand their environment, task, technology, and structure, so that they can recruit, select, train, develop, and manage the people in an organization in a way that suits both the people and the organization. Thus there are five things that exist in all organizations:

THE ENVIRONMENT
THE TASK
THE TECHNOLOGY
THE STRUCTURE
THE PEOPLE

These fit together like a jigsaw puzzle in each organization, and it is seldom possible to interchange pieces from one organization to another. For example, if you took the structure of an Oxbridge college and put it into a shoe-making factory it would be unlikely to work. So each of these five things must fit together and suit the other four. If they do not, the organization is likely to be ineffective. As a corollary, if there is a change in one of the elements it will—or should—create the need for change in one or more of the others.

The key thing which will decide what form the other ingredients take, however, is the *environment*. One factor in the environment which affects the way in which it is managed is the extent to which the input of raw materials is changing or remains the same. If the input is constantly changing, then there will be a lot of problems to deal with. If the input changes only slightly, then there are likely to be only few problems. Where there are only few problems, then jobs can be planned and instructions given in great detail, there will be very little stress and few crises in the work. The leader's job will be concerned with seeing that the work gets done, training his subordinates, ensuring that morale does not fall and overcoming problems of boredom. We can call this the *routine organization* or *situation*.

If, however, there are many problems or crises that arise in the operation of the organization, then it will not be possible to plan things far ahead, or to describe people's work in great detail, because both plans and jobs must be capable of adapting quickly to changing situations. This can be named the *non-routine organization* or *situation*. In these circumstances, the leader must focus more on the work to be done, he must ensure that his resources are correctly used, and that people are able to adapt quickly and to think for themselves, using their own discretion.

There are, however, few organizations that are totally routine or totally non-routine; most lie on a scale or continuum between the two:

ROUTINE |___|___|___|___|___|___|___| NON-ROUTINE
ORGANIZATIONS   ORGANIZATIONS

Moreover, most organizations start off at the non-routine end, and as they come to know how to run their work and as the problems get solved, so they move towards the routine end. As this happens, a different kind of leader tends to come to the fore who is better adapted to a routine organization. In fact few leadership jobs today are either totally routine or non-routine, and the good leader must be able to change his way of leading according to the situation.

THE PARISH SYSTEM AS A SYSTEM

Between this generalized picture of organizational or systemic life and the parish system of the Church of England, taken as an example of all church systems, some sparks of relevance may jump. In the first place, it is clear that we must take the parish system as a whole: we cannot radically disagree with or dismantle one dimension of it while ignoring the others. Although we have to keep this holistic view of it, it may be an aid to understanding to consider each of the dimensions separately. In order to do this it is necessary to look at the parish system as a phenomenon, not to be content with writings about it from clerical or lay pens.

The Environment

An immediate thought is that the environment of the parish system has changed beyond all recognition from the time of Theodore of Tarsus to the modern day. The move from an agricultural to an industrial economy has transformed the physical environment of the parish church in many cases from meadows to pavements, a fact eloquently illustrated by the old name and present situation of St Martin's-in-the-Fields. Moreover, as the historical and sociological perspectives reveal, the cultural and social environment has also changed considerably if gradually over the centuries.

But the faith of the Church (and a clue to its longevity) centres around the assumption that the environment is not merely a physical and social phenomenon. It is true that our perception of our environment is conditioned by our culture, but there is sufficient Christianity left in our culture to colour the natural religious view that the environment is not the sum of materials but discloses occasionally a presence that is always behind it, like the sun beyond thick layers of grey or translucent white cloud ceilings. In this theological perspective the environment is created by God, who is both active within it and yet also transcendent.

The Task

Religions are about establishing some kind of contact and relationship with the deity or deities who are invisibly present in the environment. Characteristically, their major function has been to set up a relationship of giving and receiving with divinity as variously conceived, offering material goods such as food and wine and shelter for the god in return for protection, favours, and rewards. In tangible terms this meant temples and services, including sacrifices, forming together a kind of technology of worship, organized and led by priests.

Whether Jesus intended to found a new religion or to reform an old one or to announce the end of all religions is a matter for discussion, but what transpired was in fact a new branch of Judaism—a synthesis in some ways between Judaism and higher Gentile religions—which became a discrete religion called Christianity. It established its own equivalents to temples, sacrificial services, and priests, although they were transformed by the creative spirit or genius in the new religion, which made it so much more than the sum of its parts. But Christianity was expected to be like other religions in what it did, promised, and provided. Allowing for the transformations wrought by Christianity and the general refinement of all religions, we can see that the central common activity or task of the Church as it waited for the Second Coming was worship. Of course, Christianity is about far more than going to church and taking part in certain rituals, ceremonies, or services, but the early medieval Church when it gained the religious monopoly put store upon attending regular worship in consecrated church buildings. As already noted, the parish system originated and spread when such an interpretation of the Church's task or purpose was becoming dominant. Its social acceptance by tribal and national rulers meant that sufficient resources were forthcoming to establish and endow the system so that it could run in perpetuity. During large tracts of its history attendance at church services was compulsory by law, although it always proved impossible to enforce the law.

At a very early date worship could be seen as a sacred routine, a recreation of the worship of the Temple in Jerusalem. It consisted of saying or singing the same services without variation every Sunday. Some variation had been introduced by the monastic practice of a daily cycle of services. Of course the church year, with its cycle of festivals and seasons, also varied the weekly routine, but it became a routine in its own right. In part the parish system had anchored itself to nature; the natural cycle of the year, so vivid in those agrarian shires, found a counterpart in worship—the changeless activity of eternity for which man had to prepare himself now.

The religious cycle of prayer also perhaps reflected the medieval world view that history goes round in circles, a World of Again-and-Again as it has been called. History does not move forwards, it simply revolved, so that the same patterns keep reappearing. History is seen here as ritual which the Mass fully and adequately expressed, rather than as a unique drama. The wheel of history was turning, and would bring in the golden age of Eden again. Meanwhile the round of services in the parish system was man's addition to the rhythms of nature and the music of the revolving heavenly spheres. Such worship tended to be past-centred or retrospective for the essential drama was over. It even implied a static idea of God and a cyclical view of life.

The Technology

Where the technology of an industry, e.g. brewing, is relatively un-changed there tends to be little change in structure. The technology of Christian worship in the sacraments and services is relatively fixed and has not altered much since the second or third century, a fact exemplified by the retention for the celebrant of Roman-type clothes, such as alb, chasuble, and cope. Despite what must seem to be very large changes for worshippers between different versions of services or even a change from Latin—the language of the Roman Empire—to the vernacular, there is relatively little change in the essential process of collecting, converting, and offering to God and receiving in return.

On the other hand, it is possible to interpret technology in a wider sense in the context of the Christian Church. It could be argued that the process is essentially about the conversion of people. The 'inputs' are fallen human beings, tainted fatally by original sin and destined thereby for eternal damnation, who are baptized, confirmed, and sanctified in the continuing life of the Church, and then become 'outputs' to Paradise or Purgatory rather than Hell. This conversion 'technology' has its roots in the mystery religions and reflects the concern for individual salvation which was apparently a great impetus to the early growth of Christianity. The Reformation challenged the late medieval Catholic version of that technology, but in the light of history it could be argued that what it changed was the emphasis rather than the essential nature of Catholic Christianity. Of course these differing views on the technology of conversion are still evident in the contrast between the extreme Catholic and Evangelical positions, the latter placing much more stress on the part played by the Word enshrined in the Bible in changing the raw materials of human nature into the glory of the saints. But they agreed that Christianity and Church membership imply a sub-mission to and active participation in a mysterious spiritual technology of personal salvation, which clergy were ordained to supervise and theologians to understand. In the Gospels Jesus was described as a *tekton,* a builder or carpenter, and the following prayer aptly sums up this interpretation of the Church's technology:

> O Jesus, Master Carpenter of Nazareth, who on the cross through wood and nails didst work man's whole salvation: Wield well thy tools in this thy workshop; that we who come to thee rough hewn may by thy hand be fashioned to a truer beauty and a greater usefulness; for the honour of thy holy name.

The Structure

Whether the emphasis was placed upon worship as an anticipation of heavenly life, with salvation by sacrament and adoption of an appropriate way of life, or upon individual conversion by hearing and feeding continuously upon the Word, the structure of the parish system was adequate. For it consisted at the simplest level of a man, a building, and an area of territory. Each could be altered to suit changing interpretations of the task and the technology. But the fact of the building, usually an ancient one and built in a certain shape, tended to institutionalize the worship function, just as, for example, a railway network implies trains.

The People

Who are the people in the Church of England's parish system? All kinds of answers are possible, ranging from all those resident within the parish boundaries, i.e. the entire population, to those who are active members of the congregation. Certainly beyond the active participants in the worship of the parish church and its associated organizations there is a *diaspora* of occasional attenders—'the fringers'—and the nominal C. of E. who may hire the building and the man for the rites of passage—christenings, weddings, and funerals. But the core of the people concerned are the full-time professionals, the bishops and clergy, church workers and lay administrators at national, diocesan, deanery, and parish levels, who work the system.

THE PARISH SYSTEM REVIEWED

The parish system is a form of organization and it can be subjected to organizational analysis to some extent. But it exhibits in theology and practice too many of the characteristics of a spiritual family or community to be entirely understood in organizational terms. Even so there are some sparks of relevance which at least have flashed in my own mind. I think that the physical features of the structure weight the task towards the regular pattern of worship, and the whole system—the environment, the technology and the people as well—tends to imply the maintenance of this pattern.

Church worship is traditionally regarded as *opus Dei,* the work or service for God. But the provision of church services has also been seen as a means for meeting the religious needs of the people. This brings us to the first major question mark about the system. Owing to the related changes between the cultural and social environment and what goes on in people's minds—their cast of mind and sensibility—it could be argued that the public provision of Sunday and weekday services in cathedral or parish church is manifestly not meeting the religious needs of men, women, and children today if we taken them *en masse.* One interpretation of the figures given in Chapter Two is that people as a whole do not find that the aspects of Christianity available in the parish system—notably sacramental worship and congregational membership—are meeting their religious needs. Except in a minority of cases this conclusion would not find expression in a conscious or articulate way: people just drift away, or become bored with sermons and services, or discover that they are too busy in more interesting ways on a Sunday. There is no overt disavowal of Christianity, just a growing indifference to the parochial system and what it appears to offer, coupled with a diminishing awareness of a specifically religious set of needs.

Many parishes have responded by trying to brighten up their services, or to widen their appeal to the natural family through family services or parish communions. In the process the length of the sermon has fallen from an average of 40 minutes in 1945 to about 7 minutes in 1975, and almost every service has been rewritten. Other churches have abandoned counting heads altogether as an unspiritual practice, holding that in the last resort the parish system could run with only a handful of people. Armed with the 'doctrine of the remnant' the priest could say the services on behalf of the absent people, as their representative, even though he is alone. Obviously this approach fits in more with a more Catholic theology. Once I attended Holy Communion as almost the sole member of the congregation for about six months, and the priest added a gloss on the Book of Common Prayer words, praying for the Church 'militant here on earth and'—looking at the empty seats—'triumphant in heaven'.

But the trend continues to be away from the building and the man which the parish system exists to provide at no small cost in time and money. To those who do not take the Catholic line of a representative or priestly idea of the Church, there still remains the question as to why the well-established conversion process of the Church—Catholic or Protestant—is failing to attract, retain, and sanctify those who are drawn by birth, custom, or inclination into its net. Is there something wrong with Christianity? Or is the form in which it is expressed—the parish system with all its books, rites, clothes, sermonology, special people and so on—no longer relevant to the spiritual needs of secular man in the industrialized West? In other words, as a missionary organization—something it was never designed for—and as a matrix for Christian growth, is the parish system simply out of date?

On the other side, it can be pointed out that Christianity still works for a lot of people, and the laity who support or belong to the congregations in the parish system are probably the most committed and self-consciously Christian in the history of the Church of England. To those critics who point out that the parish system almost entirely failed to train the laity because its traditional teacher methods—the confirmation class and monologue sermon—were largely ineffective for educational purposes with adults, it could be replied that an organization as large as the Church of England could not be expected to respond to the theology of the laity in a decade or even two or three decades. Indeed, being relatively insulated from the pressures of the environment by wealth and endowments, it might seem as if it intends not to respond at all, but this apparent institutional apathy is merely because theological ideas have historically taken three or four decades to permeate through the parish system.

In the light of these reflections on the fixed characters of the parochial system and its manifest failure as a structure for either mission or the education and training of the laity, it is not surprising that there have been predictions by radicals that its days were numbered, and that Babylon in the guise of hyperinflation would knock down the card house. The 1950s and 1960s saw many clergymen and a few bishops pronounce its doom in such terms. Instead, the radicals foresaw, the Church would be just people once more, meeting in house groups. All the structures would be dismantled, and the Church would be the Church. Perhaps in every British heart there is a Celt struggling against a Roman (with a pagan Saxon into the bargain). Perhaps in these radical yearnings there is a distant echo of that Celtic Christianity which fell away after the triumph of the Roman order. But no organization or formed community can roll up its history like a parchment and start all over again, just as I cannot go back to being a fifteen year old boy. That form of the Church is as illusory an idea as the 'alternative society'. Within a decade or two, as the history of sects illustrates, these informal house groups would get more organized and begin the long march from groups to sect, and from sect to denomination. Man is a social creature, and that ultimately rules out anarchy.

Thus we come back to some version or other of the parish system, that is one man, one building, and one area, with each of these units associated together and served by larger structures, such as deanery, diocese, and church. It is in the British approach, with its feeling for tradition, to modify and adapt rather than to abolish and invent. Our regimental system, for example, has survived in a much changed manifestation since the eighteenth century, thanks to some great reformers, although some regiments can be traced back still further, and the idea of the regiment can be traced at least as far back as the Roman legion. The parish system, granted similar reforms, is capable of surviving. The issue, however, is what kind of reforms are required if it is to become more effective in meeting the religious needs of people? Falling numbers are only indicators, not absolute signs of value. If only thirty people read this book I may console myself in various ways, but if I am wise I must take it as an indicator that I have failed to get through, that I have not communicated. Of those thirty, one might include a future Pope and a future Archbishop of Canterbury: as Christians rightly say, in the end it is quality and not quantity which counts. Unfortunately for us, God cares about the quantity as well as the quality!

Consider again, however, the basic simplicity and high adaptability of the parish system. It is true that superficially the building and what goes on inside it cannot be much changed. But the territory must be translated into people, perhaps 10,000 of them. And the placing of a man, a trained and dedicated pastor, preacher and priest, in such a human situation is bound to reveal to him all kinds of opportunities. We should not make haste to write off the parish system with these countless opportunities for communication, community, experience, growth, and love until we have done all we can to mend the nets.

Perhaps I can best illustrate the ways in which the parish system can be developed not just to survive but to carry music by considering four levels of it: the parish, the deanery, the diocese, and the centre.

1. THE PARISH
In terms of its essentials—a man, a building, a territory—the parish system has remained relatively unchanged. It is true that what happens inside the building on Sunday is no longer quite the same as the order

laid down in 1662, but the alterations in services are relatively minor, just as central heating and electric lighting hardly transform a medieval church building. The technology in terms of liturgiology and soteriology also remain much the same. Moreover, whatever the personality or character of the man he has to confine himself within a certain role, bounded by the expectations of his congregation, society at large, and his fellow clergy.

Within these constraints, however, there is room for considerable originality and creative action. In a sense the implicit strategy of the parish system is not unlike that of the Royal Navy at the time of Nelson. Central administration limited itself to building and equipping the ships. Once at sea an admiral could bring his fleet into the vicinity of his enemy's fleet, if possible on the windward side. Then each captain was expected to lay his ship alongside his opposite number. Victory went to the side which won most of these individual conflicts. Traditionally bishops have taken the same line with their parishes: select good captains and ensure that their buildings are in good order. Like Nelson's 'band of brothers' the vicars were also expected to find their own crew.

The story of the Church of England is in part the account of what the parish priests have made of their opportunities. Some have been useless, and a fraction of this minority in every decade have faced the equivalent of court martial. The majority have served their parishes well. A few have been outstandingly successful, although what counts as success in the parochial ministry is justifiably a matter for debate. Here I use it to mean a judgement by those who are orientated towards the situation that the man in question is actualizing its potentialities, however limited they may seem to be. Numbers at church are only one imperfect criterion of success, because they are governed so much by general factors outside the parish system. The personality or message of a parliamentary candidate in a general election may gain or lose him say ten per cent of the votes, but the outcome is determined by national swings to Left or Right. On the other hand, that plus or minus ten per cent can be crucially important in marginal seats, and even decide the next government. Within the constraints of the present social, economic, and cultural system what is needed is not so much success in the pre-Second World War sense, the kind of success at running a 'big show' like Portsea with ten curates which took you to a bishop's throne. What matters now much more is creativity.

Is the work of a parish clergyman creative? It is bound to be in so far as it involves creating and sustaining a community, and helping

Christians of all ages to grow in their spiritual life. The creativity lies partly in seeing relationships of links between unlikely people. It almost always includes a vision of what the Church is in theological terms, but it is more than that. The pastor in question looks upon his congregation with a creative perspective, seeing it like an artist considering the realities of his material with all the knots and patterned grains of various human nature. But he also sees people as in the process of becoming—unfinished, incomplete, waiting.

This picture of parish ministry appealed to individualists, those who like working on their own with maximum freedom and discretion to plan their own work, and minimum supervision. In this respect the clergyman was like the artist or the don. Indeed the system had a creative effect on the man, tending to develop in him individualism and sometimes eccentricity. The obverse side of individualism is loneliness. During the 1950s and 1960s the problem of clerical loneliness, especially in rural areas, was frequently discussed and mentioned in such reports as that written by Leslie Paul (1964).

The institution of group and team ministries constitutes one approach to diminishing the problem. There are technical differences between group and team ministries, but both imply that a large territory is being worked not by an individual or set of individuals in their watertight compartments but by a group with a leader. Dr Anthony Russell in *Groups and Teams in the Countryside* (1975) explains the difference—in the team (one benefice, with assistant clergy), the group (a number of incumbents working together)—but rightly describes these as 'polar models', for it is possible to work a team like a group, or a group like a team. In practice several of the Norfolk teams may be described as 'a team of clergy working in a group of parishes'. He traces their history from the first in 1961. Of the seventeen groups or teams the Blakeney one (1964) was the first to group smaller parishes with a large one. (Since his book went to press, however, this group has been dissolved.) The staffing varies from one to 600 to one to 800.

This method had the added initial advantage that many thought it would save money and manpower, but it has not done so on the whole. In extreme cases, where the team circulated among a dozen or more churches, the laity sometimes complained that their village or hamlet had lost their own parson. The real justification for team ministries lay not in their supposed time-saving and cost-effectiveness as in the case of a group medical practice, or in the synergy of a group working together, but in their being a means of reducing the individual clergyman's sense of isolation in the apparently God-forsaken backwoods of the country or the urban wilderness of indifference.

Implicit in the group or team solution was the idea of the clergyman spending more working time with his colleagues—planning, reviewing, encouraging, and acting as pastors to each other in meeting individual needs. Those still in the traditional parish increasingly in the postwar decades came to feel the need for more contact with their fellow clergymen, and in particular their bishop as pastor. They were looking not for praise but for encouragement. Moreover, they needed spiritual support, the reassurance that the gospel was true and that their ministries were worthwhile. The less these messages came from society in the parish, including the congregations who all too often displayed a stolid conventional faith or an openness of mind verging onto chronic doubt, the more the clergy sought them from the earthly sources of their own commissions, the bishops and other leaders among the clergy. As most elderly clergymen recall, the contrast between this picture and the situation in the 1920s or 1930s is very marked. It should not be the subject for a value-judgement: times have changed, and the parochial system as a whole has to respond to this particular change.

The postwar decades have certainly seen their fair share of creative and lively parishes, and the humility of their vicars prevents them from taking much credit for them. The Holy Spirit was seen to be at work in the situation, and usually—indeed always—there were many good people involved as the parish came alive. But the parson is more often than not the change catalyst for good or ill. It is to the credit of these outstanding parish ministries, most of them destined to go unrecorded in church history, that we owe for example the emergence of a significant number of articulate and committed people.

Within the contexts of my reports on the dioceses of York and Chichester I advocated a 'ministry by objectives' approach in the parish, whereby the larger purpose and aims of the Church (see Chapter Seven) are broken down in the local situation into tangible objectives. This idea was borrowed from the 'management by objectives' approach introduced into many large organizations in the late 1960s, which stressed the importance of participation by a manager in the decisions about what he should be doing as well as the discipline of identifying goals. Michael Wright, a vicar in Middlesborough within the Diocese of York and now editor of *Ace,* the quarterly bulletin of the Archbishops' Council on Evangelism, wrote about his experience of using this kind of basic management thinking at parish level in his book *New Ways for*

Christ (1976). In 1975 Leicester Diocese arranged a course on such management thinking at Leicester Polytechnic's School of Management. The Diocese of St Albans is already embarked upon a programme of inviting parishes to set their objectives in the context of the purpose and aims of the Church in the diocese.

The Church in Wales is also currently introducing a self-appraising programme for deaneries and parishes, along the lines of 'ministry by objectives'. The programme (quoted in Michael Wright's book) makes this important point:

> Many parishes find their resources fully stretched in maintenance work, in balancing the books, baptizing the babies, burying the dead, marrying, teaching and visiting. To extend mission further seems almost insuperable. Yet an examination of essentials and what time, money, and manpower is available can lead to the preparation and fulfilment of a simple plan of aims and objects, containing some element of growth, within a specified period.

As Michael Wright concludes:

> Management by objectives is an approach to our work that may be the servant of the gospel: it must not be the master. The basic work of worship and witness goes on, and management by objectives will not change that. It can, however, help us to examine what is essential and what time, money, and manpower are available, and to concentrate on some aspects of growth for the next six to twelve months ahead.

The expansion or growth of the congregation, traditionally among the aims of the parson, has come under some scrutiny. In a paper presented to the General Synod in 1974 entitled *Let My People Grow* (Urban Church Project, Workpaper No. 1), the Reverend David Wasdell as Director of the Project, focused attention on the following questions:

> Are the factors causing the breakdown of the Church in the city part of the given environment, or do they stem from within the churches' own life?

> Can the current programme of clergy re-deployment possibly create the needed breakthrough?

> What are the real long-term effects of holding a parish mission, a diocesan call to mission, a provincial or national campaign or using

'mass evangelism' techniques, while present patterns of ministry and church life prevail?

What is the fundamental priority of mission in contemporary urban Britain?

As a step towards answering these questions he introduced the idea of 'the self-limiting church'. By this term he meant that there are factors at work which tend to limit the growth of a congregation regardless of the size of the population in the parish boundaries. In a piece of research by the Reverend A. B. Miskin, the main findings of which were appended to the Paul Report (1964), a relationship between the number of Christian communicants, the number of full-time workers in the parish, and its population, was established. One full-time assistant adds an average of 90 communicants to the figure for a lone-incumbent parish, independent of any rise in parish population. A third worker adds an extra 81 Christmas communicants on average. (Mr Miskin confined his study to parishes of over 2,000 population.) Mr Wasdell concludes from his own research:

> In parishes of over 2,000 the single-clergy model church levels off at an average congregation of 175 regardless of parish population. The fact that large parishes tend to have larger congregations is purely the result of the deployment of more assistant clergy in the larger parishes. The self-limiting model is retained but the limits are raised slightly by increased manpower. . . . If we examine the congregation size as a percentage of its parish population, we find that penetration of the parish drops drastically with rise in population. This tendency was noted in the Paul Report, revealing itself in the decreasing pastoral effectiveness of the church with rise in population density of the dioceses. However, not until we examine the parochial level of effectiveness is the full extent of the collapse revealed. Penetration of the mini-parish (125 population) runs in excess of 20 per cent, dropping to 10 per cent for parishes of 1,500. By the time we are dealing with 10,000 parishioners, only 2·3 per cent are involved in the congregation, while the figure declines to 1·6 per cent for parishes in excess of 20,000.

These conclusions suggest that merely rationalizing the deployment of incumbents and assistant clergy will have little effect. 'While the present structure and life style of the self-limiting congregation are retained no amount of pastoral juggling and re-deployment of the clergy can create the needed breakthrough.' One way of possibly defeating the phenomenon of self-limitation is to persuade the congregation to form themselves into groups, which will then grow and sub-divide in a natural process, aided albeit by the midwifery of the clergy. In this way, it is thought, the inputs of new members, drawn in by the laity and clergy alike, will begin to exceed the outputs caused by death and lapse. Mr Wasdell stresses, however, that there is no one 'right solution'. The central principle he is asserting is that 'the structure of the Church must be appropriate to the task of the Church'. Given a missionary task, he believes that a cellular structure may be more appropriate than the self-limiting congregation. Further research is being carried out to test this hypothesis.

Behind this approach there is a long-standing history of a search for some unit or group smaller than the parish but larger than the individual. In some periods the natural family and the household servants constituted such a group, with their Christian conversation and family prayers. The Puritans sought it in their Bible-study groups; descendants of the 'classes' of Elizabethan days. The Methodists in their turn tried to establish some form of infra-parish system of groups. The 'house church' movement, such bodies as the Servants of Christ the King, and the charismatic movement in recent times have all turned with hope to the small group. All agree that depth in Christian fellowship can only be achieved in the small group.

It is possible to imagine the small group or 'cell' sub-division theory working in many parishes as a means of building up the congregation, providing—and here is the snag—the parish clergy have the necessary kind of leadership to encourage it to happen, without adopting a *laissez-faire* attitude on the one hand or forcing groups to divide prematurely on the other hand. Moreover, the underlying assumption that the task of the parish system as a whole is primarily worship would have to be radically revised. But even so it would be no panacea. At best it will mean that in the 1980s the Church of England declines less slowly in numbers than in the 1960s.

The essence of a parish priest's work is authority and freedom. He is given authority to take charge of the assets and resources of the Church of England in a certain area, authority to administer the sacraments, lead worship, preach, and to be responsible for the congregation: he is the Church of England's official on the spot, readily identifiable by his uniform. He is paid and housed. The directions as to what he should actually do are vague, although he will have acquired from his training and apprenticeship some definite ideas on what is expected from him, what he ought to do and what is possible in the contemporary situation. After that he is free—free to be positive and creative, to lead or inspire, or free to be negative, uncreative, routine-minded, and dull. If that freedom is ever removed, with it would go the possibility of job satisfaction, or—in religious terms—the hope of joy. That is not to say that he does not need supervision, but there are ways of exercising that supervision through good leadership which enhance rather than detract from individual freedom.

2. THE DEANERY

At one time there were archpriests in the Church as well as archdeacons. These senior priests had oversight of either a group of clergy in a particular area or a cathedral. By the end of the ninth century the title of rural dean and dean was being applied respectively to them. That term was borrowed ultimately from the Roman army, for a *decanus* was a section leader, holding command over ten soldiers in a legion. It appeared in the Latin Vulgate in the Exodus passage where Jethro persuades Moses to choose able men to be rulers over thousands, hundreds, fifties, and tens, to 'bear the burden with you'. The monastic world first adopted the title for one who was set over ten monks, hence a dean.

William the Conqueror's archbishop, Lanfranc, probably imported the office of rural dean to England, and by about the middle of the twelfth century most archdeaconries or sub-divisions of a diocese were further divided into deaneries. But the rural deans soon lost their lowly ecclesiastical courts, and became little more than the delegates of the archdeacons. From the reign of Edward I, wrote Guy Mayfield, 'the office to all intents and purposes disappeared until its formal revival in 1836'. The Puritans showed some interest in the rural deanery as a possible basis for a presbyterian type of church government and some bishops maintained the office after the Restoration, but Mayfield's words hold true as a generalization.

In the nineteenth century rural deans were reintroduced more-or-less as the archdeacon's local deputy, with legal and administrative functions, a view echoed in the report of the Royal Commission on Ecclesiastical Discipline in 1906. But some bishops had begun to see creative possibilities in the office. For example, Bishop Samuel Wilberforce could write to his rural deans in February 1846 in the following vein:

. . . my great object is that the rural dean should form an easy and accurate medium of communication between me and the clergy of the deanery, and still more that he should be a local centre of spiritual influence and brotherly union to his clergy.

And,

My desire is that the rural dean should carry out throughout the district committed to his charge that effective parochial visitation and inspection which the size of this diocese renders impossible for the bishop or even for the archdeacon.

In the Enabling Act of 1919 the electoral system was established whereby the parochial church councils elected members of both the ruri-decanal conferences and also the diocesan conferences, who in turn elected some of their members to the General Assembly. This fact helped to keep the rural deanery in virtual oblivion until the Synodical Government Measure of 1969. Besides interposing the deanery synod between the parishes and the diocesan synod, the latter gave the dean—shorn of the prefix 'rural'—a large role in the leadership of the Church. In theory the deans became the middle management of the Church. But attitudes towards and long-held assumptions about the role of the rural dean cannot be changed merely by promulgation in a Measure.

My impression is that of deanery synods between 1970 and 1975 about one-third remained fairly unchanged, so that the clergy and laity noticed nothing much different from the old ruri-decanal days (except the clergy grumbled that they were no longer automatically members of the diocesan conference, which they missed partly as a social occasion). In about one-third of the deaneries the opportunities of synodical government were welcomed, and there has been a successful development of the deanery synod and a growing sense of deanery identity and purpose. The other third of the deaneries fall somewhere in between these two polarized clusters.

Time, however, is on the side of the deanery in the sense that many of the activities—such as laity education, for example—which are at present attempted in the parishes could be much more effectively tackled at deanery level. Moreover, I see the deanery as the true group or team ministry, with the dean giving and receiving from his colleagues support and encouragement. It is also the natural centre for establishing aims and objectives in the various areas of the Church's purpose or mission, so that an incumbent has someone with whom he can discuss both the planning of his own parochial church council and also his own priorities over the next six months. As the relationship of trust grows, so the dean should be able to offer constructive suggestions which will not be mistaken as ill-founded criticism, over such matters as how an incumbent leads a service, preaches a sermon, or conducts a meeting. In order to provide more specialist advice where training needs are mutually agreed, the dean may well develop his own deanery team of functional specialists, who would be available for consultation in the parishes. Each deanery, for example, might have a specialist—layman or clergyman—on youth work, Sunday schools, lay education, or the conduct of worship. Thus the possibilities of the rural deanery are many within the evolving parish system, but in order to realize them the dean has to be properly selected, trained for the job and himself led and inspired by his area bishop. That conclusion leads us to consider changes in the diocese.

3. THE DIOCESE

Diocesan Size

What ought to be the size of a diocese? The simplest answer is that a diocese should be sufficiently small for the diocesan bishop to oversee the work and life of the Christian Church within it. What that means in practice, however, hinges upon the meanings of all the terms used, such as size, oversee, Church, and bishop. Is size measured in square miles or population? Does oversee imply active leadership and communication? Is the Church the sum of church-going members, or all baptized people, or everyone who pays their taxes other than Jews and infidels? Does the existence of archbishops, suffragan bishops, and assistant bishops possess any significance?

These are questions which will receive different answers in different churches for some years to come. Here I can only write against the background of three sets of assumptions. The first set concerns the nature of episcopal work as being essentially leadership and communication. The historical evolution of the diocese in the Church of England, the present state of English ecclesiastical boundaries and the development of the suffragan bishop concept during more recent decades, constitutes the second set of assumptions. Thirdly, I have assumed that the Church will encounter ever larger financial costs in relation to its assets, and so it will need great care in the allocation of its money. In organizational terms this means that the Church of England

(and all other churches) must resolutely set itself to gain the economies of size (that is the financial and practical advantages of large size), while seeking to maintain the well-known benefits for people which come from being part of a small social enterprise. That may sound paradoxical, if not impossible, but it is the quest upon which all major organizations and institutions are now embarked.

The present sizes of English dioceses range from the very large in area, such as Oxford (2,000 square miles in three counties), or population (London: 3,800,000) to the rather small, for example, Truro with a population of 394,000 in 1976 or Sodor and Man, a mere 57,000. Some reformers, intent upon rationalization, have argued for a standard-sized diocese, so that the country would be divided into uniform units. Perhaps, if our forefathers had resolutely established the principle that a diocese should be coterminous with county boundaries, the present-day results would satisfy the rationalizers. But ecclesiastical boundaries are the products of a long and complex history, which has incidentally introduced a pleasing variety and a difference of diocesan tradition which we should be reluctant to see bull-dozed into a monochrome uniformity.

Bearing in mind, however, the need for *both* size *and* smallness, there are two possible lines of advance which are not necessarily mutually exclusive.

1. *One diocese, but working in episcopal areas*

In both my York and Chichester reports on organization I recommended that the diocese in question should remain a unity but work more in three episcopal areas, each under the leadership of a suffragan bishop. Both dioceses were already divided into three archdeaconries; one had three suffragans, the other possessed two. It seemed to me that an archdeaconry was sufficiently small for episcopal leadership to be a reality, yet large enough to prevent the suffragan bishop from trying to do the jobs of his rural deans or incumbents. Besides the advantages of having a diocesan bishop to exercise supervision and to provide encouragement for the three area bishops, his central staff could provide services and administrative support for a sufficiently large segment of the Church to make them cost-effective in financial terms.

During the period when I was completing my research for the reports (1969–73) other large dioceses were moving to a similar conclusion. The Bishop of London, for example, created four area bishoprics in Kensington, Willesden, Stepney, and Edmonton. The new Bishop of

Oxford rejected a commission's report recommending the division of his diocese, and applied instead the area principle by making his suffragans responsible for two of the three constituent counties of Buckinghamshire, Berkshire, and Oxfordshire. Norwich and Canterbury made similar moves towards the same method of work.

2. *Single dioceses, but grouped together in associations*

The present large dioceses obviously lend themselves to the area principle, but what about the smaller dioceses, such as Wakefield or Lichfield? In some cases they could beneficially become episcopal areas rather than independent sees. So that every diocesan bishop had working under him not less than two and not more than four suffragan bishops, each responsible for about nine deaneries. The historic unity of the small see would thus remain, but it would share administrative and financial services with a neighbour.

Supposing the dioceses of England—or any other country for that matter—were reorganized into bishoprics of two, three, or four areas, each under a diocesan bishop as the leader of an episcopal team. It would still be necessary to group these dioceses together in a regional association, so that they could share in such matters as common projects and pursue jointly an intelligent policy over the training and placement of clergy.

At present the only organization above the diocese is the province, and there are only two provinces in England. In my York Report (1970) I proposed that dioceses should work together in clusters much more. This idea had been in my mind for some time, but I had tended to dismiss it on the grounds of my belief that the holder of an ancient and venerable see would be unlikely to accept the membership of a cluster of dioceses grouped around some city or centre other than his own cathedral town. Yet in a conversation in 1970 with Dr Charles-Edwards, then Bishop of Worcester, he spontaneously volunteered the point from his own experience, suggesting that Worcester should form part of a group of dioceses centred upon Birmingham.

Personally I am not in favour of creating six or seven new and smaller provinces, each under an archbishop, which is one proposed solution. Any organization should be kept as simple as possible, and we should be cautious about the introduction of another formal level or tier in the Church's superstructure. There is also a fatal tendency sometimes to increase the number of Chiefs just at the time when the Indians are getting fewer on the ground. My own hopes would ride with a more modest expedient, in a limited way already essayed by the East Anglian dioceses, of a form of informal association, more-or-less along the lines adopted by Oxbridge colleges who group themselves together in clusters of five or six for the purposes of admission, or—on a more historical note—the counties in the English Civil War who formed themselves into associations.

At this stage it is necessary to discuss explicitly what has emerged implicitly, namely that bishops differ in ranking order. There is much confusion over this matter, both in the Anglican and the Catholic Churches, because the principle of a three-fold *order* or status of ministry—bishops, priests, and deacons—has to be reconciled with the evident fact that not all bishops are equal in *rank*. These differences in episcopal rank are perhaps more obvious in the Catholic hierarchy, but they are also present in the Anglican Church. The tendency in the Church of England has been to emphasize the equal status of bishops (a reflection of the sixteenth century polemic against the papacy), and it may therefore find it uncongenial to take the topic out from under the dusty carpet and examine it in the light of day. As the Anglican Church stands in the tradition which values order as the essential complement to freedom, however, we might not be afraid of the principle of hierarchy as such.

Making use of the military model, we could say that the ordained ministry roughly falls into three categories: curates and junior clergy (subalterns); those of incumbent status (field officers); and men in episcopal orders (general officers). All these men are ordained, or (in military parlance) commissioned, but they differ in rank and responsibility. Owing to historical and practical factors, the first and second levels of the Church are not marked by separate services of ordination; the second level of status comes normally after a year of commissioned service. This present system is frequently discussed and criticized on theological grounds; sometimes ecclesiastical authorities even tinker with it. Doubtless the relation betweeen the ordinations to diaconate and priesthood needs further examination, but here it is the third order of bishops which chiefly concerns us.

General officers in the British Army have been divided into a bewildering number of categories in their time. Some of these titles, such as Captain-General, have virtually disappeared. Those that remain are somewhat confusing. Who would guess that a Major-General is in fact junior to a Lieutenant-General, when a Major is senior to a Lieutenant? Is a Brigadier actually a general? To clear up the anomalies of history the Americans introduced a simple classification in terms of stars, one to five, which has the merit of continental roadsigns in being universally clear. So much so that the British Army adopted the star-category system, at least on the green-and-silver signs which mark official staff cars. In inter-service or international matters it also helps to determine the level of participants who may be disguised behind bewildering displays of gold-braid and resonant titles.

If we apply the method to the hierarchy of the Church of England, a body of about 100 bishops, a division of the present episcopate into five levels could be suggested, using such criteria as their incomes, the status of their sees, and the size of their areas of jurisdiction.

*****	The Archbishops of Canterbury and York—Primates of All England and England respectively, and both provincials.
****	London, Durham and Winchester.
***	Diocesan bishops with two or three suffragans, e.g. Oxford and Chichester.
**	Bishops of small dioceses, e.g. Bradford, Lichfield, or Coventry.
*	Suffragans with area responsibility, e.g. Hull, Horsham, or Stepney.

One possible criterion for present four-star bishops is whether or not they have the right to a seat in the House of Lords, as some bishops do. It may well be one four-star bishopric should stand at the centre of each cluster of dioceses in a region. This would entail the possible inclusion of the key bishoprics in such metropolitan areas as Greater Manchester, Merseyside, West Yorkshire, and West Midlands in the four-star list, assuming that Durham embraced the Tyne and Wear region. Assuming also some adjustment of diocesan boundaries, the present (implicit) system might be changed into the following:

Five-star	The two Archbishops.
Four-star	Senior Bishops in the eight associations: North East (Durham), North West (Manchester), North Midlands (Birmingham), Midlands (Oxford), East (Norwich), West (Exeter), South (Winchester), and London.
Three-star	Diocesan bishops with two or three episcopal areas under their supervision.
Two-star	Diocesan bishops with one episcopal area or suffragan bishops in charge of an episcopal area.
One-star	Assistant or auxiliary bishops.

The star method of identifying levels of episcopal responsibility is only an aid to thinking. It is not meant to be a rigid classification, still less the source of endless arguments about dioceses—as if we were rating restaurants for a Michelin guide. Nor am I advocating that bishops should have their stars embroidered upon their mitres! The enormous merit of the star idea is that it stresses the one-ness of the episcopal order in a way in which titles such as Suffragan and Assistant—trailing their past connotations like clouds of vapour as they do—can never quite do today.

In the remainder of this chapter the word diocese will refer to a structure of three episcopal areas working together in a unity, as in the present cases of York and Oxford dioceses. The bishop of such a diocese would thus be at least a three-star man, and its suffragans two-star bishops. In practice there will be variations on the theme: for example, dioceses consisting of two or four areas. Moreover, some diocesans will have four or five-star standing. But the principles of organization evolved from the study of the three-star diocese can be applied in smaller or larger ones, provided that they are not too small or large.

Better Communication

One important development taking place within some dioceses concerns communication, for it can be argued that in the less certain or stable environment, coupled with the unpredictable opportunities which are emerging, the Church needs better communication like any other contemporary organization. The main channel of upward and downward communication in the diocese should be the diocesan bishop, the three suffragans and the twenty-four or so rural deans. In most dioceses there are already staff meetings at which the diocesan and suffragans are present. Ideally each of the suffragans should then gather together his eight or nine rural deans for the purposes of *briefing* (or passing down information and guidance) and *consultation,* or seeking facts, advice, and constructive suggestions. Then, each of the rural deans should hold his briefing and consultative meeting with the incumbents in his deanery. Thus it should be possible for the diocesan bishop to ask the suffragans to give some news, and explain the reasons for it, in such a way that every clergyman has heard it verbally either from a suffragan or dean, with the chance to clarify meanings, within a week or so. The same should prove possible for the upwards movement of communication in the consultation process.

Although this corporate method of communication has been exalted in the management textbooks into the status of elaborate organizational theory, it is essentially simple. The determination to take seriously the primacy of personal face-to-face communication, coupled with a growth in the numbers of people involved, leads an intelligent person almost inevitably to some such system. But it is not easy to maintain this line of communication in working order; still more difficult to use it aright, like a musician winning the best sounds from his instrument.

Such a system, it must be repeated, still leaves the diocesan free to communicate to the clergy. But clergy will not fully accept the episcopal leadership of suffragan bishops unless they have a larger and clearer decision-making authority within agreed limits.

By hook and by crook: Line and Staff Leadership

There is a useful distinction in organizational theory and practice between *line* and *staff* responsibility. In any organization a line of spoken communication should exist between the head and the least of its members. Each leader who stands in such a line also carries the main responsibility for giving leadership in terms of the common strategy. He is accountable for results, and he should have sufficient authority to make the decisions necessary to his job.

The staff responsibility is complementary to the line leadership. The central task of the staff man is to give specialist advice and assistance to the line leader. He does not interfere or exercise authority over those in the line. On the other hand he is individually responsible and accountable for the quality and standard of the service he provides to the organization. It is important to be clear on the distinction between these two roles.

This concept of the different functions of line and staff leadership should not cause difficulty to the Church theologian. For we owe our classic statement of the general principle to St Paul in the first Epistle to the Corinthians: 'If all were a single organ, where would the body be? As it is, there are many parts, yet one body. The eye cannot say to the hand, "I have no need of you", nor again the head to the feet, "I have no need of you".'

There is a slightly different pattern of authority in the two kinds of leadership. Today authority in positions of leadership comes in three strands: the authority of position, the authority of knowledge, and the authority of personality. To be fully effective a leader needs all three strands bound as in a single rope. Nor can or should they be unravelled in practice, although we can distinguish them in theory.

The staff specialist, although he does have an official appointment, will be dealing more with his equals or superiors in status. To get his suggestions considered and implemented he will have to rely upon that authority which 'flows from the man who knows'.

Both line and staff leaders in any organization today need also the authority of personality. This phrase can conjure up visions of charismatic persons exuding their auras of influence, and others less so gifted practising magnetic glances in their private mirrors. In the Christian context, however, it is significant that St Paul passed on immediately from his organic description of the Church, and the gifts appropriated by some of the more prestigious functions, to his moving and immortal praise of love. The authority of personality is only the authority of love, and no amount of charismatic fireworks can replace its steady and unassuming flame.

Within each diocese there should be an inner leadership team together working to meet the task, unity and individual needs (see pp. 140–1) of the body of the Church in that district. Members of such a team might perform different functions, some on the line side and some as staff specialists. But there should not be a rigid distinction between line and staff leadership: both form a whole whose parts may combine into new patterns according to the necessities of the situation.

This development of a staff is already quite advanced in all dioceses in England and throughout the Anglican Communion. Over the past sixty years a number of diocesan specialists have appeared on the scene, covering a range of subjects ancillary to the parish ministry, such as:

Post-Ordination Training	Lay Training
Further Training	Youth Work
Women's Ministry in the Church	Children's Religious Education
Laymen's Ministry in the Church	Social Responsibility
Ordinands	Industrial Mission
Family Social Work	Ecumenical Affairs
Diocesan Schools	Overseas Mission Work
Parsonages	Stewardship
Church Buildings	

Many of these functions are concerned with areas where the parish system has been notoriously weak, for example lay training and mission to those outside the Christian fold. In the traditional parish system these specialists had relatively little influence except on a personal basis direct with incumbents. They are not able to contribute towards and inform the strategy of the diocese and the deaneries. How could this part of the system be strengthened vis-à-vis those parts which sometimes had become preoccupied with maintaining the parishes, supplying the right men and caring for the buildings, on the apparent assumption that Sunday services and associated pastoral work exhausted the purpose of the Church in society? My own solution involves a development of the office of archdeacon.

In the past century several factors have been at work which have influenced the role of the archdeacon. The development of a central administration in each diocese, with a full-time staff working under the direction of a lay diocesan secretary, has reduced many of the archdeacon's traditional functions. One possible line of evolution—still open—would be for archdeacons to turn into archpriests, changing their responsibility for the administrative or temporal matters in their archdeaconries into a much more pastorally-orientated care for the clergy; and many wise and good archdeacons have naturally moved in that direction. A possible difficulty, however, arises from two other developments already noted, namely the changing positions of suffragan bishops and rural deans. Since 1900 the numbers of suffragan bishops have greatly increased. There are theological, historical, and practical reasons why it may be more fitting for a 'chief shepherd' to be in episcopal orders. Moreover, the move towards synodical government has been accompanied by an emphasis upon the rural dean as the pastor and friend to the clergy in his deanery. If area bishop and rural dean are doing their jobs, what becomes of the pastoral role of the archdeacon?

One solution would be simply to abolish them. The Catholic Church in England, for example, has no archdeacons but a priest is appointed on an *ad hoc* basis to fill the traditional role of the archdeacon at an ordination. Another solution, tried more than once in the recent past, is to combine the roles of suffragan and archdeacon in one person. A brief analysis of experiments, however, is not encouraging. It seems that there are still enough of the residual functions of an archdeacon remaining to overload a suffragan: the Bishop of Reading, for example, gave up being an archdeacon as well as an area bishop for this reason in 1973.

In my York and Chichester reports it was suggested that the three archdeacons in each diocese might become eventually the heads of separate diocesan staff teams in the fields of administration, ministry, and mission, while retaining at least some of their residual functions. Thus the archdeacon would be seen as a senior priest in a staff (as opposed to line) leadership role; not primarily as an administrator or as pastor—though he would still require both these gifts.

It is part of the leadership work of the diocesan bishop to hold together the different but complementary ministries of his area bishops, deans, and vicars on the one hand and his archdeacons and directors, advisers, and secretaries on the other.

4. AT THE CENTRE

In England during the Reformation the parish system was kept intact but severed from Rome. This meant that sovereign power resided in King-in-Parliament. As the House of Commons were a part of parliament it gave the Puritan laity a chance to try and alter the main function of the parish system from traditional worship to the preaching of the gospel. They failed in this attempt but succeeded in emphasizing the Protestant character of the Church of England.

These constitutional upheavals resulted in the position after 1660 that the monarch indeed continued to be the Supreme Governor of the Church of England but in effect the ministers of the Crown (owing their power mainly to support in the Commons) gradually acquired greater authority to act in the name of the Sovereign. In the eighteenth century these politicians relied heavily upon patronage to gain or reward supporters, and the abundance of ecclesiastical offices, notably the rich See of Durham, were used as an instrument of party politics. It was easier to make any changes required in church affairs through Whig Parliaments than Tory Convocations, and in 1717 the two Convocations were suppressed. They were not abolished, however, and still went through the motions of having a separate existence under the Crown.

Behind the restoration of the two Convocations in 1852 and 1861 lay a century or more of secularizing trends. The majority of M.P.s, while remaining nominally members of the Church of England, gradually lost interest in matters concerning the mission, doctrines, or ceremonies of religion. Moreover, the fact that Jews and Catholics, Non-Conformists and (later) Atheists, could take their seats in the House of Commons attacked the traditional belief—already stretched thin—that the Lower House still constituted the assembly of the lay members of the Church of England. In particular, the awakened sensibility of the Tractarian or Anglo-Catholic wing found intolerable the decisions of Parliament in Church matters, especially on questions involving doctrine. And what ecclesiastical issues did not involve doctrine?

The revived Convocations not only met separately but they were also exclusively clerical. In order to discuss questions of importance with the laity, such as church rates, division of sees and co-operation between clergy and laity, the Church's leaders convened a Church Congress at Cambridge in 1861, which subsequently met annually in a different city. Although it lacked any legislative power the Congress served as a useful debating forum. In 1885 a House of Laymen in each Province was created, its members elected by the Diocesan Conferences. The first Diocesan Conference met in Ely Diocese in 1866, and lay members were first introduced by Bishop Moberley in Salisbury in 1871. Both Convocations and both Houses of Laymen came together in the Representative Church Council of 1904, which paved the way for the Church Assembly as established by the Enabling Act of 1919. Thanks to the energetic efforts of the Life and Liberty Movement, the new Church Assembly received a limited legislative power. Thus it marked a limited reversion to the medieval principle of an area of legislative autonomy for the Church.

The new Church Assembly consisted of 38 bishops and 251 clergy who made up the two provincial Convocations, and 357 laity elected by lay members of the diocesan conferences. Later reforms in the Convocations led to an increase of clergy, so that by 1964 the total number of 739 was composed as follows: House of Bishops 43, House of Clergy 350, and House of Laity 346. It rested upon the emergence of a compromise distinction during the pre-1919 debates between spiritual and non-spiritual matters, with the Assembly being largely limited to the latter sphere subject to the veto of Parliament. Clauses of the Enabling Act thus stipulated that any measure concerning the Church's doctrine or rites had to be accepted or rejected in the terms proposed by the House of Bishops; that the Church Assembly had no authority to define doctrine; and that nothing in its constitution should be held to diminish or detract from the powers belonging to the Convocations or the bishops. In addition the House of Bishops enjoyed the power of veto, just as the assent of the individual bishop was still required for motions carried in the diocesan conferences.

As part of the political compromise the Convocations also continued in existence, although it had been envisaged by the architects of the Church Assembly in 1916 that these ancient bodies would disappear in the 1920s. Meanwhile the Church Assembly busied itself in legislation and financial matters. It met three times a year, and on average three days out of each five-day session went on legislation: by 1930 some forty measures had been placed on the statute book.

The General Synod came into being as a result of the Synodical

Government Measure, 1969. Like the Church Assembly it consisted of the Convocations of Canterbury and York joined together in a House of Bishops and a House of Clergy, with a House of Laity added to them. The total membership of 545 was composed of 43 bishops, 251 clergy, and 251 laity. Thus the plea for a reduction in size was met. But in what other ways does the General Synod differ radically from the General Assembly? Apart from the acceptance that the laity can contribute in debates on doctrine, it is difficult to see any substantial change by scrutinizing either the constitution or the first five years of the Synod's life. Even the two Convocations maintained their separate existence.

The Chairman of the Standing Orders Committee defined its functions as follows:

a. A legislative assembly, preparing measures, canons and regulations of statutory force.

b. A liturgical body, approving forms of service, ceremonies and versions of Scripture, and dealing with matters of doctrine.

c. A financial authority, authorizing money resolutions, approving a budget and making apportionments.

d. An administrative organ, regulating the powers and composition of 'a hierarchy' of subordinate bodies and the appointment of certain of their staffs, as well as its own.

e. A deliberative forum, constitutionally empowered to express an opinion on any 'matters of religious or public interest'.

By keeping the Church Commissioners as a separate body, with clear terms of reference laid down in an Act of Parliament, the nation ensured that the Church's wealth should go directly and only towards the parish system in the form of clerical stipends and the maintenance of bishops and archdeacons. So that the General Assembly and its successor were not given the power of decision over the direction of the main central funds.

The fact that most of the money is committed anyway to the parish system leaves the General Synod with relatively minor issues of financial administration to debate rather than allocation of funds according to real policy decisions. For the major policy decision seems made and institutionalized. The General Synod's instrument in this remaining area of discretion is the Central Board of Finance, which actually pre-dates both Synod and Assembly, having been established in 1914 on the recommendation of the Archbishops' Committee on Church Finance, which reported in 1911. The decision was taken at the time by the Archbishops and a good many bishops to relate the Central Board of Finance directly to the diocesan finance boards, and not to the Representative Church Council (the two Convocations and their associated Houses of Laymen), which the bishops clearly mistrusted. The Church Assembly took over the Central Board of Finance, but an attempt to raise by appeal a Central Church Fund of £5,000,000 for it had brought in only about £250,000, and so the Board had to rely upon the dioceses for its income. (The Central Church Fund appeal of 1919, incidentally, had been initially opposed by Archbishops Davidson and Lang because they disliked the implication that a strong central organization would be set up to run the Church.) By a compromise decision one elected member from each diocese was also a member of the Central Board of Finance.

A Commission set up by the Church Assembly in 1921 reported after three years of discussion that the funds of the Ecclesiastical Commissioners should be regarded as the central treasury of the Church of England, and not devoted entirely to the stipends of clergymen:

> Unless the hands of the Commissioners are set free and their funds made available for other purposes, it will not in our opinion, be possible for the Assembly to deal successfully with the large central problems which confront it, and for which financial assistance is urgently required.

The merger between the Ecclesiastical Commissioners and Queen Anne's Bounty in 1948 was a small step in this direction. But the level of fear and distrust of centralization and bureaucracy has been high enough to prevent any merger between the Church Commissioners and the Central Board of Finance.

The official programme on the inauguration day of the General Synod (4 November 1970) declared that the opening of the first session 'starts a new era in the government of the Church', and expressed the hope that the 'renewal of church government may serve the renewal of the Church'. Sir Kenneth Grubb, the last chairman of the Church Assembly's House of Laity, commented in his autobiography *Crypts of Power* (1971):

> A change of Church government, it must be repeated, will not of itself revive the appeal and power of the Gospel, but if it proves a good

change, it may provide new opportunities if the Church and its members are spiritually alert to seize them.

Although those who have experienced membership of the old Assembly and new Synod agree that it was a 'good change', the remainder of the expectation remains to be realized. In 1972 the Standing Committee in a published report said that it

> makes no apology for its preoccupation in the past year with the need to marshal the queue of business coming before the Synod and to bring some order into it. This has been a necessary task and will continue to be so. But we are well aware that this approach to the problems of determining priorities is secondary to a much more fundamental issue with which the Synod and the Standing Committee must get to grips. The question, baldly, is whether the General Synod is simply to respond to the initiatives of others, or whether it is to set itself to the task of taking an overall view of the needs of the Church in the present age, and to determine the priorities in its own life and work in the light of its assessment of those needs.

Yet the Standing Committee still looked back with satisfaction in its report *The First General Synod* (1975), identifying only one area for improvement:

> Communication between the different levels has, so far, been the greatest single weakness in the working of the system of synodical government. Much is being done, and much more needs to be done, to remedy this.

Certainly communications can be identified as a major area for improvement in the work of the central institutions of the Church of England. In any very large organization that requires perennial attention. It is not merely a question of upwards and downwards communication between the various levels of the parish system—national, diocesan, decanal, and parochial. The General Synod and its staff exist as the centrepiece of various institutions and agencies, mostly based in London, which are expressions of the whole rather than the parts. The parts depend upon these central bodies to make possible the most effective forms of lateral communication or cross-fertilization. For example, the specialist in youth services at national level should be the person responsible for communication between diocesan staff specialists in his area, so that every diocese learns about a good development without that traditional long-time lag while the grape-vine slowly does its work.

Is the parish system as a whole static and unchanging? In this chapter I have set out to show that there are changes already happening, and an even greater potential for development in the future. The chief issue about the synodical system of government which has emerged, primarily as a reformed piece of legislative and financial mechanism, is whether or not it can sense the direction of all these changes and give an active corporate leadership to the whole parish system. In other words, will the synods and the bishops succeed in giving *purpose* a priority over *maintenance,* with all that that involves in self-imposed change? As Clifford Longley wrote in *The Times* in July 1975:

> The Archbishop of Canterbury, Dr Coggan, remarked forcefully not long ago that the Church of England was a synodic church, as well as an episcopal church; the relationship between the two had not been settled. . . . The past five years has seen almost a revolution on the episcopal benches, as a succession of new and younger men have taken their seats among the dwindling band of the old guard. They have produced a house of bishops which is talented, articulate, and vigorous. . . . But that does not mean that the question posed by Dr Coggan has been answered. Leadership is more than a matter of a good relationship with the led. It implies a corporate sense of direction as well.

6

The Pastoral Ministry

One essential ingredient in the parish system is people to do all the jobs necessary to maintain it. The people in question are of course drawn from the clergy and laity. In Chapter Three the relationship between clergy and laity was explored, and any rigid differentiation of role and functions eschewed. The clue to manning the parish system in the next thirty or forty years may well lie in modifying that traditional differentiation while retaining those valuable distinctions of vocation which are implicit in any corporate theology of the Church.

In this chapter I want to set out how this can be done, using the Church of England as a case study. The principle of 'distinction but less differentiation' may well apply in other ways to many other churches, especially those which are exposed by the institution of a married ministry to the full rigours of inflation. Perhaps the problems that inflation creates for the parish system are invitations to a new era of creativeness. Is it not fortunate that the changes which the straitened financial circumstances of the churches will make inevitable over the next two decades coincide with the emergence of the laity? But the difficulties of locating, releasing, refining, and channelling the lay resource are such as to prevent us falling into a facile optimism.

THE FULL-TIME MINISTRY

At present the main burden of running the Church of England as a parish system falls on the shoulders of the full-time professional clergy. On 1 August 1976 the broad picture of the 12,056 Church of England clergy employed in the parochial system was as follows (statistics supplied by the Church Commissioners):

Dignitaries (including 45 beneficed dignitaries)	357
Beneficed incumbents (including 148 Team Vicars and 95 Group Ministry members)	8,276
Non-beneficed clergy of incumbent status (including 309 Team Vicars)	1,019
Assistant Parochial Clergy (Curates)	2,175
Other non-parochial diocesan clergy (industrial chaplains, etc.)	229

Deployment of the Full-Time Parochial Ministry, 1 August 1976

The approximate figures for clergymen outside the parochial system are:

Chaplains (armed services, hospitals, prisons)	591
Serving overseas	1,437
Retired on pension (as at 1 July 1976)	4,155
Missionary Societies and Religious Orders	316
Employed outside the Church	776

Deployment of Non-Parochial Clergymen, 1 August 1976

The older 1971 figures issued by the Church of England's statistical unit are still of value because they could relate the number of clergymen to the number of people in the parishes.

On 31 December 1971 there were 9,591 incumbents in the Church of England (compared with 10,298 in 1965). Some 2,667 of these vicars or rectors held livings where the total population was less than 1,000 people; 928 parishes contained 10,000–20,000 inhabitants, while only 96 vicars worked in parishes of 20,000 or more, and they were supported by 261 assistant clergymen. Thus the bulk of Anglican vicars (5,844) worked singly or in teams in parishes of a population size between 1,000 and 10,000 people, with the help of 2,838 of the 3,314 assistant clergy available. It should be remembered, however, that these figures are based upon the 1961 census; there has been an overall increase of population since then from 46,196,000 to 48,854,000 in 1971, and to over 49 millions at 30 June 1976. On the basis of the 1971 figures for the existing clergy and population trends, the Statistical Unit of the Church of England forecast in 1972 that by 31 December 1974 the Church would need 16,215 parochial clergymen, i.e. 3,310 more than it possessed at that time. Since then, however, it is worth noting that the national birthrate declined sharply by about 7 per cent in 1972 and 1973.

One method of rationalizing the system—powerfully propounded in the Paul Report (1964)—would be to redeploy the clergy in terms of population. This is already happening to some extent. The 2,667 livings with populations of under 1,000 people in 1971 have already been reduced, and the activities of diocesan pastoral committees in amalgamating parishes continue apace. Moreover, diocesan bishops have agreed upon a quota system for the deployment of deacons according to their populations. But there are some sociological factors to be considered. It could be argued that the unit of a parish is not a territory but a community (in old days, with distance between villages, they could be synonymous), and that parishes cannot be therefore plotted simply by numbers. Secondly, wherever a man is placed he is not going to be able to build up a congregation beyond a certain size of perhaps two or three hundred people, and so it does not matter much if that congregation is in the midst of 900 people in a county town or 12,000 people in a city precinct—indeed, better 200 out of 900 in Little Barster than 50 out of 12,000 in Southdon, S.E.13.

But there are counter-arguments to these two points. First, it may be part of the Church's mission and ministry in contemporary society to be a bringer of community, even in situations where the possibilities of developing it seem daunting. Secondly, neither the clergyman nor his lay congregation can see their vocations solely in terms of what happens in church or amongst themselves, ignoring their environment. If they do ignore it they are possibly experiencing a counterfeit form of Christian common life. For fellowship and service are not alternatives: there can be no fellowship without service in a common task, nor can there be any true service without fellowship. Therefore the principle of relating the deployment of clergymen to the population is a sound one.

That principle, however, only tells us how to allocate or share out the number of clergymen we have. To attempt to determine the ratio of clergymen to population needed in a theoretical way would be a largely subjective and valueless exercise. So that we cannot conclude that there must be, for example, one full-time clergyman to every 10,000 or every 20,000 people. It is better to consider the total number of men available for the parochial ministry, the number of established incumbencies, the membership of the Church of England, and the national population. The first three sets of figures have been gradually falling while the latter has been slowly rising. How can the Church of England move away from its present strategy of pragmatic response to institutional decline imposed upon it by its environment towards one of preparing for a positive parish mission in the 1985 to 1995 period? Part of the answer must lie in looking through the creative perspective at the parochial ministry, opening up and developing it in a way hitherto only dreamed about. But that is not an easy answer, it must be repeated; it requires a ten per cent higher performance by everyone in the Church: bishops, diocesan staff, rural deans, parochial clergy, lay men and women.

Central to my proposed policy is the concept of a ministry team based upon the deanery territorial unit. The dean would be the leader of a ministry team in his area, which would include an average of 15 to 25 full-time clergymen in 1975–85, dropping to 5 to 15 in 1985–95. In the ten years between 1965 and 1975 the Church of England's establishment of incumbents fell by 2,000 incumbents, a staggering reduction achieved by normal retirements and the amalgamation of parishes. By 1985 the fall should be about the same, giving the dioceses a total of about 6,400 incumbents facing a population of some 50 millions in England and Wales. Obviously each incumbent must become part of a wider ministry team in the deanery, living alongside other contributors to the national pastoral work of the Church of England. Integrated into the team, for example, would be overseas clergy, semi-retired clergy, part-time ordained men, lay readers, lay professional church workers and short-service ministers. Each of these categories needs some further discussion.

OVERSEAS CLERGY

Just as the National Health Service relies upon a large body of temporary immigrant labour so the parochial system should welcome clergy from the Anglican Communion for two or three years of service. In 1971 some 1,576 clergymen ordained in England were at work or resident in other provinces and dioceses of the Anglican Communion. At any one time we should expect to find about 1,000 clergymen from the Anglican Communion at work in one capacity or another in this country.

SEMI-RETIRED CLERGY

'Retirement' is not really a New Testament word or part of the Christian idea of vocation. A true priest can no more 'retire' from his work than an artist, sculptor, or writer can. The divine compulsion is renewed, the spirit does not grow old. Of course bodies and brains do, and there are bound to be many clergymen beyond the statutory retiring age of 65 years who can do nothing but exercise their ministry through prayer. But there are a large number of clergymen who are still active. Although they may not feel able—even if called—to emulate the example of Theodore of Tarsus, who became Archbishop of Canterbury at the age of 68 years and held the office for twenty strenuous years, or Pope John XXIII, or even those two stalwart nonagenarians who still held Anglican incumbencies in 1971, they are quite capable of ensuring that a church has its own service of Holy Communion on Sundays. With a large number of semi-retired clergymen (over 2,000 in 1971) there should be no want of celebrants. Indeed we may envisage a time when every deanery maintains a house for a semi-retired clergyman, precisely so that he can contribute such a light service and continue happily within the living and active fellowship of the deanery team.

Would semi-retired clergymen welcome such opportunities? The Provost of St Edmundsbury (the Very Reverend John Waddington) led an enquiry in 1975 into the desirability of the diocese using more efficiently its active retired clergymen at a time when the number of full-time priests was diminishing. Just over half of the retired clergy in the diocese of St Edmundsbury and Ipswich replied to the questionnaire. Nearly all said that they were prepared to co-operate in a scheme whereby they could be attached to a parish or group of parishes for Sunday duty and receive a mileage allowance except when fees were payable, as during an interregnum. Of the 108 incumbents who answered a related questionnaire, only ten implied that they would not want to have the services of a retired priest at no expense to the parish. Of the others a few incumbents had reservations as to how 'active' a man might be. At the same time there was a warm welcome for the suggestion that a retired priest might regularly visit elderly people who were house-bound. The majority of the incumbents considered that payment to retired priests of a mileage allowance similar to that paid to readers should be a legitimate charge on the diocesan stipends fund. It was announced that a 'Who's Who' of retired clergy was being prepared, and rural deans and any other interested parties would be able to receive copies from the Provost. Without waiting for an official diocesan scheme some parishes are already trying out Mr Waddington's idea and providing the travelling expenses.

AUXILIARY PAROCHIAL MINISTERS

The A.P.M. as it is called should not be confused with the 'worker priest' movement of the 1950s, which was essentially a French Catholic phenomenon aimed at evangelizing the secular wastes of industrial life. The incipient theology of the laity nipped in the bud similar experiments in Protestant countries. The A.P.M. is the child of inflation. Its forerunners were the various theological programmes, notably the Southwark Ordination Course, which prepared men for the full-time ministry by a combination of evening classes and residential weekends while they continued to earn their daily bread. As inflation hit the Church of England in the 1970s bishops began to ordain men to serve in parishes while they supported themselves in secular full-time or part-time employment. The numbers of those recommended or conditionally recommended by the Church of England's selection conferences was as follows:

1970	17	1973	64
1971	31	1974	70
1972	75	1975	90

In 1974, 45 men were ordained to the auxiliary ministry, 36 of them being aged 40 years or over. Many dioceses have now set up or joined in training programmes for such men, and are quietly encouraging more vocations.

LAY READERS
Traditionally the laity have been involved in the administration of the parish church, as churchwardens, parochial church councillors and sidesmen. Within the liturgy they acted as servers and members of choirs, the latter role being opened to women and girls from about 1950 onwards. In addition there was the office of lay reader, which was (and is) essentially a preaching ministry. But it lifted the lay man or woman out of the administration level and into the strata of spiritual ministry, and so it deserves special consideration.

Shortage of ordained men fit to fill the many vacant benefices in the early years of the reign of Queen Elizabeth I led to some being held in plurality, and others not being filled for years at a time. In both cases services had to be taken and there was often no ordained man to do this. This gap in the Church of England's ministry was filled by the licensing of Readers, and Archbishop Parker's *Order for Serving Cures Now Destitute* gives the duties assigned to a Reader in some detail.

The principal incumbent was to depute a deacon 'or else some honest and grave layman who as a Lector or Reader shall give his attendance to read the Order of Service appointed: except that he shall not, being only a Reader, intermeddle with christening, marrying, or ministering the Holy Communion, or with any voluntary preaching or prophesying; but read the service of the day with the Litany and homily agreeable, as shall be prescribed, in the absence of the principal pastor or someone pastor chanceable coming to the parish for the time'.

This venture into a Lay Ministry seems to have been discontinued as a result of the religious and political troubles of the seventeenth century. It was, however, a realistic response to pastoral need and when in the nineteenth century similar problems of shortage of clergy arose, the precedent created in the sixteenth century helped to ensure that the 'Lay Reader' was restored as part of the ministry of the Church. By 1904, 2,375 men were licensed as Readers and their work and witness were responsible for the decision not to proceed with the establishment of the

minor order of sub-deacon, but instead to extend and regulate the office
of Reader.

An extract from the report of the Joint Committee of the Convoca-
tion of Canterbury (1904) explains the circumstances which forced the
Church to expound the responsibilities laid upon licensed laymen. The
Reader's services were urgently required

> in country parishes where two or more churches are held by one in-
> cumbent. Under the present conditions of clerical incomes we foresee
> that such cases are likely to grow more frequent, and the difficulty of
> meeting them with our present resources more serious. For the
> temper of our country people makes them cling persistently to their
> own buildings and their own immediate surroundings. If a church in
> a hamlet is shut, they will often cease to attend public worship at all
> or go to a Non-Conformist Chapel, rather than attend another
> church than their own. It is important that while an incumbent is
> engaged in one of his churches, Morning or Evening Prayer, or such
> other services as a Reader may take, be said in the other (p. 77).

In these circumstances the Reader was permitted to read all of Morning
and Evening Prayer, except the Declaration of Absolution, in either a
consecrated or an unconsecrated building. The Reader also under the
Bishop's Licence was to be allowed to preach, though it was envisaged
that licence to preach in a consecrated building would only be given
with great caution. These licences were, in fact, granted on a wide scale
and the ministry of Readers played a vital role in all dioceses. By 1921 it
became necessary to think in terms of an Office of Reader as one which
needed regulation on a national scale and a Central Readers' Board was
set up on the recommendation of a Joint Committee of Canterbury and
York Convocations.

By 1937 there were 4,381 Readers licensed in the Church of England
and shortages of clergy and money to pay them continued to press the
Church towards further extensions of the content of the Reader's
ministry. A joint committee of the Convocations of Canterbury and
York reporting in 1938 urged that the Reader should be allowed, in
exceptional circumstances, to administer the cup and read the Epistle at
the Holy Communion service. Perhaps not the least contribution made
by this committee was its clear assertion of the Reader's having a contribution of his own to make as layman to the total ministry of the
Church. It was the first authoritative rejection of the earlier presupposi-

tion that the Reader would, of the nature of things, be someone called in only in the event of there being no clergyman available.

In 1969 the Reverend B. D. A. Spurry carried out a research study at St George's House, Windsor, into the attitudes and role of Licensed Readers in one diocese, with a comparative investigation in half of another diocese—a total of some 300 Readers.

Only 22 per cent of those who completed the questionnaire expressed or implied that they were satisfied with the current situation. 78 per cent in one way or another had criticisms to make. There were no special 'pockets of discontent'. It was expressed in all age groupings and professional groupings. The main discontent was with the status still being assigned to the Office of Reader as a 'stop-gap' ministry. A high percentage complained that they were openly regarded by clergy, churchwardens, and people in the pew as a regrettable necessity and were valued only in as much as they were able to 'fill in' when a 'proper' minister was not available by reason of sickness, holidays, interregnum, or shortage of staff in a parish. This image they rejected as one which belonged to the past. They insisted that the ministry they exercised as laymen was vital and significant and deserving of recognition in itself. . . .

The second major criticism was directed at the limitation placed upon Readers who were licensed to a particular parish under a particular incumbent. Supervision was seen by all to be desirable and many paid tribute to their incumbents and the use they made of their Readers. At the same time many parishes in desirable residential areas tended to accumulate a number of capable Readers, who were not being used as widely as they might have been because such parishes often were those best able to pay for the services of full-time assistant clergy. There were areas in which the services such Readers could supply would be invaluable. Yet the extent to which they were actually used depended upon others learning of their availability and making an approach for their services through the incumbent. The situation of being dependent upon the incumbent in exercising a ministry was particularly frustrating where the Reader found himself with an incumbent who did not wish to share his ministry with lay-helpers, or was of a theological persuasion that was plainly in opposition to his own.

One solution often suggested is that a permanent Diaconate should be created, which would give the present Reader a status within the hierarchy of the Church's ministry. It would be chiefly a preaching and teaching ministry, but might include welfare and administrative Church workers. Yet Mr Spurry's findings did not support such a course:

> The evidence of my survey is that this would not be the best way forward as far as the Readers themselves are concerned. Just over 5 per cent of those who were dissatisfied with the present state put forward this as a possible solution. 9 per cent thought in terms of training as Auxiliary Priests. Over 15 per cent made a positive statement of the value they set upon their witness as laymen speaking to laymen:

> 'We are Lay Ministers not Imitation Clergymen.'

> 'Readers are ready-made link men with the man in the street.'

> 'We are not "stop gaps" . . . substitutes for the clergy, but . . . have a special and complementary ministry.'

> 'The essential lay character of the Reader Ministry must be maintained.'

> 'A Reader's main witness is in his everyday secular work.'

> 'A specifically lay witness . . . should be one of the greatest assets of a Reader.'

> 'Essentially Readers must be *Lay* Readers not second-class clergymen.'

> 'It would be a pity to remove Readers from their instant identification with the "world" by making them into Deacons.'

> 'A Reader's value and strength to his Church should be that he is truly a Layman and remains such.'

These quotations highlight the convictions Readers have that the ministry they exercise has its value as a lay contribution and that the Church would be the poorer if it were hived off into an order of the ordained ministry about which most churches seem to be confused. In 1975 there were 6,328 men and 263 women licensed as lay Readers. Clearly it is a matter of vital importance that their ministry is fully recognized and effectively deployed.

There is no doubt that the Church of England has neglected the potential of the office of lay Reader. Canon T. G. King, writing in *Readers: A Pioneer Ministry* (1973), the best modern book on the subject, concludes with this 'new vision' of the parish system manned primarily by voluntary ministers:

It must be remembered, however, that Readers are a lay ministry, and that their functions are limited to the Ministry of the Word. To provide the full ministry of both Word and Sacraments in any parish requires at least a priest. This means that paid clergy will have to be replaced either by large numbers of voluntary priests, or that the duties of Readers will have to be extended in some cases to include the sacramental duties of priests.

It will be claimed that there is nothing new in this main proposal, for the Church has already embarked upon a policy of ordaining men to serve as voluntary priests. This is true, but it needs to be emphasized that it has not seen these as entirely, or almost entirely, replacing the professional clergy, but only as a supplement to them, so that full-time paid clergy would remain the normal ministerial provision for most churches. It is doubtful whether in the face of the accelerating inflation of these days the Church will really have the money to implement such a policy. . . .

If the parishes were maintained mostly by voluntary ministers, the job of the professional clergy who remained would change radically, and amongst their main functions would be the seeking out, training, both intellectually and practically, and organizing of voluntary ministers. This they would do over a wide area, and so would function very much as supervisors and fathers-in-God. Such a change in policy would also rapidly free the Church from excessive money-raising and enable it to concentrate upon an outward-looking ministry.

Canon King saw the possibility that lay Readers might be commissioned to administer Holy Communion during the intervening period before this voluntary unpaid ministry—which the Readers in their long history have indeed pioneered—emerges in sufficient numbers. For my part I see the deanery pastorate of the future, headed by a dean with a core of full-time men and women about him, and included in the team both auxiliary priests in charge of small churches and also lay Readers, suitably licensed, acting as pastors in neighbouring churches with the help of a semi-retired priest. The deanery of tomorrow will thus show a variety of forms of the pastoral ministry, depending upon the gifts or talents that are available.

LAY PROFESSIONAL CHURCH WORKERS
The Church Army, Anglican religious orders, deaconesses, lay and

social workers all contribute to the ministry of the Church of England in diocese and parish. Their numbers are comparatively small:

	1972	1974
Church Army Captains	189	187
Church Army Sisters	162	133
Deaconesses (full-time)	94	93
(part-time)	24	23
Women Lay Workers (full-time)	241	238
(part-time)	128	75
Social Workers (excluding Church Army Sisters and Members of Religious Communities) (full-time)	204	155
(part-time)	59	58
	1,101	962

Professional Lay Workers (Church of England)—1972 and 1974

Of course not all of these are deployed in the parishes. Many run hostels or homes of one kind or another. But even a few hundreds constitute an important source of ministry in the parishes. Again I suggest that they should be based upon the deanery rather than the parish, so that the particular gifts are used in the most flexible way possible.

A SHORT-SERVICE MINISTRY

An experiment which might be worth trying, however, would be the ordination of young men and women to the diaconate for a two-year period rather along the lines of the Voluntary Service Overseas or Peace Corps programmes. Four months of that time would be spent in training, and the rest in a parish. At the end of the two years the young men or women would take up their secular careers. Certainly the experience of the British Army with the national service and short-service officers who passed through Eaton Hall and Mons Officer Cadet Training Unit in the 1950s and 1960s has overwhelmingly confirmed the value and feasibility of such a programme. Indeed its success has brought about some major changes in the training of regular officers in the early 1970s, including the shortening of the traditional Sandhurst two-year course.

By 1980 there could be some 500 young men and women holding temporary orders as deacons. It should be part of their terms of service that they should serve their 20 months in whatever parish they are directed. Consequently many of them will work in the parishes which exhibit the worst symptoms of social decay and lost opportunities.

SUMMARY

Various trends in the complex process of secularization have conspired to work against the laity playing a full share in the theological and spiritual life of all the churches at their various levels, or—more accurately—to slow down the process leading towards such participation. For example, the move in the Church of England towards a more sacramental stance cuts down the need for lay Readers and Sunday School teachers. Moreover, the tendency of the clergy to see themselves as a profession leads many to regard the potential lay contribution as amateur or second-rate. (The same process can be observed in social work since about 1960, when professionalism set in.)

Thus the ordained Christian is pushed towards becoming more a professional individual like his lay middle class counterpart. He rarely sees himself as essentially the leader of a team of lay pastors or ministers. He finds fellowship with other professional individuals in his own and other churches. Meanwhile the lay Christian also becomes more professional, in that his service to his neighbour is usually paid work done through his job. He feels less involved in the spiritual, pastoral, or social work of his parish or locality, leaving that to the ordained or lay professionals.

All these trends have to be deflected into more fruitful directions. The concept of the deanery ministry group or team, each person with an individual area of responsibility, is already on the way. Already also there is a growing sense that auxiliary forms of lay ministry, so potentially rich, have yet to be called into existence in the quantity and quality that the situation of the 1980s will require.

What matters most about the ordained and lay ministry in the parishes is not its quantity but its quality. There is a strong vocation from God which draws a person to respond to the needs of the Church through the old but ever new functions of the pastoral ministry. We cannot turn back from the provision of a full-time ministry. It is vital, however, that the smaller number of Anglican clergy in the 1980s, as in all churches, should be well led, wisely deployed and generously supported. Provisions to these ends should be set in motion now: tomorrow is too late. For the ordained ministry is perhaps the most precious human resource possessed by any church. It is a time for creative thought and experiment. The churches have a comforting range of options open to them, but they require hard thought and research. Like the steward in the parable, the Church of England will only be condemned if it does nothing to increase the spiritual returns on that most valuable resource of all—the working lives and daily time of its best servants.

7

Church Leadership

From the preceding chapters it is plain that the Church requires good leadership if it is to do its work effectively. At a time when the parish system in all churches is coming under strain its spiritual and practical agenda is increasing: there is more to do with less resources to do it. Moreover, the turbulence of the environment, coupled with the all-pervading mist of a continuing secularization, creates its own problems for the churches and can lower morale. It also opens up sites of opportunity, if only we have leaders—lay and clerical—who are able to see and respond as architects, builders, and stonemasons of new initiatives. Thus the Church needs leaders as perhaps never before in its history. But what is leadership?

THE NATURE OF LEADERSHIP

Three major theories about the nature of human leadership can be fruitfully distinguished. The first of these, and by far the most commonly held, may be called the *qualities* approach. According to this theory men and women are either born with the silver spoon of leadership in their mouths, or not, with the corollary that those who possess the inborn or inherent qualities of a leader will naturally emerge as the head of any group in which they are placed, regardless of the situation. They are born to lead.

The earliest research workers in this field tended to share this assumption that leadership consisted of a certain pattern of inherited or acquired personality traits, and therefore they set about trying to produce a definitive list of qualities. Much to their surprise they found very little agreement among the legions of writers upon the topic. Each list seemed to be subjective, telling the reader more about the author's own temperament and beliefs than about leadership. For example, in *Social Psychology*, Professor C. Bird in 1940 looked at twenty-two experimental studies on leadership and found that only 5 per cent of the qualities appeared in four or more of the studies. In fact there was a bewildering number of trait names from which the student of leadership could make up his portfolio. Two researchers in 1936 listed some

17,000 adjectives for human personality.

The lack of agreement among research students has contributed much to the present tendency towards dismissing altogether the personality and character of the leader from all discussions on leadership. Yet we do know that leaders tend to possess and exemplify the qualities which are required in their working groups. Courage, for example, may not make you a military leader, but you cannot be one without it. There is also an impressive testimony, not least from world authorities on management such as Professor Peter Drucker, that *integrity* is a core quality of good leadership. Lord Slim defined integrity as 'the quality which makes people trust you'. And trust is in short supply today, not least within the churches.

Applying the qualities approach to the Church we could say simply that leaders in the Church—ordained or lay—should personify the qualities of a Christian. This is clearly the approach taken in the New Testament. They should be men and women of faith, hope, and love, with warm hearts, clear minds, and compassionate hands. Above all they should convey the ethos of the gospel in their own lives: in morality above suspicion and firm in spirit. They should be good listeners simply because all Christians ought to be good listeners. But these characteristics will not in themselves make a person a leader in the Church.

A second general theory about leadership may be called the *situational* approach. Those who held it believed that whoever became the leader in a small group depended upon the situation in which it found itself, including the task immediately confronting it. Professor W. Jenkins, an investigator who reviewed 74 studies in leadership in the *Psychological Bulletin,* (vol. xliv, 1947), concluded:

> Leadership is specific to the particular situation under investigation. . . . [There are] wide variations in the characteristics of individuals who become leaders in similar situations and even greater divergences in leadership behaviour in different situations. . . . The only common factor appeared to be that leaders in a particular field need and tend to possess superior general or technical competence or knowledge in that area.

But there are drawbacks also to this 'Admirable Crichton' theory as we could call it. It is unsatisfactory in any group for leadership to change hands like a football passed from 'expert' to 'expert'. Secondly, further research has shown that technical knowledge, important though it is, does not qualify a man to lead. We all know 'experts' who are useless as leaders.

A third theory or approach may be called the *functional* understanding of leadership. The best way to grasp it is to look for a moment at the *needs* present in the life of any small group. First, we may discern the *task need,* that is the necessity experienced by the group to achieve the purpose for which it has come together, its *raison d'être.* Secondly, there is the need for group cohesiveness, for social harmony, partly as an essential requirement for the completion of the task and partly as an end in itself. This we may call the *group* or *team-maintenance need.* Thirdly, there is an area of need present in the life of a group which springs from the lives of the individuals who compose it. Many of these *individual needs* are met through participation in small groups: the needs for status, recognition, and worthwhile work, are three examples.

These areas affect each other. To look at it negatively, if there is a group which does not achieve its task, then this will affect the team maintenance area. Disruptive tendencies may increase, morale will go down, and individual work satisfaction will also be affected. If the personal relationships within a group are bad, this affects the performance of the task, and again it will affect the individual members. Conversely, if a group achieves its task, then morale rises and the personal welfare of individual members is enhanced. Thus, for good or ill, the three areas overlap and interact upon each other. This relationship can be illustrated by the simple model of three circles, thus:

Interaction of Needs

In order that these needs may be met, certain *functions* have to be performed by the leader. In relation to the task, for example, he has to define it clearly, make a plan, allocate work to individuals, control work on the job, and evaluate the performance. In team maintenance, the leader has to set or maintain standards of discipline. Discipline in this sense can be best understood as the invisible bonds which bind a group together. He has to encourage. He has to reconcile any differences which may threaten to diminish the harmony and the working efficiency of that group as a team. For the individual, he has to be aware of any particular problem which may affect the work of a member on the common task and his relationships with others in the group.

The degree to which the leader shares these functions with members of his group varies according to the organization and its purposes. But some degree of participation must happen in groups of more than three of four people, for there are just too many functional contributions required in the three areas of need for any one person to provide them all. A senior leader may cope with this fact by delegating an entire function, such as the training function. Or he may treat each function as a cake and share its inherent decision-making requirements in different proportions with group members, according to such varied factors as their knowledge and experience, the philosophy of the organization as a whole concerning people, his own personality and the constraints imposed by the actual situation. And so the *situation* still exerts an influence on the relationship of leader and group members.

Leaders are never the same: they always possess a unique personality and character, a distinctive way of doing things and sometimes a particular flair which they only half understand themselves. Moreover, leadership is an aspect of human relationships, and it therefore cannot escape the mystery which perhaps characterizes all inter-personal life. Yet we can confidently generalize that a leader tends to be: (i) a particular sort of person (*qualities*); (ii) one possessing knowledge both about the given technology and also more general knowledge and experience of how people work together as partners in common enterprises (*situation*); one who (iii) is able to provide the necessary functions to enable the group or organization to achieve its task and to be maintained as a working unity (*functional*), and to do this (iv) in the right ratio or proportion with the contributions of other members of the group or organization. This portmanteau sentence can never be a definition, but it does highlight some of the features which appear to be common to the practice of leadership in a wide spectrum of working spheres.

Such an understanding would win the assent of a social psychologist, but it leaves out the important dimension of moral values. The general word most often used to indicate this dimension in the mind and character of the leader is integrity, which means moral probity as well as wholeness or integration. The importance of integrity in the field of human relations at work is testified by the definition of it already given as 'the quality which makes people trust you'. One only has to reflect upon the symptoms of lack of trust between management and employees in the sphere of industrial relations to realize how vital is integrity to any understanding of the leadership needed in contemporary society. Without trust, which is the by-product of integrity, the social science of leadership collapses into an armoury of gimmicks, alternately adopted and discarded by cunning, cynical, or confused men.

But trust has to be two-way. Dr Max Warren, former secretary of the Church Missionary Society, described in his autobiography how he found out early in life that Christian leadership is 'the acceptance of responsibilities on the one hand, and on the other a complete trust in the capacity of others in the same team to be responsible—to be ready to let others, in their several fields of activity, be themselves leaders'. Things could get done if he inspired other people and remained always ready to learn from them.

SOME NEW TESTAMENT IMAGES

In social science various models of leadership, organization and communication have been advanced, such as the author's diagram of the overlapping three circles. A visual diagram such as that one can be invaluable, because—as the Chinese proverb says—'a picture is worth a thousand words'. In the New Testament the same truths are conveyed by word pictures or images. There are two such pictures which are especially important for a Christian understanding of leadership: the images of the *shepherd* and the *servant*. In their Latin forms these have come down to us in the descriptions of the Church leader as a *pastor* and *minister*.

In the course of time the pastoral image has shrunk in significance, so that it is used now mainly to describe the clergyman's activity of responding to the needs of individuals. But the picture of the shepherd and his flock suggested much more to the inhabitants of Palestine in the first century A.D.

First, the shepherd would have to lead his flock on a journey of up to twenty miles a day in search of sparse vegetation for grazing.

Characteristically he would walk in front of the flock, literally leading them in the right direction. Thus the 'sheep' of Psalm 23 sings of his shepherd: 'He leads me beside still waters'. It is difficult for us to imagine this aspect of a shepherd's work, accustomed as we are to seeing fat white sheep grazing in hedged green fields or fenced hillsides. But when I lived in Jordan, as adjutant of a Bedouin regiment in the Arab Legion during 1954, I can well remember meeting such shepherds in the dry riverbeds and stony hills between the Dead Sea and the mountains of Judaea. The urgent task of leading the flock to the next pasture was ever present to such semi-nomadic herdsmen in the time of Jesus.

Secondly, the shepherd maintained the unity of the flock. This would often include both sheep and goats, doubtless a source of considerable inner squabbles which the shepherd would have to resolve. Moreover, the stealthy approach at night of a predator such as a wolf or jackal, or the sudden rush in daytime of human raiders from another tribe, could scatter the flock. The good shepherd kept his flock together, maintaining its unity at night by watching over the gate in the dry-stone wall of the fold. Having spent nights alone in the hills near the Dead Sea, where hyenas still prowl, and seen the armed shepherds ready to defend their flocks, I can well appreciate this aspect of a shepherd's work in the hill country of Jordan.

Thirdly, the shepherd cares for the individual sheep. He calls them by name; that is, he knows them as individuals, each with a particular idiosyncrasy. He washes their cuts or sores, and dresses them with oil. He makes sure that an individual sheep has its share of water and food. His stick and weapons give each a sense of security. The good shepherd will risk his life to save a sheep; he will search the gullies and ravines to find the lost and trapped stray.

Besides possessing the character needed to face the dangers of the open country, and the love or attachment which springs from ownership as opposed to the lesser interest of a wage-earning hireling, the shepherd needed to be proficient in the technical skills of his occupation. Knowledge and experience, gained through family conversation and apprenticeship and long days spent in the hills, equipped him to be a shepherd. It is interesting that the Greek word for 'good' in the sentence 'I am the good shepherd' is *kalos* and not *agathos,* meaning skilful or expert rather than good in the moral sense.

An obvious limitation of the pastoral image, however, is that the shepherd is human and personal while the sheep are animals, having nothing to contribute to the three areas of the journey-task, the maintenance of cohesive unity, or the meeting of individual needs. Historically the laity have been identified as the sheep in the image. Consequently it has bred a passive attitude in the lay people of the Church, a dependence upon the appointed pastor seen also as the father figure of an infant family.

Yet this deficiency in the pastoral parable of leadership is perhaps corrected in the New Testament by the juxtaposition of the *servant* image. When Jesus took basin and towel to wash the dusty feet of his disciples, thus symbolically meeting their individual needs, he made it clear that he was doing it as an example so that they too would act in response to each other's needs.

The essence of service lies in the meeting of human needs. In the foot-washing incident the need in question was a minor physical one. But the New Testament invites us to extend the principles to include the major individual needs, such as the needs for food and drink, safety, personal acceptance, and friendship, to name but a few. Moreover, by a further extension, the Christian disciple experienced the constraint of Christ's example to meet the team maintenance needs of the Church as a whole, rather than its individual members. As Jesus maintained the unity of the Twelve when they split into two factions over who should occupy the best positions in heaven, so the Christian leaders 'edified' or built up the Church, for example, by reconciling the potential disunity of Jewish and Gentile converts.

The foot-washing episode may be construed as an invitation to the disciples to share in the work of meeting the task needs of the new community. Certainly the existence and nature of such a task would have been opaque to them at the time, if only because they were caught up in the emotional distress of losing a man whom they had come to love. Moreover, the foot-washing action would not have made the point so clearly about sharing in the common task as it did concerning the response to individual needs. Only a leaping spark of creative thought would connect a slave's service to feet of flesh with a leader's contribution to the purpose and movement of Christ's 'Body', the Church.

According to St John's Gospel, Jesus had foreseen this particular shortcoming in the servant image and supplemented it with a much warmer and larger vision of his relation to the Christian follower-leaders: 'No longer do I call you servants, for the servant does not know what his master is doing; but I have called you friends, for all that I have heard from my Father I have made known to you. You did not choose me, but I chose you and appointed you that you should go and bear fruit and that your fruit should abide; so that whatever you ask the Father in my name, he may give it to you. This I command you, to love one another.'

Besides its possible equation of leadership with the meeting of task, group maintenance and individual needs, the foot-washing incident speaks to us about the *status* of a leader within the Christian frame of reference. In contrast to the civil and religious leaders of his day—lording it over their subjects, dressed in rich purple clothes and occupying the special seats at social gatherings—Jesus held up the image of a slave naked to the waist, kneeling in a lowly manner, obedient to the will of his master, and without position of honour or hope of earthly glory.

This teaching of Jesus about the status of a leader must have seemed absurd to the upper classes of the day, just as it has proved to be 'impracticable' to many leaders, both civil and ecclesiastical, in the later Christian centuries. Yet there is some evidence that only such a leadership will work with people. There is something in us all which responds to the quiet and essentially humble leader, who possesses an inner sense of dignity in whatever circumstances he finds himself.

One translation of a saying by Lao-tzu, who is thought to have lived in China during the sixth century B.C., suggests that other men of insight in the ancient world had observed that only leadership offered in the form and spirit of a servant is truly acceptable to mature human nature:

A leader is best
When people barely know that he exists,
Not so good when people obey and acclaim him,
Worst when they despise him.
'Fail to honour people,
They fail to honour you';
But of a good leader, who talks little,
When his work is done, his aim fulfilled,
They will all say, 'We did this ourselves'.

Taken together, the images of the leader as *shepherd* and *servant* complement each other. The activity of a good shepherd in leading his sheep in the right direction, maintaining the integrity of the flock and caring for its individual members, gives us a functional understanding of Church leadership. But standing alone the pastoral model can engender the assumption that the followers—in this case the laity—are a flock of sheep, walking lumps of mutton. The servant image, however, exemplified in the foot-washing incident, stresses the fully personal nature of the followers, and invites them to participate in the work of leadership by performing the functional activities essential to the progress and unity of the group. This work the disciples were to do in the spirit of Jesus as he knelt to wash the dust of the day's journey from their feet.

LEADERSHIP IN THE PARISH SYSTEM

Comparing the parish system with any other organization, bishops and clergy clearly occupy the role of leadership. In this respect they are in the same role as officers in an army, managers in a business or senior officials in the trade union movement. May I repeat that the 'parish' originally encompassed parishes and dioceses, so that parish system is a comprehensive term for the whole lot. The word 'diocese' itself comes from the Greek verb meaning to keep house, or to manage, administer or govern. The Greek *oikos,* a house, which gives us the middle letters of our word, links 'diocese' with such cousins as 'economy' and 'ecumenical'. These latter terms also centre upon the image of the large household in the Graeco-Roman world. The word bishop, an English version of the Latin *episcopus,* descends from the Greek name for one who literally 'watches over'—an overlooker or overseer.

The origins of episcopacy as the chief method of governing the parish system are far from clear. The Acts and Epistles refer both to 'elders' (*presbyteroi*) and overseers (*episkopoi*), sometimes implying a distinction between them and sometimes a common identity. Certainly the early development of the Church was not neat or tidy, and some time elapsed before the three-fold orders of bishops, presbyters or priests, and deacons emerged into the light of history. We can only speculate about how it happened, but the fact that it happened is indisputable.

Doubtless a major factor in the evolutionary story was the deaths of the apostles in the closing decades of the first century A.D. It would be natural if the need was felt for a small group of men—smaller than the widely dispersed elders and deacons—to move into the psychological gap left by their passing. It would be equally natural if the apostles, either corporately or individually, made some provision for their successors by selecting and training suitable men. All good leaders take such steps. These successors may have been found among the general body of presbyters and deacons, or they may have been selected from the younger men who were attracted or drawn to working directly with the apostles as personal assistants. Owing to the egalitarian nature of the Church, however, such nominees would still have to win acceptance from the congregations, even in the areas which looked upon that particular apostle as their founding father.

The authority of this second generation of senior (not necessarily in age) leadership could not duplicate that of the apostles. The authority of the disciples comprised the three strands in a unique degree: they had been *chosen* by Jesus personally; they possessed a direct *knowledge* of him as personal companions and eyewitnesses; and, thirdly, their *personalities* had been enthused by the Holy Spirit at Pentecost. At best the authority of successors could reflect that unrepeatable authority of the disciples. They could be *chosen* by those whom Jesus had chosen, or be presented as such. They could receive by communication the *knowledge* or tradition concerning Jesus. And they could be men who exemplified the graces or fruits of the Holy Spirit in their *characters* and domestic lives. Hence, while still falling short of the apostolic standing, a bishop came to be seen as a person in the Church who did or should possess the most authority which could be expected in a Christian leader, and who had a universally accepted right to exercise leadership within a particular geographical area.

BISHOPS AS LEADERS

The bishop of an English diocese has international, national, and regional responsibilities, besides his work as a diocesan bishop. The international aspect of his role is deeply rooted in the traditional belief that he is primarily a bishop of the whole Church. If we accept that there is something called the whole Church, which is more than the sum of its individual parts or churches, then it is understandable that bishops should be responsible for promoting or maintaining the unity of this whole. How they do this when only the idea exists and not the reality is another matter. But the office of a bishop commits him to contributing to the task, team maintenance and individual needs of the whole Church as a universal phenomenon.

Thus he should have a world-vision of the purpose of the Church, and become involved with all other bishops in working out how to serve it more effectively. His understanding of the unity of the Church should rest upon a vision which is universal in scope, and his pastoral care for needy individuals should be aroused by suffering in the remotest corner of the earth. 'Will you shew yourself gentle, and be merciful for Christ's sake to poor and needy people, and to all strangers destitute of help?', he is asked by the consecrating archbishop. 'I will so shew myself, by God's help', he answers.

Consequently the bishop may sometimes be a corrective to the various ills of particularism such as afflict the body of the Church. There is a tendency for congregations, deaneries, and dioceses to become entirely parochial in their thinking. Families, tribes, and nations naturally tend to care for their own poor and sick first, and to preach the virtue of a charity which begins and ends at home. The family assumptions of the Church and its close alliance with the natural family may lead some members to urge a similar policy in the name of Christ, and the bishop as a universal shepherd has to stand out against this attitude. His three-fold concern is not limited to a particular Church or Communion, still less to his given district. He leads the diocese in its relation to the universal Church; he walks and speaks in the diocese as the representative and spokesman of the whole Church.

The national responsibilities of the bishop spring from his universal and local positions. It is natural for bishops in a nation to associate together both to take decisions at a national (or provincial) level touching the Church, and also to negotiate with or influence the rules of the state. Taking into account the relation of Church and world in the theological apprehension of God's purpose, it would be difficult to separate these two aspects of the national episcopal role, even in theory. In practice they are even more confused by the legacy in England that Church and State are but the two faces of the same coin—the community of England under one earthly Head. Attenuated though it may have been by the rising tide of secularization, together with the pluralities of Christian denominations and the import of other religious faiths, there is still a good deal of reality in the concept. It is symbolized by the method of appointing bishops in the Church of England, and by the presence of the bench of bishops in the House of Lords.

These larger responsibilities, however, should not disguise the fact that the bulk of a bishop's time is spent in his diocese. The idea of a bishop without a geographically-defined area of responsibility strikes us as odd these days, although it was not so in the Middle Ages when bishops acted as senior civil servants. Both the Pope and the Archbishop of Canterbury have remained diocesan bishops, and therefore we may conclude that a territorial responsibility belongs essentially to the office of a bishop. The needs of his diocese for his leadership and personal company stand at the head of a diocesan bishop's list of commitments.

The role of the diocesan bishop is central because all other jobs undertaken by ordained ministers in the diocese relate to it in some way or other. The diocesan remains actively responsible for the functions set out above, but he has to share his leadership with other ministers. Their work is an extension of his 'cure', as in the case of an incumbent, or else supplementary to it. Besides sharing in his general pattern of functions, albeit at a lower level or in a more limited district, or specializing in one of them, the ordained minister naturally participates in the bishop's sense of responsibility.

Originally the word suffragan meant a bishop considered in relation to the archbishop or metropolitan, by whom he might be summoned to attend synods and give his suffrage. The word suffrage in this context meant not only support or assistance in a general sense but also the giving of votes. Thus all diocesans were bishops suffragan to the metropolitical or archiepiscopal sees. By the late medieval period, however, the phrase also described a bishop appointed to assist a diocesan bishop in a particular part of his diocese. Thus some English towns were first sees (or seats) of suffragans in the Middle Ages, such as Horsham and Lewes. By virtue of his episcopal orders a suffragan bishop should have some regional, national, and international concerns and responsibilities. In practical terms this means that he will be absent from his particular part of the diocese for a percentage of his time. But his main task is to exercise episcopal leadership in his area, and that responsibility entails helping the clergy and laity to plan together in terms of their common task.

LEADERSHIP AND PLANNING

Three men were travelling together in a railway compartment:

> The first sat with his back to the engine watching the trees and fields receding into the distance and thinking about the course of events which had brought him where he was. The second, facing the engine, saw the landscape grow and flash by while he considered the object of his journey and what he was going to do.
> The third man said 'This is a very comfortable compartment; it is very gratifying to travel first class.'

This parable which appeared in *Sociology, Theology and Conflict* (1969) was written by Bernard Babington Smith, lately Senior Lecturer in Experimental Psychology and Fellow of Pembroke College at Oxford University, to whom I owe the valuable distinction between purpose, aims, and objectives as advanced in this chapter and discussed more fully in my book *Training for Decisions* (1971). Mr Babington

Smith suggested that *planning* has a quite different significance for the backward-looking and forward-looking passengers:

> If one faces the past and thinks in terms of cause and effect, planning becomes a matter of considering the possible courses of action. Thus a determinist planner must produce the possible sequences of events flowing from the present state. He may assess the value or desirability of the various possible outcomes, and it will be for someone to choose which to try to follow (whatever such choice can mean to a determinist).
>
> Another way of planning, one which I should like to associate with a forward-facing outlook, may be derived by expanding ideas put forward earlier. If one 'faces the engine' one cannot deal in terms of facts or events, but must accustom oneself to using symbols, and principles and generalizations. On this basis planning takes on a distinctive character. Facing forwards one can state the principles or standards which will guide one's actions towards an objective. The resulting planning will be more like navigating by compass or stars than like following an A.A. route.
>
> If these two types of planning, both of which may be encountered in ordinary life, are typical of travelling with one's back to the engine or facing it respectively, what about the man whose concern is in the present? I suggest that for such people planning is uncongenial and unfamiliar, and that it is among such that are those who, when things go well, live for the present, but are liable to be overwhelmed in the expedients of 'crisis management' when things go wrong. By 'crisis management' I mean a state in which action is reaction to sudden and unexpected change. When there is no planning, all changes come as sudden and as unexpected . . . .
>
> In practice, of course, it may be advisable to have at one's disposal all three outlooks referred to above so that they may supplement each other. But I have observed that a man who has developed one of the three methods described may not be aware of other possibilities and may seek to persuade others to follow his example. In short, some individuals tend to face forwards and think, live and act in terms of purpose, or to face backwards and see life as an inevitable succession of effects of causes, or to think in terms of the present and of observable concomitant variation.

It is not very difficult to identify the three men in the story with different attitudes in the Church of England or any other church. Supposing, however, a church leader and his fellow members choose to face forwards, how can they break down the general task of the Church to more tangible or concrete forms? The word *task,* which has been used more than once, implies work usually imposed by a teacher or employer or by circumstance, and it has acquired the overtone of something hard or unpleasant that has to be done. In speaking about human enterprises I have found that *task* is a useful general word for the ends to which they are working, with the added advantage that it introduces the savour of necessity, the sense that this *must* be accomplished. Of course this feeling of compulsion may stem from the circumstances, as when a prisoner is compelled by his taskmaster to sew mailbags, or it may be internally generated in the mind and spirit of the individual or group, as in the cases of artistic or religious vocation where a subjective feeling of 'it must be done' possesses a person.

One way of breaking down the task or mission of the Church is to divide it into purpose, aims, and objectives—three related levels of thinking about the future:

1. *Purpose*
The word *purpose* stands for that for which anything is done or made, or for which it exists. In one of its uses *end* means much the same, as in the celebrated definition of the Scottish Catechism: 'The true end of man is to glorify God and enjoy Him for ever'. But the word *end* evokes the concepts of the temporal and spatial limits, or ending and termination, so that we can also say that death is the end of a man. Thus *end* is a very general or inclusive term, implying the final limit in time and space, in extent of influence or in range of possibility. Moreover, *end* introduces the idea that the ultimate state of anything—if only we could know it—defines for us its purpose. Yet the last state of anything in time may not coincide with the full development of it in terms of realized potentiality. Even so, the suggestion that the last state of anything discloses its true nature is a contribution to our understanding of purpose.

We need to enlarge the implication of the phrase 'last state', however, because it can suggest simply *being* or a state of satiation and rest. Yet our idea of perfection, especially where life is concerned, may necessarily include *doing*. If we think of the perfection of a bird, for example, we cannot help imagining it in flight. We must continually challenge the ancient assumption that somehow *being* has a kind of essential superiority over *doing*. We can recognize the abstract distinction between them, but in practice we cannot divide them. Does the bird carry the wings, or do the wings bear the bird?

There are two ways of talking about the purpose which the Church is there to serve, ways which can be seen as contradictory but are in fact complementary:

(i) in connection with God's purpose for the whole world—the purpose of evolving mankind, human history, or the created universe;

(ii) in terms of relationships—the love of God and man, this two-fold love being focused in the person of Christ, in whose life the Church is called to share.

Although contemporary theologians sometimes speak mainly in terms of (i) above, it can be argued that (ii) is essential to the formulation of the Church's purpose, if it is to escape the pitfalls of a secular utopianism. Equally, (ii) above without (i) can become pietistic, and the static thinking implicit in it can lead to an immobile fixed Church. Putting it another way, the Church is called to be both fully a spiritual family, its members joined to one another and to God by the bonds of love, and also a working organization with a real task to accomplish. The 'family of Christ' experience is part of what it has to share with the world; shared endeavour towards a common end is necessary to deepen and enrich the Christian fellowship.

In discussing purpose in any large corporate body it is inevitable that the language will be general and abstract. We should not expect some sacrosanct formula or arrangement of words, still less a precise academic definition. But the above two aspects would have to be present in some form or another, as guidelines or hallmarks, in any expression of the Church's purpose. Otherwise the statement would fall short of the consensus of theological reflection which each generation receives from its fathers and refines in the crucibles of its own experience.

The presence of these two essential themes and the variety of words employed, both to marry them and to convey them to others, may be illustrated by the following statement by one bishop. In 1970, at the beginning of my organizational survey of the Diocese of York, I asked the then Archbishop of York, Dr Donald Coggan, to give me his understanding of the purpose of the diocese. Unless I knew what the Diocese was trying to do and be, I explained, it would not be possible to review its organization and communications in such a way as to suggest improvements. Some days later the Archbishop sent me a brief essay, which included his understanding of that purpose set out clearly and simply as follows:

> Briefly, I would say that my vision for the Diocese in the 1970s would involve (i) such a training of the people of God in the Diocese in worship and in the knowledge of the faith as would enable them, (ii) to reach out with an infectious faith to wholly untouched or only nominally Christian people within the Diocese, and (iii) to have a world-vision of the purpose of God, with a strong conviction that they are deeply implicated in making it a reality.

It is a useful exercise for the reader to see if he can put the purpose of the Church more succinctly than this sentence by the present Archbishop of Canterbury, bearing in mind the need for the two complementary ways listed above to be present in it. But there is no one right answer. Purpose cannot be pinned down neatly in words. We need to turn it constantly before our eyes, with many reformulations and new ways of putting it, so that the light flashing from the facets of the simple truth penetrates into the depths of our minds.

2. Aims

The word *aims* signifies purpose broken down into more definite time-and-space categories. A university, for example, might have 'the promotion of learning' as its purpose; but 'to teach' and 'to research' will stand prominently in its list of aims. Thus, by specifying the activities of teaching and research, we are helped to understand *how* a university goes about its purpose. The concept of a single purpose (learning), on the other hand, helps us both to see *why* the university is engaging in those activities, and also to grasp the distinctiveness of a university in comparison to, say, a secretarial college.

The Church of England Synodical Government Measure (1969) mentioned four such areas of purpose or aims for the Church—pastoral, evangelistic, social and ecumenical. On reflection, however, this list seemed to me to be incomplete, and in my York and Chichester reports I added three other areas. By prefacing these areas with active verbs they are expressed as aims:

Worship—to offer to God worship of the highest standard possible in a given situation and worthy of the Church's knowledge of his nature.

Pastoral—to care for individuals, both within and without formal church membership, especially those in 'sickness, sorrow, or adversity'.

Evangelistic—to invite and attract nominal Christians and those untouched by Christianity to share in the Christian faith and life.

Social—to serve society in its gradual movement forwards in the pursuit of its own legitimate ends, and to relate them to the Kingdom of God.

Ecumenical—to promote the unity of the Church in prayer and action.

Financial and administrative—to make fullest use of all the resources of people, money, and materials entrusted to the diocese, not only in the cause of efficiency but also to the glory of God.

Educational—to equip each member of the Church with the knowledge and skills appropriate to his or her Christian responsibility.

3. *Objectives*

A middle-aged manager, somewhat out of physical condition, went on a residential course in the Lake District. At the beginning of a path leading up a hillside towards a mountain he complained to the instructor that he could never ascend it. 'Look at that gate up there', came the reply, 'do you think you can make it to there?' 'Yes', the manager answered. 'Right, let's get there first, and then decide if we can tackle the next stretch.' Some months after the course the instructor received a letter from the manager, in which he wrote:

> The mountain climb really magnified the most important point for me. At one point on the climb I did not think I was going to make it, so as you suggested I looked just a few yards ahead and not at the mountain top; that objective did not seem so hard to achieve. That climb is a constant reminder to me now in all the jobs I do at work.

This story illustrates a general human need in all groups or organizations to break down aims into the more limited *objectives*, which are sufficiently distant to challenge us and yet near enough to encourage our easily-daunted efforts. An objective is a highly definite goal or target in time-and-space, a concrete incarnation of purpose and aim. The images of the archery *target* and the football *goal* remind us of the characteristics of an objective: it is within sight, it can be touched, and there is instant feedback of results, for you can see whether or not the arrow thuds into the coloured canvas face of the target or the ball finds the back of the goal net. As the mental aptitudes of most people tend towards the concrete, visible, and proximate in terms of time and space, it is natural for them to enjoy the pursuit of short or medium term goals rather than to contemplate the abstractions already mixed with aims and still more with any statement of purpose.

Of course not all the work of a Christian enterprise—or any organization for that matter—can be expressed in terms of objectives. Yet this is not an argument against having *some* objectives. The setting of some such goals or targets in order to achieve more fully each of the seven aims, and other aims which may now emerge, can have tonic effects upon both the leader and the local Christian community. This enhancement of the quality and direction of work in fields which lend themselves to the setting of objectives may overflow into other areas which are less amenable to such planning.

Purpose, aims, and objectives are not separate entities, but they should fit inside each other like a nest of tables. Or, to change the analogy, they are a Jacob's Ladder which enables a group to reason downwards or upwards from the general to the particular. The first movement (downwards) helps to answer the question *how?—How* are we going to achieve this purpose? Answer: By pursuing these aims. Then, How are we going to pursue this aim? Answer: By accomplishing these objectives. The second movement (upwards) enables us to answer the question *Why?*—Why ought we to tackle this objective? Answer: In order to do something about this aim. And why this aim? In order to fulfil the purpose of which it is one element, facet or area.

LEADERSHIP AND APPRAISAL

In all kinds of groups and organizations objectives or standards tend to be established, and the subsequent performance reviewed in the light of them. For a person working on his own, such as an artist or writer, both these processes can be carried out internally. Having grasped his purpose and explored his aims, the artist can decide what his next piece of work will be. Moreover, he will learn to appraise his performance against his own high standards. But even artists or writers find it useful to discuss their plans with others, and to learn from the comments of fellow artists about their work. For those who are working with others in a corporate enterprise, however, the setting of objectives or standards and the appraisal of performance ought to be social activities: they should be done together.

There are some common-sense reasons for both practices. Groups and organizations need someone to help them to break down their sense of purpose and their large aims into the more manageable targets or standards. Providing that the working situation allows for sufficient time and the group members possess enough relevant experience, the wise leader will seek to involve his team in the decisions about what to do next, or—if the objective is already given—how to do it best. For the more that people share in decisions which affect their working life, the more they feel involved and responsible for the outcome.

This is a good argument for a leader sharing as many decisions as possible with his team, or with an individual member of that team as in the case of delegation. But should the leader discuss his tentative or proposed objectives and plans with *his* superior? Again, there are obvious and common-sense reasons why he should do so. First, if you never tell your superiors what you intend to do they are powerless to help you. Secondly, as the old adage says, two heads are better than one. A searching discussion of probable objectives with a superior should result in higher quality decisions. In important matters it is natural for us to test our plans with the help of an outside but involved superior, and to seek his personal and professional support.

A performance appraisal should centre upon what has been done or not done, how it went or why it did not happen and what are the lessons for the future. The prospect of such appraisal discussions at regular intervals can arouse fear if we identify appraising with criticizing. Christians have inside themselves the seeds of a fear of failure, and those seeds can begin to grow as they become more aware of the enormity of their common task and their own individual and corporate (and organizational) shortcomings. Therefore the positive values should be drawn out first, and then the areas for improvement discussed.

The enemy of such appraisal is always fear—fear in the giver and fear in the receiver. Consequently the work of the Church is not always properly evaluated and improved. Perhaps it would help to diminish that fear if we could grasp that the doctrine of the Last Judgement is not a threat but a promise. As persons we *need* to be judged; we need someone to look at our work and to affirm the value in it while pointing out the possibilities for improvement. A God who did not judge or appraise us (to get away from the picture of a criminal court) would miss one of our deepest and highest personal needs. As a thirsty animal needs water so we need our work to be evaluated by God, so that we can receive our payment for good results in the coinage of joy and have also the opportunity of discovering new possibilities for better service.

But it is a common experience that some people do have the power by what they say about our work to uplift or dispirit us. Within the

Hebraic-Christian tradition we may relate this influence to the gifts of blessing and cursing, which were present in the prophets. 'Blessing then becomes an expression of the power of charity', writes Professor Emmet in *Function, Purpose and Power* (1958). 'It no longer has to be connected with particular ritual words and acts, though these may have their place on occasions. The ancient Hebrews were right in thinking that blessing had to do with a heightening of vital energies, but it is not just vitality. It is like the increased vitality which comes from release from anxiety and self-consciousness through loving absorption in the task at hand, or in the person before you. . . . For the individual this may bring renewal out of dejection; and in social relations it may bring that raising of vital tone we call morale.'

The power of blessing is expressed in the appraisal interview by both appreciating the value of a person's contribution and by constructively discussing what has not been accomplished or service that has fallen short of agreed standards. In the graceful company of that 'still more excellent' gift of love, we should not expect this inner power or gift for appraising the worth of work to be manifested in extraordinary ways. We all know the quiet blessing which happens to us when someone shows a genuine interest in our work, and actually listens to what we are trying to do and be, and then makes some creative suggestions for our future. Alas, such natural appraisers are as rare as physicians in a plague-ridden city.

Lastly, it should not be supposed that one person is an appraiser while another is essentially the appraised. That may be true in a particular interview situation, which requires a certain fidelity to roles. But we are both followers and leaders; we are called to bless as well as being blessed. It is part of the humility of a Christian leader that he is willing to receive personal encouragement from his team members, and their solicitations about his own individual needs. In the right place and at the right time he should also be open to critical comments upon his leadership from his own superiors and his colleagues as well.

SUMMARY

Leadership is an important principle in the Christian enterprise, as in any other, but it is by no means the whole story. It is only within the context of other positive developments in an organization of community—structure, communications, training, morale—that good leadership becomes really effective. A wise organization, while never leaving everything to its leaders or blaming all misfortunes upon them, learns to value good leadership as an essential resource.

There is a harmony between the main social psychological theory on the nature of leadership and the images (or primitive theories) of the biblical era. Together they give clear guidelines to Christian leaders. But the biblical and early Church concepts about the need for planning, which means thinking forwards in terms of purpose, aims, and objectives, is perhaps less obvious, and they may seem to owe more to the nineteenth century doctrine of progress than a theology of the Kingdom of God. But the image of the manager in the form of the steward is present in the New Testament, and responsibility for making the most effective use of resources of time, money, and buildings by planning is written into the charter of Christian leadership by its founder.

Many working groups have to choose between effectiveness in their common task and enjoyable human relationships. At some stage in our lives we have to experience this as an *either/or* situation in order to understand. Do we want success with conflict, disagreement, and unhappiness or else an easy and pleasant climate of warm mutual acceptance with low task results? We know which alternative Christ chose. But groups and organizations, especially those made up of christianized people and those financially insulated from the effects of low task performance, can easily opt for the unity and happy fellowship alternative. This may be particularly true if people live as well as work together, for example in a cathedral close. As one diocesan bishop said to me recently, 'the sin of this diocese is niceness'. It is perhaps almost natural for those who hold consciously or unconsciously the view that the Church is *only* a spiritual family to put the maintenance of the group—good human relationships—first and to play down the demands of the common task equation.

That stark *either/or* is the fundamental choice facing the Church of England and indeed the Church today. By choosing the first alternative the churches will find themselves in a painful period of readjustment; old moulds or patterns of established relationships will be disrupted, and the structures will be shaken to their very foundation. By choosing the second alternative, the churches will enter into some long reaches of quiet and peaceful decline, like painted canal boats gliding down a nineteenth-century backwater. But the reward will be less schism, less disagreement, less threat, and less discontinuity with the beloved past. The clergy will love the bishops who will love the laity who will love the clergy. . . .

Of course a deeper reflection on the three-circles model suggests that in the last analysis this is a false dichotomy (like all temptations). There is a third alternative. Only progress in the common purpose of the Church can build up true Christian fellowship. Or, to put it the other way, really good relations between people are those which enable them to work together towards common aims and objectives. Within this kind of climate a bishop or dean can appraise the work of a parish clergyman in such a way that trust and relationship are built up rather than destroyed. Consequently in any situation a balance has to be struck between the three circles. The willingness to give appraisals in the light of agreed plans and to be appraised—much more difficult—is a sign that the bias in traditional church leadership towards the group and the individual is being at last balanced by an orientation towards the common purpose.

It is not easy to give such leadership, especially as the Christian leader may have become hooked upon the warm social rewards of popularity, approval, and love which the churches have traditionally imposed upon their people-oriented 'pastors'. The pastors of tomorrow must lead their sheep across raging torrents—and they must go through the waters first, or else the flock will not follow. Niceness is not enough.

8

Further Training: A Change Agent

Leaders are not either born or made. Many people have in them a potential for leadership which has to be developed by a life-long learning process of experience and reflection. Until about 1955 it was assumed that a clergyman who had completed his theological college course and post-ordination training (such as it was then) had been wound up like a clockwork mouse, and would run down slowly until the end of his ministry without benefit of any further training. It is true that some colleges ran 'refresher' courses, as they were called, for their alumni. These one or two week courses were part-holiday, part-reunion and part-seminar. The syllabus tended to be drawn exclusively from the traditional subjects of academic theology. They did not deal with leadership or the churches as complex and delicate systems intelligible only in terms of purpose.

Between 1960 and 1970 there was a vast expansion of post-experience management education in all countries. This decade, for example, saw the establishment of the London and Manchester graduate business schools. Organizations of every kind began to send their mature managers or executives to courses or conferences. Adult education, which had hitherto been the cinderella of the academic world, suddenly blossomed within the context of working life. In the early 1960s the training bandwaggon really began to roll in organizations, and received a further powerful impetus from the Industrial Training Act (1965).

Behind this sudden burgeoning of activity lay a very general realization that education and training were no longer something you completed once and for all at twenty-one or twenty-two, it was a lifetime process. Changes in society and technology, changes in the level or even direction of a person's career, meant that his knowledge could be soon obsolete and his vaunted experience out-of-date. The organization itself had to become a learning organism, and it could only do that if its members were as highly trained as possible, not only in technical ways but also in such areas as leadership, corporate decision-making and creative thinking, and communication. For size in organization,

although it might in theory produce more economic products or services, in practice posed such problems for people working together that
in some cases even those benefits were in jeopardy. By the mid-1960s
many organizations had decided that training at all levels—from the
board of directors downwards—could contribute towards the solution
of the problem of how to operate organizations of all sizes more effectively and with the maximum satisfaction for the people participating in
the enterprise.

The churches were sufficiently cut off from the realities of their own
changing environment and the rest of organizational life to lag about a
decade behind these developments. By the late 1960s, however, many
clergymen in, for example, the Church of England were talking about
the need for further training, which they also sometimes called 'in-
service training'. By then there were a number of further training
courses available to clergymen, usually provided by private enterprise
organizations rather than the dioceses or the Church itself. Some of
these courses, notably the College of Preachers (which gave further
training in sermon-craft—a widely recognized area of pastoral
weakness), had acquired a sort of semi-official status. But a rash of
other offerings, such as 'clinical theology' (a mixture of psychiatry and
theologizing), remained on the fringe. By 1969 a clamour had arisen
that the Church of England's Advisory Council for the Ministry should
take on the chore of cataloguing and 'co-ordinating' these courses, to
which it replied—not without justification—that first it would have to
increase its establishment before undertaking this responsibility, not a
welcome idea in a period of retrenchment. It was then hoped that the
British Council of Churches would assume responsibility, possibly in
conjunction with the Church of England. For by this time other
churches had accepted the need. By 1970, for example, the Methodist
Church had adopted the policy that a minister would have three weeks
further training in every ten years of his ministry.

Thus the Church of England at the centre saw the problem posed by
the development of a variety of further training courses as essentially a
bureaucratic one of getting more staff. The staff in question would
presumably list and circulate information about the courses available.
After one or two experiments with the thorny problem of evaluation,
which was tied up with the question of which courses would be supported from central funds, the Advisory Council side-stepped that issue
by leaving it to diocesan bishops to decide what courses they would
patronize with men and therefore money.

AT DIOCESAN LEVEL

The chief responsibility for the selection, training, and deployment of the ordained ministry in a diocese lies with the diocesan bishop. In a large diocese more than one bishop will share in that main responsibility. Each such diocese, however, needs a senior man as Diocesan Secretary with special responsibility for the staff functions relating to the selection, training, and deployment of the ministry. But it should be stressed, again, that he and his team would be only staff advisers: the responsibility for what happens within the ordained ministry still rests squarely on the shoulders of the bishops. As already concluded, it might be appropriate for this office to be filled by a clergyman with the title and status of archdeacon.

The growing case for further training, supported by the success of some of the pilot ventures, led some dioceses—it is true—to appoint a person with staff responsibilities in this sphere. Owing to the state of play at national level and the lack of a senior member of the bishop's staff meeting to support them, the task of these pioneers has not been an easy one. As a contribution to the development of their important role, I would suggest the following duties as a possible framework:

1. to work with the Diocesan Secretary (Ministry) to establish the training needs of the clergy and lay ministers in the diocese;

2. to list and evaluate all courses available regionally or nationally for clergy, and to ensure that the suffragan bishops and rural deans have up-to-date details of them;

3. to explore the opportunities within the diocese for the attendance of clergy and others on relevant secular courses, e.g. at polytechnics;

4. to interview all those who go on courses both before and after to make sure that they as individuals and the diocese as a whole gain maximum benefit from them;

5. to teach on some of the regional and national courses, and to conduct some research in depth into one aspect of further training.

The grouping of dioceses into local associations on a semi-informal basis would certainly help to multiply possibilities for further training. The ideal is to provide each clergyman with the right 'learning experience' and the right time as his ministry progresses. To come near that ideal some form of local association would be a considerable advantage.

AT NATIONAL LEVEL

Any policy for further training has to reflect an agreement about priorities. Perhaps the major priority at national level is for courses based upon the staff college principle. The Church of England has already taken the first hesitant step in that direction, and rightly so. For a staff college should provide training for those who will immediately occupy staff appointments, such as diocesan secretaries or directors and members of central departments or agencies. More widely, it may give to clergymen at a key point in their ministry the chance to think deeply about the theology of the Church in relation to the realities of organizational life. In the later years of their ministry such men may become bishops or deans as well as others who have not attended staff college courses. Perhaps they will retain their vision, including the understanding of how organizations ought to work in practice.

The reasons for a leavening of such men and women in the churches is obvious. For the Church as a body has to react faster and more effectively to the environment's challenges; it needs flexible joints and a good nervous system. Otherwise it will become like a dinosaur—a large bulk and small brain—heading for extinction. But good communication implies a better relationship: it requires a new vision of the English parish system as more like a body, a whole made up of interacting and interdependent parts. This view has to struggle against the established assumptions of a thousand years that a church is a collection of independent units which are loosely associated together for certain minimal jurisdictional and financial purposes.

In order to grasp the need for and role of a staff college in any large organization it is necessary to consider the father of them all, the Army Staff College at Camberley in Surrey. As Brian Bond describes in his *The Victorian Army and the Staff College, 1854–1914,* published in 1971, the Staff College (like the profession of nursing) was born in the lamentable confusions of the Crimean War, when an army led and organized as if it was about to fight once more the Napoleonic Wars of fifty years ago almost crashed to defeat. The young British officers of the post-Waterloo generation at least realized that the military world of the 1850s had changed from that of the 1800s, and they had to subject themselves as students to the most searching study of war.

Various reforms of the British Army's system and organization, such as those of Lord Cardwell after the Franco-Prussian War in the 1870s and Lord Haldane's in the first decade of this century, increased the effectiveness of the Staff College. That illustrates an important principle, namely that organizational (or structural) reform and further training must go hand-in-hand if either are to be effective—one without the other is largely barren. It is tempting to draw an analogy here between the purchase system in the Victorian Army with the freehold system in the Victorian Church, but that must be resisted here.

In terms of this analogy the Church of England in 1960 was roughly in the position of the British Army in the 1870s, except that the changes it was encountering were not the concrete and concentrated ones of reversals in the field, but the almost imperceptible and slow transformations within an increasingly secular society. The Church also needed a staff college to help it to respond appropriately to the changing elements in its social environment, in the light of its essential purpose.

In an attempt to clarify the possible functions of a staff college, I wrote an article entitled 'A Staff College for the Church of England', which *Theology* published in May 1962. It began with a brief account of the aims, content, and methods of the Camberley Staff College, and moved on to consider what a church equivalent might look like. Because some later developments stemmed from this article, it is reproduced here in full:

During recent discussion on post-ordination training, the phrase 'staff college' has been used more than once. Few people, however, seem to know what it means. Some use it as synonymous with 'a college for post-ordination training'; others mean by it a college for training staff members for a particular department or activity. Therefore, before discussing whether the Church of England needs one or not, we must first determine what functions a staff college fulfils.

The parent of all the staff college experiments in industry and the Civil Service is the military staff college at Camberley. Some, such as that of the British Oxygen Company, have actually been founded by former members of the directing staff at Camberley. It would therefore be apposite to describe the college at Camberley, and the needs it meets within the army.

The staff course, which lasts for a year, is attended by some sixty young officers who have been selected by examination and interview from a very large number of candidates. The aims of the course are 'to fit them for second-grade staff appointments and, with further experience, for command of units of battalion size and upwards'. The syllabus designed for these ends falls into two broad interrelated

parts: the study of the way that large units achieve their aims in warfare, and an analysis of the staff officers' work in connection with
these operations.

The study of warfare begins with a revision of tactics up to battalion level, and then goes on to the use of brigades, divisions, and armies in the different phases of war. The young officer comes to see the
army in a new way, as a developed complex organism, designed to
respond as a body to such situations as the enemy might impose
upon it. Within this common vision, the functions of the various services and arms become meaningful, and the problems of co-
operation receive a fresh significance. It might seem odd that a young
officer still under thirty years of age should spend his time working
out how he would withdraw a division of 40,000 men over a river at
night in face of the enemy. Such a study is necessary, however,
because he might be responsible for working out in detail a general's
plan for this kind of operation, and it is therefore essential that he
should—unless he is to be a mere automaton—understand in some
degree the problems involved. This formulation of an understanding
or vision of the brigade, division, and army through the study of their
action or reaction in given situations, which is required for efficient
and effective staff work, also serves as an excellent theoretical introduction to the job of commanding these great bodies of men. For
at the same time as the function of a large unit within the army group
becomes clear, so the role of the commander takes shape.

During their study of warfare, the course members become aware
of the need in any large army for some form of general staff to act as
the nerve-centre of the 'body', to co-ordinate its various 'members' in
the common task. They consider the necessity of communication,
both 'scalar' (from general to private) and 'lateral' (group to group,
unit to unit). Planning for operations, administration, and training
are considered in detail. These are studied not only within the context
of the officer's vision of the modern army, but also within the
perspective of military history. It is against such a background that
'staff duties' in the narrower technical sense of the term are learnt.

It is interesting to note that the principal unit of instruction at
Camberley is not the individual but the small team or 'cadre' of ten
students and a directing staff instructor. All the work—discussion,
exercises, role plays and post-exercise analysis—is done in these
groups, which are called 'syndicates'. These are composed as far as
possible of members of different parts of the army, and include

foreign and Commonwealth officers. The Staff College lays great store upon a group's ability to teach itself, and few 'DS (Directing Staff) solutions' (in the worst sense of the word) are offered to course members. Moreover, the Staff College provides an opportunity for young officers to form personal relationships with each other which endure when they meet and work together on the staff and as commanders. In other words, it creates fellowship at a key level in a great organization.

From this picture some idea of the function which a staff college in the Church of England might fulfil begins to emerge. For there is a real sense in which the Church is 'like a mighty army'. It has its hierarchy of organizations from parish to province, its discipline and officers and its own form of warfare to which we are committed at baptism. The Church of England also has its staff officers, ranging from the chairborne clergy in London to the diocesan staffs grouped loosely around the Bishop. To these we might add the staffs of various training colleges, lay administrators, and extra-parochial officers. A carefully selected number of these staff jobs should be occupied by men who have been given training for them. For they are the hidden 'nervous system' of the Church of England.

The students at such a staff course might start with a study of the Church as the 'body of Christ' and the ways in which it responds to the concrete situations and needs of the world. The structural organization of the Church of England would be reviewed in terms of the total work of the Church. This classification of the nature and purpose of the deanery, archdeaconry, diocese, and province, with all their ramifications, would serve not only as the first step in staff training, but also as a theoretical introduction to the roles of rural deans, archdeacons and bishops.

Working together in small teams of eight with an instructor, course members would then study, with the help of sociologists and management consultants, the present function of the staff within the Church of England. Thus would include an analysis of the duties of various staff appointments within the economy of the Church. From this investigation, groups could evaluate, and if necessary modify, the suggested programme of training. This specialized work might also include subjects such as the sociology of large organizations, methods of personnel selection, office management, lateral and scalar communications and ecclesiastical law. To balance these practical group investigations some lectures on more general topics such as recent church history and world politics could be added to the course.

It might be worthwhile to point out at this stage that this course is radically different from anything offered in the Church of England at present. St Augustine's College, Canterbury, which is officially described as 'the Central College of the Anglican Communion', is not a staff college. For example, a quarter of its number of residents should be ordinands. Only a very few Church of England members go there. Contacts with the faiths of Asia and Africa, general lectures and thesis-writing occupy its time. It could be described as a vague centre of Anglican missionary and ecumenical research. None of its great possibilities have been actualized yet.

There would be many difficulties in establishing a staff college within the life of the Church of England. Foremost amongst these would be the antagonism of a large number of clergymen. To a certain extent this is due to the fear of 'the organization' becoming an idol, and efficiency coming to matter more than people. Perhaps the suggested syllabus of the staff course, which includes a study of the dangers and pitfalls in large organizations, might allay this fear. The same fear was present when C.A.C.T.M. week-ends (based on War Office Selection Boards for Officers) were introduced. Yet few would now suggest going back to the old haphazard methods of selecting ordinands.

Against all these hesitations are set the very great needs in the Church of England for a staff college. In the preface to his *William Temple, Archbishop of Canterbury,* F. A. Iremonger points to the administrative burden which shortened the Archbishop's life, and the possible remedy. His words are applicable today. 'But human memories', he wrote, 'are notoriously short, and the Church still lacks its G.H.Q., that department devoted to planning and strategy—by whatever name it may be called—of which the need is constantly and continuously felt in the day-to-day work of our National Church.' To this we might only add the need to train the men who might serve on such central and diocesan staffs in the best and most imaginative way possible, so that when they after further experience are called to high office within the Church of England, they will be able to use to its maximum effect the staff which they find at their disposal.

The 1962 *Theology* article evoked no response, except one letter from a retired clergyman living in Cyprus saying that he had thought of the idea in the 1920s! It is true that the Paul Report (1964) advocated a staff college, but it was lost among the concluding list of 62 'principal recommendations' and then subsequently dropped in the Morley Committee's revision of Paul, which appeared in 1967.

But in 1966, inside the steep grey walls of Windsor Castle, the doors opened of what *The Times* called 'a most exclusive, discreet and unusual kind of hotel'. St George's House lies in the jumble of medieval buildings to the north of St George's Chapel, up against the castle wall. All the labyrinth of chapter property had just been restored at a cost of more than £300,000, raised mainly from industry and commerce. And St George's House had been created out of two seventeenth century canons' houses to be a residential centre. The Dean, the Very Reverend Robin Woods, called it 'a genuine attempt by the Christian Church to enter into dialogue with the secular world'.

The Dean, who had served as a Second World War army chaplain and also as an archdeacon under Bishop Leslie Hunter, intended St George's House to be a place for lay discussion at weekends. But, as a secondary aim, he planned to hold courses on weekdays for senior clergy in the 40 to 55 age group.

In January 1968 the staff of St George's House (which by then included myself on a year's sabbatical leave) already had plans for the first of a series of ten-day courses for newly-appointed bishops, archdeacons, and senior Church officials. But the Dean had read and kept the *Theology* article on the need for a staff college course for those in the 30 to 40 age bracket. After much discussion in the various advisory committees on policy, it was agreed during 1968 that St George's House would mount the first four-week staff college course in the following year.

A variety of people contributed to the planning of the course syllabus, including some bishops and the heads of staff colleges and business schools. From Norman Leyland, then Director of the Oxford Centre for Management Studies, came the necessary advice and confidence to invite the 22 participants to spend time in the six months before the course in preparing a written project.

Some twenty dioceses nominated men for the 1969 course, and the Methodist Church also agreed to send two ministers. The dozen or so bishops, including the present Archbishop of Canterbury, whom I interviewed personally in the pre-course preparation, without exception grasped the point of the course, made constructive suggestions about its content and showed wisdom in choosing their man. Lastly, they and all other senior church leaders who were approached co-operated fully with course members in their project work: answering questionnaires and giving generous interviews. Their interest and support was a source of great encouragement.

The first course in summer of 1969 began with a survey of what was happening in the world. Much of the work took place in syndicate discussions, but in the first phase there were lectures by sociologists, experts on local government, contemporary historians, scientists, and lecturers or consultants in management studies. There were also visits to Camberley and Henley Administrative Staff College, and even a session on 'management by objectives' at the Urwick Management Training Centre in neighbouring Slough.

In the second phase the course reconsidered the nature and purpose of the Church. Dr Coggan commented upon the first group of syndicate reports, and gave his own views. Professor C. F. D. Moule, then the Lady Margaret Professor of Divinity at Cambridge University, spent more than a week with the course, leading Bible studies and discussions on such topics as leadership and decision-making in the experience of the early Church.

The last phase was occupied by studying the ways in which the purpose and aims of the Church could be more effectively achieved in the world revealed by the lectures and discussions of the first week. Present proposals and experiments in altering the Church of England to meet the contemporary situation, were subjected to a critical review. The presentations of projects, in both small group and plenary sessions, occupied much of this time: put together, these studies covered a considerable range of important topics which needed research. The course ended with a comprehensive and challenging summary by the Dean of Windsor.

Since 1969 two courses based on that approach have taken place at St George's House each year. In 1972, as part of his studies for the M.A. degree in Organization Studies at the University of Leeds, the Reverend H. W. Moore (a member of the first Windsor course) wrote a research thesis on the evaluation of the first five Mid-Service Courses. His study embraced the expectations of some twenty diocesan bishops who sent men on the course, as well as the men themselves. Naturally there were possibilities for improvement, but Mr Moore reported 'an overwhelming assertion of confidence and appreciation for the M.S.C.C., by course members of all five courses, and by the bishops who send men on the courses'.

Nor were the courses barren of what Mr Moore calls 'organizational outcomes', but the picture is less uniform here. The research findings showed:

1. Many cases where the diocese and course participants were deeply involved in creative activity stemming from the course;
2. Other cases where the diocesan bishop recognized immediate benefits and had plans for the future of which the course member was not aware;
3. Cases where the course member was 'going it alone';
4. Other cases where the member felt 'flat' and let down because nothing had happened in response to his efforts, and to his report on the course to the bishop who sent him on it.

Readers with experience in general management or professional training at the higher levels will recognize this pattern. The way forward lies partly in better communication between the senior man (or sender) and the course member, and partly in encouraging senior leaders to pay more attention to the post-course application of results (and therefore also to the pre-course period of study).

In my mind one of the aims of the course was to serve the staff college function of preparing men for staff appointments and, with further experience, for senior leadership positions. It is true that four or five of the 119 men (less thirteen Free Church ministers) who attended the first five M.S.C.C.s have become suffragan bishops or archdeacons, and another is now a diocesan bishop, and also that others may yet become bishops or archdeacons in the next decade or so. But there is a possibility that the full potential of the original staff college idea is not being realized. For few of the men coming on the course have moved into staff appointments. Only eight out of the twenty bishops (i.e. those who replied to Mr Moore's questionnaire sent to 36 diocesans) gave as one of their reasons for choosing a man for the course that it was the basis for increased responsibility. In order to clarify this issue the bishops were asked:

a. When you are considering men for posts of responsibility under your jurisdiction, do you take into account attendance and results at the Windsor Course?
b. Do you refer to St George's House when considering men from outside your diocese?

To the first question fifteen bishops replied Yes and five bishops said No. To the second one, four bishops replied Yes and sixteen said No. 'On this evidence', concluded Mr Moore, 'it appears that for appointments within the bishop's jurisdiction, M.S.C.C. attendance and results are seen as important, but for appointments from outside they are not. Further data, about criteria used for considering the appointment of men from outside the diocese, would be necessary in order to fully understand the situation. The matter is further complicated in that St George's House does not issue reports on men's work or achievements at M.S.C.C. Therefore unless a bishop takes steps to inquire of St George's House, the only results he has to base his judgement on are the thesis, what the man himself reports, and any visible change in his performance. . . . The view already expressed that the system of appointments is fairly chaotic and irrational in the eyes of many members of the Church is not contradicted by the data, but there is evidence that in some quarters there is a consistent use of M.S.C.C. and by implication therefore other courses, as a basis for choosing, developing, and appointing men for particular posts. That "cloud the size of a man's hand" may be encouraging to some.'

Although the Windsor Course of 1969 took root in the Church of England, its staff college aspect has perhaps lost ground to its 'mid-service' refresher role. But, as Mr Moore's study reveals, the former has not disappeared entirely from view. The position is roughly that of the Staff College in the British Army during the 1860s. Certainly a Staff College concept is needed for improving the vocational preparation of those 150 bishops, 800 rural deans and 500 or so clergymen holding national and diocesan staff jobs in the early 1980s.

Nobody wishes to see the ordained ministry lose its original identity of humble service after the example of Christ. The fears that a staff college would stimulate the ambitious, or create a professional *élite* proud of its difference from the other clergy, has certainly hindered developments. The danger is that the necessities working *for* a staff college and the fears working *against* it will produce a compromise which can easily become a form of unreality. This situation can only be prevented by a deeper spirituality.

Put plainly, it is necessary to trust the clergy. The expressed fears that the clergy are prone to ambition in the worst sense, or that they are naturally jealous and envious, merely reveal the assumptions of the speaker about human nature: they expose *his* doctrine of man. 'Most of the evils of mankind have no other cause but false suspicions', said St

Augustine in a sermon: 'could we but *know* one another, we should be less tempted to say to ourselves "I alone am good".' In the transfigured Church, wrote St Augustine, it will not be like that, for 'the hearts of all will be transparent, manifest, luminous in the perfection of love'.

Better pay and housing conditions, and the reform—as yet incomplete—of the stipendiary and pensions systems in the direction of fairness, coupled with changes in the social status and finances of the hierarchy, have obviously diminished the need for a Victorian scramble for preferment. The majority of clergymen, like all Christians and people of good will, simply want to 'fulfil their ministry' (to use the phrase of the author of the First Letter to Timothy) in the most effective way possible. They desire only to be returned empty to their Maker. It is unfitting for them to go about touting for jobs or promotion. Therefore there must be a fair method of making appointments to both line and staff positions of responsibility. And each clergyman should have the opportunity of regularly discussing his service with an area bishop and possibly his diocesan as well, secure in the knowledge that the bishops know their occupational interests, talents, and temperament on the one hand, and are in touch with all the current or expected openings at diocesan, regional, or national levels on the other hand.

In such a Church a staff college course would be a natural organ, one among a plurality of other courses in further training. Moreover, like the Armed Services, there would always be routes to senior positions for those who had not attended staff courses. Equally many of those who did go on them—perhaps a majority—would make their major contribution as deans or vicars of large parishes. Not one of them would have a crozier in his suitcase by virtue of being selected for a staff course. Rather, the Church would make heavier demands on their dedication and love.

AT SUPRA-NATIONAL LEVEL

In the 1962 *Theology* article I mentioned St Augustine's College, Canterbury, which was said to be the central college of the Anglican Communion. Besides pointing out that it was in no sense a staff college for the Church of England, being a place where senior members of the Anglican Communion came from all over the world for a period of study, I recorded my impression that it was not going well, in a tentative conclusion that 'none of its great possibilities have been actualized yet'. Within two or three years after those words had been penned the college was disbanded and the buildings were eventually allocated for the use of a London theological college (who recently vacated them owing to the shortfall of ordinands).

Although I have no first-hand knowledge of this case-study in expensive missed opportunity, my inquiries suggest that it sprang from a basic failure to be clear about the *aim* of a central college for the Anglican Communion. The imaginative and potentially valuable idea collapsed because of this fundamental failure in thinking. Thus the students came and wrote their long theses and listened to lectures in a kind of organizational vacuum. Neither they nor their research work was seen as part of a general development programme for the Anglican Communion as a whole.

Fortunately a good idea does not grow old, nor should one false start be held to prove that it does not work in practice. The error here lay not in the idea but in the design and guidance of the project. In other words, it should be taken up again.

In organizational terms, I would see it as a college which men and women would attend at roughly the one-star level of episcopacy or its staff and lay equivalents. The object would be to explore the workings of the Church in the world at the international level, with special reference to the Anglican Communion. But it would be a training course rather than a conference house. Course members would spend three months based at St Augustine's College, carrying out an advanced study of world society, politics, and economics. They would also explore the making of policy in the churches. Each person, as at Windsor, would prepare and present a project on some aspect of the Anglican Communion in its changing social and ecclesiastical context. The academic standard of this interdisciplinary work would be exacting enough to be stimulating and challenging. The establishment of such a college may well come high on the agenda of the Anglican Consultative Committee or possibly a Lambeth Conference in the near future.

In the wider ecumenical context there are a number of colleges or centres, such as the Ecumenical Institute at Brussels (which receives financial support from the Church of England amounting to £2,000 a year), the Anglican Centre in Rome, St George's College in Jerusalem, and the Ecumenical Institute for Advanced Theological Studies also near Jerusalem. Quite what all these colleges, institutes, and courses actually do and how they do it needs some careful study and evaluation which to my knowledge has yet to happen. Looking at the world level and taking into account all the churches, it would be natural to expect a pattern of about ten major colleges to emerge, each with some special field of study within the context of a world-vision of the purpose of God for humanity.

SUMMARY

The Church of England, in company with other churches, has responded slowly and only partially to the need for further training for its clergy as well as its laity. In part this delayed and muted reaction was the product of a healthy scepticism about the value of more 'talking-shops', but in part it merely revealed again a degree of organizational torpor which proved unacceptable. Gradually, however, the emphasis began to shift away from clergy communicating with each other in the form of those listless committee meetings or conferences where they all passively listened to lectures, towards training which promised to improve effectiveness in the parochial and diocesan situations.

Faced with the welter of courses and programmes which emerged for the clergy, many of them poor in quality and uncertain in character, it was easy for the Church authorities to take a pragmatic and permissive line, without formulating any kind of policy at diocesan, national, or international level. Indeed without training themselves the authorities were incapable of forming such a policy. Fortunately for its long-term prospect, the Church of England was rescued from that *impasse* by one of those creative accidents in its history, in this case the combination of events and people which led to the first staff-college type courses at St George's House, Windsor Castle.

'Rescued' is of course a word used in faith rather than from experience. An objective evaluation of the Windsor courses would suggest that—partly because of external factors in the organization as a whole (the standards of leadership and staff work at the centre and in the dioceses) and partly because of the internal difficulties of grafting a staff college onto an ancient institution like St George's Chapel with a particular sociology of its own, expressed in other concerns and interests—the experiment still falls short of the original vision. But that is to be expected. It will take one or two more decades before the staff-college principle is fully working, and its fruits are nourishing the Church at large. Yet the necessary interaction between theology, theory, and principles on the one hand and churches, practice, and experience on the other hand, centred upon a college and providing the necessary education for those who might be called to other leadership positions later on in their ministries, has at last been inaugurated.

Such a college should train men in the 30 to 40 years age group. It should of course be duplicated in every continent for the indigenous Anglican churches. For more senior men already in leadership positions of one-star episcopal level throughout the Anglican Communion, however, there is a need for a central college. Despite the understandable desire to stress the international nature of the Anglican Communion by placing such a college in, say, Africa or Canada, most Anglicans throughout the world would still feel that Canterbury has the right ambience to be its location. The college should be seen not as a solitary star on top of the Anglican Christmas tree, but as one among a small galaxy of ecumenical centres or institutes which have an official existence and a proper purpose within the context of the world Church.

9

Members at Work

The secularization of the churches means that clergymen and laity alike feel that the focus of Christian thought and action must be the world. There is much public impatience with anything that smacks of church-centredness. Theology and books about the churches must be 'relevant'. The churches are bidden to be healthy extroverts. Taken literally, of course, this policy is at best superficial. For without changing themselves and their members the churches have little to offer the world. And without a degree of introspection those changes cannot be made. Therefore the churches are called to be neither extroverts nor introverts but ambiverts.

With this qualification, however, which most readers will admit, the churches still have to work out what they are doing as corporate bodies in and for the world—even if they do not see themselves as wholly of it. In general terms they have given two sorts of answers. First, they are producers of lay Christians who will live and act as leaven or salt in the lump of the world. Secondly, as corporate bodies they are capable of social and political action for the good of the world. This latter aspect will be discussed in Chapter Ten. Here it is the former thesis that will be considered.

THE WORLD

The Old English *weorld* is made up of two words: 'age' and 'man'. So it means literally 'age of man' or 'course of man's life'. From this derivation springs the first group of meanings clustered around the idea of *human existence:* the early state of human existence, experience of life, this present life and its pursuits and interests, especially (in religious use) the least worthy of these affairs or conditions. As such it was used for secular (or lay) life as distinct from religious (or clerical). In 1648 the Society of Friends were applying the term to those outside their body. Worldliness was the name given to devotion to worldly affairs to the neglect of religious duties or spiritual needs, the love of the world and its interests and pleasures. The world here is the present state of existence.

The second cluster of senses forms around the idea of the *earth.*

'World' here means the universe or a part of it, the material universe as an ordered system. By extension it is used about a group or system of things or beings associated by common characteristics considered as constituting a unity. Thence it means the sphere within which one's interests are bound up or one's activities find scope: the sphere, in other words, of one's action or thought. Thus we can talk about, for example, the world of sport or the world of music; indeed there is also the world of religion and the churches.

Finally, world stands for the *inhabitants of the earth,* or a section of them. It is the human race, the body of living persons in general, society at large, or people. This is often the sense that authors and church leaders have in mind when they speak about the world. Secularization, it must be repeated, is largely the story of the rising value of the world as the earthly state of human existence, with the value of the unseen heavenly state correspondingly falling in the other scale.

In our confused cultural situation what should the Church—or rather the 99 per cent who are lay men, women, and children—be doing in the world? One popular answer has been the notion of a lay apostolate.

A LAY APOSTOLATE?

In commenting upon the statistics of declining membership of the Catholic Church in a national newspaper early in 1975, Derek Worlock, now Roman Catholic Archbishop of Liverpool, pointed to the rising value of the laity in the new 'missionary' situation of Christianity in the West:

> Since the Second Vatican Council the Church has stressed the need for the clergy and laity to be involved in decision-making. Senates of priests, diocesan and parish councils have been set up. In May 1972 new regulations were issued governing the appointment of bishops. Widespread consultation of both priests and laity has been built into the process and our Laity Commission, with the express approval of the bishops, has issued guide-lines to explain how the new process works and to prepare laity to exercise their role responsibly.
>
> However, matching accusations with figures and facts is not the best method of evaluating the health and *effective apostolate* [my italics] of the Christian community. The Church must strive always to intensify its efforts to live and spread the teachings of Christ.
>
> The most significant change is almost certainly the development of lay responsibility in a Church where in the past responsibility for

word and action was usually the prerogative of the clergy. The importance of the priest's role is no less today. The development of the layman's role has meant an extension to the work of the Church.

But what is an *effective apostolate*? Many clerical writers since 1945 have taken it to mean that the laity will somehow win back the lost ground of church membership. With instruction and leadership from the clergy, it is thought, the laity will transform themselves into missionary apostles, planting the seeds of Christianity anew in the polluted wastelands of secularized society. After all, the laity are there; they live and work in the secularized environment, rubbing shoulders with half-believers and unbelievers. The laity must come to the rescue of Christendom as its front-line evangelists. So argue the armchair strategists.

But such writings betray a lack of awareness as to what it is like to be a lay Christian today. They stem from the habit of looking at the laity from the top of an ivory tower using only the theological perspective glass. The chief fact about the modern Christian laity as a whole is their apostasy, not their apostolate. This hard fact has to be grasped first. The abandonment or renunciation of the Christian faith is running at record levels. The 'mighty army' of Christian conscripts of the pre-1914 era, willing to battle in the trenches against the spiritual foes of Western secularism, has long since died or departed. Their sons and daughters have mostly wearied of the struggle and laid down their arms, or quietly made themselves scarce.

True, there is an army of lay Christians still left, small enough in comparison with those conscript hosts of church-going days but large relative to the dwindling corps of the ordained ministry. But these lay forces are not one hundred per cent Christian; they are all influenced or infected in varying ways and degrees by the all-pervasive influences of secularization. If you contemplate the memoirs, diaries, or biographies of lay men published during the thirty years after 1945 (for example Robin Denniston's *Party Living* or Lord Eccles' *Half Way to Faith*), the effects of secularization are obvious. What secularization means in this context is that Christians become more like secular men and women, while secularized people (because of the progress of secularized religious ideas in the form of values) become more like Christians. Thus, to pursue the military metaphor, the secular forces are occupying salients of Christian ground while the depleted Christian divisions are moving into much smaller pieces of secular ground.

What then is the fighting all about? Why bother to convert anyone to a set of beliefs, especially if the Christian laity only half hold them themselves? What stands out is Christianity as attitudes and action, and by this criterion unbelievers can claim to be as christian as professed Christians.

Such questions open up a more fundamental one, which lies outside this discussion, namely: Has Christianity lost something of its converting power to change human selfishness into love? Whereas St Augustine or John Bunyan tell us of lives re-centred, the story of declining church membership seems to suggest that Bible and sacraments, worship and sermons, prayer and association with other Christians are failing more often than not to conquer self-centredness. Church leaders have consoled themselves and their followers too easily with reasons drawn from the sociological and historical perspectives for the decline in church membership. They have failed to sense the radical challenge to Christianity. Had they done so in time we might have seen far more drastic and self-sacrificial changes in the period between 1955 and 1975. Only in the mid-1970s did the underlying unease and doubt about Christianity itself begin to surface in the writings of some theologians, secure at least in their academic sanctuaries.

The secularization of Christians and the christianization of seculars makes it extremely unlikely that (were they present) all the shining good deeds of Christians, individually or corporately, would now convert the recipients or beholders to Christian belief, although they may serve to husband the present store of deistic religious or semi-religious faith. In a world where martyrdom has become a frequent occurrence, even heroic self-sacrifice by Christians would not produce that result. It only further converts people to the common quasi-religious humanism of the secularized majority. The Christian candle of theological faith no longer shines in darkness; in an electrically-lit room it flickers as an 'optional extra' on the groaning dinner table.

The definition of what is a Christian becomes problematic in such a society. Those who profess to be Christians hold a very variable ideology, ranging from a highly sophisticated theology to a collection of beliefs and half-beliefs not readily distinguishable from the much wider majority of those who hold less specifically the Christian religion. Even those who both profess to be Christians and also can speak articulately (or rationally) about their faith, however, are unlikely to be effective as apostles or missionaries, because they are constrained by the roles they occupy.

Role is a cardinal concept in sociology already mentioned in Chapter Three, and it needs no further definition. The idea that a clergyman is constrained by his social and ecclesiastical role is fairly familiar, but it is less commonly noted that the laity are also role-bound in the same way. Clearly all those who occupy a role are subject to expectations and both inner and outer controls. The public expects a certain form of behaviour from a role occupant. For example, we do not expect a policeman to stop our car in the street in order to tell us a joke: if he did so we would probably react with surprise, disbelief, or downright anger. The middle classes who occupy professional roles—such as doctors, teachers, or civil servants—are expected to restrict themselves in what they say and do to their particular role. C. S. Lewis expressed it well when he said that he thought it wrong for Christian lecturers to take money for supplying one thing (culture) and use the opportunity thus gained to supply a quite different thing (homiletics and apologetics).

The Christian layman meets people in the context of role relationships, such as teacher-student or doctor-patient. Even friendship is a social role; it leads to an emphasis upon what the friends have in common, usually with a tacit agreement not to argue about what divides them in the contentious areas of religion and politics. But evangelism is an attempt to change the mind of another person, and that is increasingly frowned upon in a tolerant society.

Paradoxically, there are probably still more doors open to the ordained minister for specifically Christian proselytizing. The much despised dog-collar betokens a man whose role includes talking about God and Christ; people expect a clergyman to do so, and are unlikely to interpret it as 'preaching' (although they may not understand or accept what he says). This conclusion does not mean that the lay theologian can say nothing. Both on account of his reputation as a Christian outside his role and—more difficult—by what he says within the limits of that role or roles, he or she can communicate with others about Christianity.

But such communication, however, remains veiled and even enigmatic—reminiscent of the way in which Jesus spoke by parables. The work of a Christian author illustrates this aspect of the lay vocation. The *Times* obituary in 1975 of R. C. Hutchinson, author of sixteen novels, made that point:

Contemporary European history and the European condition were prominent both in his mind and in his work. Committed writing, required of authors under some political régimes was, in his view, foreign to the novelist's art but he thought that, broadly speaking, a story lacked artistic shape if it did not imply some moral assumptions. His own philosophy was a Christian one, but he was too sound a craftsman to fall into the trap of engaging himself in didactic writing.

Valuable though it is, such speaking in parables is not likely to lead to a mass return to Christianity.

A THEOLOGY OF VOCATION

If we set aside the model of the lay Christian as an apostle, travelling through life *incognito* and proselytizing his neighbour to Christianity, church membership, or both—what remains? There is of course the idea of lay ministry in the sense of meeting the needs of needy individuals. Such Samaritan service will always be an expression of the life of Christ in an individual or a group, and it is done as an act of pure giving without hope of any reward, even gratitude. But in our social capitalist society, which is developing throughout the non-Communist world, the State undertakes much of this provision through the social welfare services, Besides, many in the christianized but secular majority have a record of personal compassion which can stand beside that of most church members.

Part of the answer lies in the concept of vocation. This phenomenon has been curiously neglected by religious writers, and it is still commonly used with reference to the clergy or the monastic life. But it is quite central to the understanding of the Christian's life in the world. For that reason I wrote an article upon the subject, entitled 'The Doctrine of Vocation' in *Theology* (July 1964), which I shall quote in full here (without the footnotes) because I have not come across anything else since then which tries to relate the natural and spiritual levels of vocation in quite this way:

The biblical doctrine of vocation has its roots in the Old Testament. For the Hebrews God's 'call' created the world and man: the divine 'word' summoned into existence that which was not. If we step outside the human speech metaphor we could then say that each man's vocation consists primarily of his creation as a unique individual, with a pattern of characteristics bestowed on him by nature and nurture. His basic response to God the Creator should therefore be to realize his potentialities. The sign of this natural 'worship' may well be that urge for self-fulfilment, often only a diffused concern or anxiety, which lives by nature in many modern hearts.

Although this understanding of vocation is only just beginning to stir in the Church of England in the effort to apply a money image (stewardship of talents) to personality, it has been present in a non-theological form for some time in secular thinking about careers. The Vocational Guidance Association, for example, who test and advise over 1,000 people each year on the choice of a career, is founded on the assumption that vocational work is that in which a person can exercise and fulfil his aptitudes. The V.G.A. is a remarkable example of how natural theological insights and scientific method can be married together to meet a real need in our society.

The editor of a recent symposium on careers, Robin Guthrie, contrasts this creative understanding of vocation with the apparently negative teachings of the church, and goes on to link the choice of work on the basis of aptitudes with a general philosophy of life, which can be summed up in the words 'self-fulfilment'. Christians might well be suspicious of this phrase, carrying as it does a possible Pelagian interpretation (that the 'self' is the sufficient agent of fulfilment), and suggesting an inward-looking self-centred ethic which is in fact contrary to a right love of oneself. One might prefer the biblical word 'joy', which Professor Tillich interprets as the overflowing sense of fulfilment, and contrasts it with the 'sorrow', or 'the feeling that we are deprived of our central fulfilment'.

Another way of looking at it is to say the 'fulfilment' theme is only a partial apprehension of the biblical doctrine of vocation. The distinctive New Testament understanding of vocation is summed up in the words of St Paul to the Corinthians: 'It is God himself, who called you to share in the life of his Son Jesus Christ our Lord' (1 Cor. 1.9, N.E.B.). The apostle saw this co-inherence as essentially creative—'if anyone is in Christ he is a new creation' (2 Cor. 5.17, R.S.V.). For him the Christian life, which began when the individual accepted his involvement in the cross and resurrection of Christ, consisted of growth into the likeness of Jesus Christ. This was not, however, a destruction of God's primary creation of the person: rather the salt of the Spirit of Christ brought out in each man his true flavour.

St Augustine and Martin Luther both wrote on the creativity of Christian vocation. It is reputed that St Augustine, pointing to the consecrated elements on the altar, said to his congregation: 'There,

there is the mystery of yourselves'. Luther in *The Liberty of the
Christian Man* described the Christian's calling to be 'another
Christ' to his neighbour. Perhaps the basis of the Reformation lay in
Luther's insight into the creative power of God's call.

Participation in the life of Christ leads to a greater willingness to
share in his response to need. This brings us to the third main strand
of the biblical doctrine of vocation. In the human experience
recorded in the Bible God 'calls' through the perception of need.
Vocation in this sense is not a voice in the night but a steady preoccupation with a particular need. Often the need is personified in an individual—St Francis' leprous beggar or Dr Barnardo's first tarpaulin
orphan.

Usually these crucial encounters form only the clear peaks of a
cloud-covered mountain range of experience. Dr Albert Schweitzer's
dramatic calling in 1904 through the perusal of an article entitled
'Les besoins de la Mission du Congo' is well known, but the long
search for a field of truly personal service which preceded it, the dis-
appointments and renewed waiting for the Master's summons, often
escape notice.

In the case of Glubb Pasha, the incident which, by hindsight,
turned out to be the opening of a lifetime's ministry to the needs of
Jordan's desert peoples, in fact initiated the period of reflection in
which the vocation took shape. As a young officer, John Glubb
witnessed a Bedouin tribe, complete with camels and flocks of sheep,
crossing the Euphrates over a bridge he had built. He wrote later that
'the pageant of the Shammar crossing the Ramadi bridge, and the
reading and study to which it led me, decided the course of my life.'

It is interesting to note the creative aspect of this calling through
needs. Growth of personality takes place in response to needs which
appear to be beyond us. It was as if God creates within us the power
to be the kind of person who can meet the needs he confronts us with.
A capricious girl is transformed, for example, into a mother who is
able to love her mentally afflicted child with depth and constancy.
Power comes in the situation.

The presence of creation at every point of the Christian doctrine of
vocation illustrates its underlying unity. If God the Father is connected in theology with the work of natural vocation, God the Son
with the new creation through *'koinonia'* with Christ, and God the
Holy Spirit with 'inward moving' of the heart, coming to us through
our environment and especially from the perception of need, yet it is

in reality the one God who calls us, for the Three Persons of the Trinity are totally involved in any calling of man at any given moment. At this stage the doctrine of vocation merges into that of the Trinity.

In this article I have concerned myself for the most part with the theology of vocation and how human experience and Christian doctrine illuminate each other. Belief and action are two sides of the same coin, however, and I believe that it we could reach a clearer understanding of vocation this would affect what is done in theological colleges and lay training centres, parishes, universities, and schools. It seems to me that a theology of vocation opens to the Church some tremendous opportunities for a genuine ministry to the world at the centre of life, and not simply on its boundaries.

I would urge this need for a theology of vocation and a study of its relevant application especially at this time when much energy is being spent on 'church-centred' conversations with ecclesiastical blocs and parties, and little dialogue takes place with those 'religionless' folk engaged in working out their vocations in a secular world. Of course we need a 'boundary' ministry; of course talks with other believers about our vocation as Christians are necessary; but we also share a common vocation with our neighbours as men and women. To be of any use in our dialogue with other people we need, as part of ourselves, a clear and whole understanding of the vocation of man. Only then shall we be able to co-operate effectively as fellow-callers of men.

In her book *Function, Purpose and Powers* (1958), Dorothy Emmet—then a professor of philosophy at the University of Manchester, linked up the idea of vocation with creative originality, those inner powers of mind and spirit which can both fulfil functions or roles in organized social life and also discern and serve purpose. Should not vocational groups, which include such people, for example, as religious communities (and, it might be added, a church congregation) become models for society at large? Commenting upon Dante's vision of the life of heaven, she declares that 'in the end it is the fulfilment of vocation':

> Is it fanciful to see here a vision of a society of people rejoicing with and for each other in the fulfilment of their vocations? And they recognize and rejoice in the independent contributions of those of whom they had disapproved on earth.

There is one obvious objection, it will be said, to all this: it is too pretentious. Most people have no concern whatever to work from some mysterious inner urge, and if 'vocation' is to be connected with the idea of an individual doing something creative and original, most people in fact do not have vocations; they simply have jobs. And if they do their jobs so as to perform a useful function in society, what more can be asked? In fact the world's work may be said to depend on people doing their jobs according to the norms expected of them, and if they all started wanting to be creative and original, where should we be?

There are, I think, three observations which can be made in reply to this. First, the following of a vocation need not and should not take a person right outside regard for role and function in relation to other people. Secondly, quite simple people, who can live and work in such a way that they contribute to the 'intelligent good sense' of a society which can not only carry but also encourage its creative people, are likely themselves to grow into something a good deal more than mere mediocrity. Thirdly, vocation may not only be connected with the power some may have to devote themselves to a particular kind of creative work, though that is an important part of it.

It may also come as the call to John Smith to accept himself as John Smith and live his individual life as well as he can; and this living of an individual life is something not exhaustively absorbed into his various social roles nor measured by his social status. This would be a kind of vocation concerned with the centre of an individual's own life, and if there is a growing point there, it may be able to survive changes, and sometimes even the losses, of functions and roles in various social groupings. This is something which the creative worker also has to learn; and if he learns it, he will not collapse if for any reason he loses the chance of doing the kind of work round which, in another sense, his vocation may have been built.

These thoughts suggest that vocation is the best focal point for any discussion of the Christian life in the world. It blurs the distinction between life in the world and life in the Church for both become or grow into a unity, as two eyes are joined in sight. Growth, creativity, original-ity, and first-time decisions in finding new ways into the future are the keywords, but they are not always the properties of individual vocations. The Christian should think of himself as an individual person rather than as a personal individual. In other words, he may pursue a lonely vocation, like a Carthusian monk or even an author, but he is essentially a member of a vocational society called the Church. His ship may be parted by the provisional realities of time and space, but it still belongs to a fleet. Indeed, many Christians will find themselves out of contact for periods over a lifetime, for one reason or another, with Christian community, especially if they are pioneers. Therefore the pattern of Christian spirituality may become more self-sufficient.

This development arises as more Christians see themselves, to employ a biblical military analogy, not as line or staff officers or as regimental soldiers in the parishes, but as in some other relation to the Church as parochial system, with the built-in assumption about purpose already described. The evolution of armies provides us with plenty of images, ranging from the light fast-moving auxiliaries of St Paul's own day who were called in to help the regular Roman legions to the guerrillas, commandos, and paratroopers of our own time.

Perhaps the best word, however, for a significant number of Christians—ordained and lay—today is that they are pioneers. A pioneer is one of a body of foot-soldiers who marches in advance of an army to clear and prepare the way for the main body, and thus he serves as a good symbol for all those who go out in front or begin some enterprise, be they explorers, workers or initiators. Thus he is closely related to that other military figure, the scout. Or, in modern conditions, the soldier may find himself operating in plain clothes as an agent, with all the temptations of becoming in an alien society a double-agent.

Pioneer, scout, or agent, they may work out of touch by necessity with the main body of the churches, but they have a vocation in relation to it. Certainly they will be far more exposed to the realities of the changing environment, including perhaps an infernal version of the Cold War. Moreover, they will frequently feel confused. As Daniel Boone, the famous scout, once said when he was asked if he was ever lost in the tractless wastes of Kentucky, 'I can't say I was ever lost, but I was once sure bewildered for three days'.

Therefore the model of a Church where the clergy teach or prepare the laity for some sort of mission needs to be modified. In the churches of the future the clergy as the officers or office-holders in the corporate Christian enterprise will spend much more time listening to the experience of the laity, each of whom is seeking to create an authentic Christian life for himself in his own piece of the woods and possibly to open up trails which other Christians may follow with profit. In the rest of this chapter I shall try to clothe this generalization with some flesh by taking just one area of the Church's mission as an example, namely laity training. It happens to be a particularly good example for several reasons. First, it does concern the Church in the world, the general theme of this chapter. Secondly, laity training stands fairly close to the parish system, the main investment in time and money of all churches. Thirdly, pioneers in this field are still confronted with almost limitless possibilities for their experiments, innovations, or trail-blazing. Moreover, just to discourage them, the territory is littered with bones—mine included—of pioneers who failed to get the message back to the main body.

TRAINING THE LAITY

The diligent reader of Chapter Two will recognize in the last remark a reference to the relative failure of Canon Harold Wilson and his team of voluntary workers to persuade the main body of the Church of England to use the parish life conference method to give many thousands of its laity what might be called first-aid adult education in Christian vocation. Seen through the various perspectives—historical, sociological, and church organizational or political—that failure of the main body to deviate from its traditional preoccupations is certainly intelligible. It was rather like asking a horse-drawn army led by Crimean generals to change itself suddenly into a highly mobile mechanized force.

That particular lack of organizational response, however, has turned out to be to the general good. For it exposed the need for a new kind of leadership, supported by much better staff work and a more effective system of two-way communication. Although the development of these strengths is far from complete (will it ever be?) the lineaments of them are already sufficiently clear to believe that relevant research (*alias* scouting) and potential significant projects (*alias* pioneering) are far more likely to be discussed and adopted ahead of schedule than in former times.

What matters here is the span of time which separates the first announcement of a good idea or a breakthrough in practice from its general acceptance by the main body. The larger the organization the longer it usually takes. We can chart the time fairly accurately by taking examples of ideas which were subsequently taken up by the main body and then seeing how long elapsed while they sat on the shelf waiting to be noticed. The staff-college idea, to take one example, took seven years to move from published idea to pilot project stage, and is of course still a long way from full implementation. By 1985 that interval of time should be down to one or two years. Apart from those ideas that are eventually accepted, usually by some extraordinarily meandering route composed of the 'old-boy net', pure chance and some providence, there are many that deserved to live and be developed or built upon. Of course there are other pioneers and experiments which fail and do not deserve to be taken up, although even they produce a negative knowledge—'Not that way'. Unlike science, where a significant piece of work is soon spotted in the journals, the Church is not yet possessed of a good if varied communication system for such ideas and experiments, nor proficient in its use. But there are signs that it will develop one in the next decade or so. (This fact contrasts sharply with the heavy over-communication in other areas of the life of the churches, as the contents of any vicar's wastepaper will reveal.)

Parish life conferences may still have their place. In a sense they were a Ford Model-T: capable of mass production, very good and rather basic. There are dioceses which are still producing them, and wisely so. But there are other designs since 1960 which must merit our attention in this chapter as examples of pioneering efforts that deserve to be studied, adapted, and adopted throughout the Church of England, the Anglican Communion, and all other churches. First, I begin at the Rolls-Royce end of the market, St George's House at Windsor.

St George's House, Windsor: A Case Study in Pioneering Enterprise
St George's House has already received some notice in this book with regard to its clergy training activities. Here the focus is upon the other half of its role as a centre for lay studies. As the first Director of Studies there in 1968 and 1969 I am able to write about this aspect of its work at first-hand, and indeed I have done so comprehensively with respect to the series of conferences on Business Ethics and Ethics in Management Education in *Management and Morality* (1974). But having been so involved in St George's House it seems to me wiser to make up this case study from extracts taken from an article by Margaret Duggan, which appeared in the *Church Times* in February 1976:

> St George's House is 'a place where people of influence and responsibility in every area of society—e.g. in industry, commerce, the professions, politics, science, the arts, and the Church—come together to explore, to develop and communicate, freely and frankly, their ideas and anxieties. It is a place where the values and standards of individuals and institutions can be brought into sharp focus, and where the influence of spiritual experience on material affairs can be assessed and developed.'

That is one of the declared aims of St George's. The other is 'to be a place where the clergy of all denominations can come together for short or long courses adapted to the needs of the various stages of their career. Using the understanding gained in the total work of St George's House, and calling on other knowledge and experience, the courses are designed to illuminate ministerial responsibility and functions in the context of modern conditions.'

It all began as a glint in the eye of Robin Woods, now Bishop of Worcester but then Dean of Windsor. St George's Chapel, the home of the Knights of the Garter, had a marvellous church, a generous complement of canons' houses, an able chapter, and a rather indeterminate function.

The enormous energy of Dean Woods had to find some large purpose. He was inspired by the original concept of the Noble Order of the Garter which Edward III founded in 1344 and in which twenty-five secular and combative knights and twenty-five religious and administrative canons were to meet in equal partnership for the good of the nation. Could St George's be renewed as a meeting-place for Church and State in a new way? Could it become the place where those who faced both secular and religious responsibility could find mutual help and a special sort of further training?

The ideas started formulating almost as soon as Dean Woods got to Windsor in 1962, and he received enthusiastic support from the Queen, Prince Philip, and the entire Noble Order, who met specially to consider it. Space was to be found by 'rationalizing' the row of over-ample canons' residences along the north wall of the castle, reducing them to manageable and modernized houses, with enough space left over for St George's House with thirty-five bedrooms, two seminar rooms and the necessary offices. It took £300,000, and the money was raised in the course of three appeals. The house was opened in 1966, and its reputation—and perhaps its influence—has been growing ever since. . . .

Beginning this year, St George's hopes to hold consultations to examine 'whether a change of attitude requires to be initiated in our society towards the value and virtue of the activity by which we in this country principally earn our living; and, if so, how that change of attitude might be effected.' When one puts this in the context of our country's economic plight, and also of the Archbishops' appeal, few intellectual activities would seem more relevant—providing that it leads to action.

The resultant action of more of St George's high-level discussions has to be taken on trust. Because of the necessary confidentiality, most of the reports of the consultations are confined to the people who took part in them, except for rather generalized short accounts—which say almost nothing—in the St George's *Annual Review*.

One suspects that St George's is not very good at communicating anyway. It is the one area of expertise—for all its available impressive resources—in which it seems to be deficient. With all this high-powered thinking going on, it does seem rather unbelievable that there are not a few carefully cut and polished jewels that could be judiciously slipped into the media to the benefit of both the nation and the Church.

But I am assured that results express themselves more subtly: that, when people come together to discuss ethics in public service or relations between people at work, any development in the form of a code of practice or improved employee participation in decision-making is a matter for the individual initiative of those taking part. These things—which are largely a matter of changing and developing attitudes—do happen, but slowly and quietly, and without St George's House appearing in the list of credits.

Apart from the various consultations on aspects of work and management, and meetings of special groups like Members of Parliament and trade union leaders, and individual organizations like IPC Newspapers, Esso Petroleum and Renault making use of St George's facilities and resources to discuss their way of working (and paying generously, which helps to subsidize the clergy courses), there have also been consultations on the care of the dying, and on training the laity to communicate the gospel; and a meeting between ecologists and international and political lawyers to discuss man's responsibility for the ocean, including those areas which don't come under any national jurisdiction. Canon Verney has also started inter-faith consultations which bring together Buddhists, Christians, Hindus, Jews, and Muslims to tackle huge questions about the nature of man and his world responsibilities.

The two functions of St George's House—the clergy training courses and the consultations—are distinct but, in the persons of the staff, constantly interact. The experience and the insights that Canon Verney, Canon Dyson, Major Adams and Admiral Mason (the Warden) glean from their secular ploys are fed into their

ecclesiastical ones, and vice versa. They make a skilled team. Each of
them has his own very individual contribution and enthusiasm to im-
part; but they are primarily enablers, making it possible for very
good minds of very wide experience to think creatively together, and
at the same time enabling a growing number of the clergy to find their
own renewal to take into their ministry.

   Few projects that the Church has begun in the past few years have
turned out to be so creative. It is something of which to be proud.

   In a nation the size of England there is a need for one more centre like
St George's House. In my York Report (1970) I suggested that the
Archbishop of York and Dean of York should establish a similar conference house in that city, possibly modernizing St William's
College—a timbered medieval building which stands close to the
Minster—for that purpose. Scotland, Wales, and Northern Ireland
could set up their own meeting places along these lines. Looking further
afield, all provinces of the Anglican Communion and all churches which
retain a historic link with their parent nations could consider making a
similar provision.

   For reasons of space it is not possible to describe other pioneer
developments in this one field of lay education or training at such length
as St George's House. But there are several which deserve notice. They
illustrate the principle that a creative innovation must be adapted to its
purpose. It would be no good multiplying conference houses like St
George's House indefinitely, for it is designed for a specific and relatively limited task. Other tasks or groups of people will need other kinds of
provision, as the following examples briefly noted here illustrate.

The Institute of Christian Studies
The Institute of Christian Studies was established in 1970 under the in-
itiative of the Reverend Michael Marshall, then Vicar of All Saints'
Margaret Street (now Bishop of Woolwich), in his parish in the West
End of London. Its purpose was defined as 'to provide the necessary
resources to begin the task of lay education in the Church of England',
and it was given the support of the Archbishop of Canterbury and the
Bishop of London as well as of many leading churchmen and scholars.
In 1973, over 200 people took part in its programme of lectures and
seminars. The original home of the Institute in the old choir school of
All Saints' has been replaced by a much larger building on the opposite

side of Margaret Street. The new Institute building provides a lecture hall for 150, as well as seminar rooms, library, chapel, and refectory.

The Institute of Christian Studies is designed to provide an evening classes type of academic or semi-academic education in theology and cognate subjects for those living in London. It stands in the tradition of the Church Tutorial Class Association mentioned in Chapter Three. Certainly there is a need for this form of lay training, and a big city provides a sufficiently large catchment area to make such a project viable. Again I would suggest that every major city throughout the country and the world should consider establishing an institute or centre for adult evening classes and courses in the Christian faith and life, should they not have one already. As Bishop Marshall's experiment reveals, quite often these centres could be grafted on to city churches. But they must be in the city centre or near to it, and not look like retreat houses (which serve a different purpose) that have strayed into the suburbs from the countryside.

Oxford Institute for Church and Society

The Oxford Institute constitutes a different but not unrelated approach to lay training or Church development. The Institute was founded in 1974 with the following purpose: to provide and co-ordinate resources of adult education and specialist training for those concerned with the Church's task in society; and to promote and co-ordinate different forms of study and research by which social institutions (including the churches) may better identify and explore key issues of human responsibility in our society. The Institute is not a building, but an institution working amongst a number of supporting bodies, both providing their resources to one another, and from them to a wider public in the churches and in society generally. The constituent supporting bodies are: the Diocese of Oxford; Ripon College, Cuddesdon (an Anglican theological college); the Urban Ministry Project (a further training scheme for clergy working in urban situations); and Culham College of Education (a Church of England teacher training college).

The resources of the Institute are described as follows: 'The Institute deliberately sets out with few "normal" resources, of staff, buildings or income. The staff is provided by our sponsoring institutions. Our centre is a study in St Margaret's, the Oxford Study House of Ripon College, Cuddesdon. Much of our work is planned to be self-financing. But we are able to operate on a wide front because the sponsoring bodies make their staff, buildings, and other resources (e.g. audio-visual) available to us. In addition, participating institutions, and others who simply support us, are offering to assist our work. From this it will be clear that many skills contribute to the Institute's resources. These resources are available to a range of groups. They are available first within the Institute and its institutions; then to local groups in the Oxford area; finally to wider regional and national scene. The Institute is entirely ecumenical and deliberately works with as wide a range of people in society as is possible.'

The idea of associating together these four rather different sponsors in a combined effort to establish consultations and research in the general field of adult education and training is certainly a creative one. Moreover, such schemes which promise to make better use of existing resources rather than the establishment of new cost centres are far more likely to win acceptance in the contemporary economic climate. But of course it remains to be seen whether or not the Oxford Institute or any other developments along these lines can really deliver the goods as far as lay training is concerned. The combination of a wide spread of interests and limited resources could lead to a comparatively small contribution to the progress of lay training programmes in the churches within the diocesan area of Oxford (Buckinghamshire, Berkshire, and Oxfordshire).

The London Medical Group

The London Medical Group is a creative piece of pioneering work of a different kind. It is especially interesting because it reflects the realities of secularization in society, consequently the content of the education involved is to do with values and professional ethics rather than theology or Christian moral conduct as such. Yet the authorship of the successful development of one area of professional medical training is Christian, and it owes much to the active support of chaplains at the London teaching hospitals.

In June 1963 the London Medical Group was inaugurated by the Reverend E. F. Shotter who is still the present director of Studies, as a response to the growing need for a forum for the open discussion of moral issues in medicine by medical students and others professionally involved in clinical training. In its first year the Group organized four lectures, but by 1965 the programme included 21 lectures and symposia available to all the students in the twelve London teaching hospitals.

The 1975–6 brochure describes the LMG as 'an independent, non-partisan student group for the study of issues raised through the practice of medicine which concern other disciplines. LMG has no members; lectures and symposia are addressed to medical, nursing, and other health students in the twelve London teaching hospitals and are open to all students and others professionally interested. . . . The multidisciplinary Consultative Council gives advice on both topics and lectures and includes representatives of other disciplines, such as Philosophy, Sociology, Moral Theology, and Law, as well as Medicine.' The 1975–6 programme included details of 35 symposia, 10 lectures, and three study seminars and an annual conference. The topics discussed in the symposia (by panels specialists, predominantly senior doctors and consultants, as a preliminary to a wider debate by the student audiences) included Abortion, Rape, Exorcism, Battered Wives, Pornography and Violence, Incest, Human Guinea Pigs, The Ethics of Industrial Action in the Health Service, Alcoholism in the Young, Organ Donation and the Future of Transplant Surgery, Guilt and Foetal Experimentation. In other words, taken as a whole the symposia covered virtually all of the medico-moral problems. Dr Cicely Saunders, the Medical Director of St Christopher's Hospice, also lectured on the Nature and Management of Terminal Pain and conducted some small clinical rounds.

Since the inception of the LMG other similar student Medical Groups have been set up in Edinburgh, Newcastle, Sheffield, Glasgow, Bristol, Birmingham, Liverpool, Manchester, and elsewhere. All these now belong with the LMG to the Society for the Study of Medical Ethics, which publishes a quarterly called *The Journal of Medical Ethics*. All this progress has been achieved by demonstrating that medical ethics has an autonomy of its own, as a discrete area of study within medicine. The whole endeavour has been aimed at helping doctors, nurses and medical-social workers to assess for themselves the moral issues inevitably involved in their sphere of work, and future progress depends upon it remaining firmly anchored inside the medical profession. Yet clearly members of the Church have made and are making an important, if background, contribution to this extremely significant and worthwhile enterprise. In many ways it stands as an example to the Church of what can be done, given limited material resources but much creative imagination. Perhaps more important still, it is a model of how it should be done.

SUMMARY

Within the Christian tradition the attitudes to the world are at best ambivalent. Within that ambivalence the values have decisively shifted in favour of a 'world-affirmation' rather than a 'world-negation' stance. The Church has abandoned at an intellectual level its medieval world view of a cyclic picture of history, made up of a retrospection towards the past and an attempt to recreate it, coupled with a baptized version of the natural cycle of the seasons called the Church's Year which could be revolved endlessly like a Nepalese prayer-wheel. Instead it embraced the heightened value of the secular world in the culture around it, and in particular the nineteenth century exaltation of society and the concept of progress. In this changed world-view it is clear to all thinkers of all churches that the laity occupy a position of key strategic significance for the future of the Church.

With the enthusiasm of converts, some ordained leaders engendered some quite false expectations about the laity. They saw the lay people as being like a mighty army who could be mobilized to save the institutional Church, just as they had once seen the ecumenical movement as the panacea for the failure of the churches to hold their members. But they saw a mirage. There is no evidence at all that even a better theologically-educated laity could halt the decline in church membership and attendance, or stop the process by which baptized Christians become—in Matthew Arnold's words—only 'light half-believers in our casual creeds'.

That conclusion, however, does not alter the fact of the strategic significance of the laity in the world. It means only that we should think of the laity in the 1980s and 1990s more as a few thousand Spartans rather than as serried hosts of the Medes and Persians. Moreover, just as the laity must share more in the pastoral leadership and ministry exercised in the parish system in a proportion of their time, so we should accustom ourselves to thinking of the clergy as spending a proportion of their time in an essentially lay type of situation, in particular exploring the middle ground that lies between explicit Christian belief and practice and the pattern of moral values implicit in the contemporary human scene. To do so while remaining faithful to their orders will involve them in all kinds of tensions. But these are the tensions of the lay Christian today. To be under tension means to be stretched. Perhaps it is that experience which we all need, although we do not always want it. The spiritual cost of living has gone up.

A clearer and deeper theology of vocation is the best rallying point for the laity in the world. It forms a bridge between our natural selves, with our innate abilities, and the quality of response to life and its

Creator which we call spiritual. A sense of vocation in both the general and particular senses should grow as our lives are spent. This growth can be called creative; it is a form of becoming in which we have to participate that serves as the best model for the development or becoming of the Church.

In the changed circumstances of the next two or three decades, more and more Christians will have to feel their way forwards as individuals, seeking the creative possibilities or opportunities in their environment. They will need the penetrating vision to see that problems are only solutions in disguise, plus a talent for innovation or improvisation from existing but under-used resources. To go ahead from the main body or to live outside the city wall is never an easy job. In the past comparatively few individuals or groups have ploughed these lonely furrows. In the future many more will have to do so, as the laity are transformed from regulars to irregulars who are trained to think out for themselves the implications of their vocation in first-time situations.

In this vision the Church becomes more a matrix for such experiments, complete with that essential of a matrix type of organization, a really effective set of communications systems (lateral, upwards and downwards). For the work of research and experiment, scouting ahead for new trails and digging new roads, is all to no avail if the main body of the Church—symbolized by the universal parish-diocesan-church system—is incapable of either listening or learning on the one hand, or on the other communicating to its pioneers where it would like to be going.

Taking one field as an example—lay education and training—and only a few English experiments within it—St George's House, Institute of Christian Studies, Oxford Institute for Church and Society, and the London Medical Group—it is clear that the Church does not lack those essential resources of new life which we call creative thinking, the urge to innovate and to do something original and relevant. One issue is whether or not the main body of the churches as organizations fashioned mainly in the nineteenth century on older foundations can adapt themselves fast enough to keep up with their trail-blazers. Bewildered scouts and a lost army looking for each other in a jungle of over-communication is not an attractive sight.

Can the pioneers do their work effectively in the other areas of the Church's purpose apart from lay training? Are there signs of a creative policy of maintaining the parish system at far less cost in order to devote a significant sum of money saved thereby to supporting and developing agencies designed to help the laity to fulfil their vocations in the world of the 1980s and 1990s? Until we see that happen we need not assume that the theology of the laity is earthed in the organizational realities of the churches as corporate bodies.

10

Church and Society

In this chapter the focus is upon the relationship between the churches as corporate institutions and society, rather than the leavening influence of Christian individuals and groups. As I hope that I demonstrated in Chapter Nine, that is not a distinction to be pressed too far. Of course churches and their social environments both differ so much that it is virtually impossible to generalize. Each case has to be studied. But some wider observations are possible because societies in the 'global village' are beginning to become more like each other. This similarity is more than skin-deep; the shifting pattern of values I have called social capitalism is spreading fast as the dominant philosophy of the non-Communist world. Indeed the differences between the two blocs may turn out to be more those of emphasis than kind.

The churches also have become more like each other. For example, the Catholic Church in England in the past decade has adopted the vernacular for its worship and sought greater participation from its laity—steps that bring it more into line with the Church of England. The growing similarities in their concepts of the Church's role in society is even more marked than those external signs. In particular, most churches draw upon the writings of contemporary theologians to support the emerging view that their fundamental purpose in secularized society ought to be mission. But what is mission? Again I shall use the English situation to illustrate the difficulties—and opportunities—facing those church leaders and members who seek to translate the idea of mission into practice.

THE CHURCH OF ENGLAND AND MISSION
Compared with the practical and political issues arising from the necessity of running the parish system, and matters concerning the ordained ministry, mission strikes many Anglicans as rather a vague, possibly un-English and even strangely disturbing word. The vagueness lies in its roots. From the Latin verb 'to send', mission literally means the action or the act of sending. Therefore its most general sense is a sending or being sent to perform some function or service. In systematic

theology it described the sending of Christ or the Holy Spirit by the First Person of the Trinity. In ecclesiastical usage mission meant the action of sending men forth with authority to preach the Faith and administer the sacraments. Thence it gained its chief religious sense today: a body of persons sent out by a religious community to convert the heathen, or to spiritualize various classes of people.

In the beginning the English were examples of the heathen in question, whom missionaries sent from Ireland and Rome duly converted. After the victory of the Roman missionaries over their Celtic rivals and the official conversion of the Saxons, the work of dividing England into dioceses was completed. Meanwhile missionaries from the young Church sailed from these shores to take the gospel to other parts. Not until the nineteenth century did an awareness of the unchurched urban masses begin to invade the thinking of the Church of England in a powerful way. By this time, paradoxically, the British Empire was reaching its zenith, opening out field after field of heathens who needed the gospel—whether they knew it or not.

The enormous challenge of these countless millions of heathens led to the founding of many more missionary societies, such as the Church Missionary Society (1799) and the Universities' Mission to Central Africa (1857). This overseas missionary work was left almost entirely to free enterprise societies, most of them formed by the Evangelical and Anglo-Catholic parties rather than by the bishops and dioceses of the Church of England as such. The same immobility of the Established Church on the home front helped to push the Wesleyan missioners into setting up their own separatist Methodist Church. Yet as the nineteenth century progressed the Established Church did respond to the growth of the evidently godless working classes by such organizational means as creating new dioceses and building 'mission' churches. Moreover, it gave birth to free enterprise home mission societies, such as the Industrial Christian Fellowship (1877), the Church Army (1882), the Church Lads' Brigade (1891), and the Children's Special Service Mission.

Mission often included medical and educational work, both at home and overseas. To these were added responses to social need which often arose from them but fall into neither category, for example Dr Barnardo's Homes for Waifs and Strays (1866) and the National Adoption Society and Unmarried Mothers Comprehensive Service (1919). But the official belief remained that England was in principle a Christian country, if not longer a purely Anglican one. Therefore bishops of the

National Church did not see themselves as front-line leaders in a missionary enterprise. Nor did either the bishops or Anglican clergy as a body play a major part in the medical, educational, and social reforms which culminated in the vision of the Welfare State.

The deep influence of the changing balance of values which produced the phenomena of secularization altered this picture in a variety of ways. Medicine, education, and social work became autonomous fields, and the connection of religion with them grew more tenuous. The fact that men, women, or children were healed, taught, or helped in material or social ways was less likely to be taken by them as evidence of the truth of Christianity. At least on the home front, Anglican contributions in all these spheres tended to develop in quasi-independence from attempts to convert individuals, groups, and classes to Christianity and the Church of England. The latter evangelistic type of mission became standardized in the form of special courses of religious services and sermons held in parishes, universities, or cities. Many Evangelicals, however, now maintained that *all* services and sermons should be aimed at the conversion of individuals, besides all parish visits and even all conversations. By contrast the Anglo-Catholic movement came to place much more weight on changing society into a Christian order, whose economic and social aspects owed much to their particular image of Medieval Christendom in England.

The gradual tendency to disentangle Church and State which gathered momentum after 1832, and the slow, slight, but significant shift of the conservative Broad Church majority towards the assumptions and values of the more Catholic wing of the Established Church led to a growing emphasis on society and social reform. For example, 16 out of 53 episcopal appointments between 1889 and 1913 went to members of the Christian Social Union, founded at Oxford in the former year. By 1900 it had 1,436 clerical members. With leaders such as Henry Scott Holland and Charles Gore (later Bishop of Oxford), it had a considerable influence. Bishop Wand, for example, who was an Oxford undergraduate at about this time, declared that 'it opened one's eyes for the first time to the implications of Christianity in the whole industrial field'.

The first president of the Christian Social Union was the great Cambridge biblical scholar Westcott, then Bishop of Durham. The theological college which bears his name at Cambridge today illustrates the convergence of the concepts of a professional training for the ordained ministry, grounded on the liberal scholarship of the nineteenth century, with the Broad Church-Catholic orientation in theology and churchmanship. To varying degrees this process has taken place in all theological colleges, although the more extreme Evangelical and Anglo-Catholic ones fought vigorous rearguard actions up to the late 1960s.

Meanwhile the nation has moved into an era of social capitalism, where one set of values (comprising the values of society, the individual, and the natural environment) is rising in the scales against the value of money and profits. Although the majority of churchmen remained politically conservative, believing in a slow evolutionary development of social capitalism, a minority of Anglo-Catholics and a few Broad Churchmen, such as Archbishop William Temple, espoused the socialist promise of a more rapid advance. But these Christian Socialists should not be confused with the latter day radicals who wanted to see the Established Church voluntarily stripping itself of wealth and privilege as a means of commending the gospel to the nation. Both conservative and socialist Broad Churchmen would have none of this radicalism, either because they were not very much interested in evangelistic 'outreach' or else because they believed that such a course would prove utterly fruitless as far as England was concerned.

The Church Assembly can be summed up as the institutional legacy of the Broad Church movement. So unfamiliar today is the Broad Church movement that it is worth recollecting its flavour and tenets. In a recent book about Dr Thomas Arnold, the famous headmaster of Rugby School, E. L. Williamson comments upon the party in these words:

> The name seems to have been chosen to describe the tendency of the liberals to favour toleration of religious differences and to de-emphasize the importance of formal doctrine. In sharp contrast to the Tractarians and other High Churchmen, the Broad Church party was generally receptive to the findings of modern Biblical criticism, favourably disposed to proposals for reform of the Church in the direction of increased lay participation of its government, and deeply concerned that the establishment be maintained. Along with Coleridge, Dr Arnold was unquestionably one of the important sources of this movement.

Among those deeply influenced by Dr Arnold were Archibald Tait, Archbishop of Canterbury (1868–82) and Frederick Temple, Archbishop of Canterbury (1896–1902). The latter's son William, who led the Life and Liberty Movement, regarded Arnold as the greatest

Englishman of the Victorian age.

The spirit of the Broad Church body of opinion (which is still very much alive) was personified by Dr A. P. Stanley, the great Dean of Westminster (1805–81), the first biographer and greatest disciple of Thomas Arnold. His biographer, R. E. Prothero, wrote of him in 1893:

> The great object of his life [was] to show that Christianity is at once real and universal; that it does not belong to one set of persons, or to one institution, but to all; that not only religious, but secular, occupations fall within its sphere; that it ought to raise its voice, not only in the pulpit, but in education, in literature, in Parliament, in legislation, and in every question where there is a right and wrong. . . . He regarded the supremacy of the Crown, and, as its only intelligible translation, the supremacy of the law, as 'a rare blessing of God'. He looked to the civil power to restrain the clergy in legislation as well as litigation. . . . The Church of his vision and of his historical studies was essentially unexclusive and comprehensive, an ample fold in which all citizens of every shade of Christian belief might worship together. If he had not Arnold's vehement abhorrence of 'priestcraft', he was a zealous champion of the rights of the laity, and a strong opponent of all sacerdotal claims on the part of the Anglican clergy. . . . Stripped of its accessories, the issue seemed to him nothing less than the question whether the Church of England was then, and was to continue to be, a national institution.
>
> *(Life*, vol. 1, pp. 384–5)

After 1920 the influences of secularization slowly wore down the concept of mission as the spiritualizing or converting of individuals, groups, the working class, or the nation. In the Established Church, the Evangelicals held on to the understanding of mission as the conversion and sanctification of the individual. The Broad Church and the more moderate Anglo-Catholics, who merged into a nameless majority to keep the Establishment in being, successfully frustrated the hope of many reformers that the new Church Assembly in 1920 would free the Church of England from its identification with the establishment of the nation. These reformers had wanted it to speak with a supra-class prophetic voice, in order to hasten the birth of a truly Christian society. Although the Church Assembly did set up various committees to advise it on social and industrial matters, it never saw itself as the leader of mission, be it one of evangelistic outreach or of a socialist revolution.

After 1832 the Church of England lived in an era of secularizing reform which ate holes into its monopoly of religious influence in the universities and schools. In the Catholic tradition, which the Church of England perpetuated, education stood closely associated with mission. Indeed a pre-secularized age would have found a distinction between Christian indoctrination and education a meaningless one, for revealed and discovered truth were but two faces of the same coin. The secularization of knowledge changed the situation profoundly. Gradually universities and schools established their freedom from the Church's doctrinal teaching activities.

In the case of England the fact of Establishment retarded this process in the ancient universities and schools. While the Broad Church disciples of Dr Thomas Arnold set about reforming many of the existing public schools, both the Anglo-Catholics and the Evangelicals founded new ones. Moreover, the Church of England spent millions of pounds in building schools and teacher training colleges. In 1974, for example, there were 27 teacher training colleges associated with the Church of England, which catered for nearly 20,000 students and produced about a sixth of the nation's teachers. Besides providing buildings and equipment, the Church had given £3 million in grants to the colleges since 1944. Presumably this investment represented a belief in the continuing association of mission and education in a secular age.

The Education Act of 1944 secured instruction in Christian religion and some worship in State schools, but more explicitly Anglican teaching could be given by the parish clergy in Church of England Schools. These arrangements were favoured by the Broad Church majority as a satisfactory expression of the living Establishment, and by the more Catholic-inclined clergy as an inherited method of mission. The Sunday School movement in the nineteenth century developed in a separate way, especially among more Evangelical quarters, as another way of associating mission (seen primarily as conversion) with the education of the young.

Gradually another possible ally of mission identified itself: the ecumenical movement. As we shall see, it grew from a root belief that the heathen in the mission fields would be more likely to accept the Christian faith or gospel if they were not confused by the rivalries and confusing claims of the European churches. The theory was also applied to the home front, but with less conviction because the majority of English churchmen still did not regard England as a mission field.

At one stage in history the spiritual and organic unity of all Christian churches in England might have powerfully served the work of conversion, and it may yet do so. But by 1960 serious doubts had crept in. Successes in the ecumenical progress, such as the Church of South India (1947) and the World Council of Churches (1948), seemed to produce no visible advances in the missionary enterprise. At home the ruling Broad Church majority had always been lukewarm about the premisses of the ecumenical movement, and they disliked any scheme which might imply the loss of the Church of England's identity, especially the spirit and letter of Establishment. Both conservative Evangelicals and extreme Anglo-Catholics could be relied upon to oppose union with specific churches on theological grounds, while joining together to reject schemes which revealed a Broad Church underestimation of dogmas or doctrinal systems as such. Not unlike medicine, education, and social work, however, the ecumenical movement has become somewhat separated from mission, so that it came to be pursued more as an end in itself than as a means.

WORSHIP

In Christian theory mission and worship are so closely related that they can be seen as one. But in this context worship means the various services held in the churches and cathedrals. Many contemporaries see little or no connection between mission and worship. But St Paul clearly thought that what happened at Christian assemblies could have a positive or negative influence even on an 'outsider or unbeliever'. Visiting a service such a person, wrote St Paul, might 'say that you are mad' or else 'falling on his face, he will worship God and declare that God is really among you'.

In the Anglo-Catholic city parishes of the 1880–1930 period the priests regarded themselves as missionaries to the working classes who had been 'lost' to the Church at the Protestant Reformation and under the Puritans—or so they believed. They thought that colour, movement, light, and incense in church would play a missionary role in winning back the poor. The policy did not work if the test of time is applied, but at least it reflected a passionate belief in the power of worship to touch the heart of the outsider or unbeliever.

Historically, most of the energies of the Church of England with regard to worship since 1920 have gone into reforming the Book of Common Prayer (1662). With the swing towards making Holy Communion the central Sunday service marches a spate of revisions of its contents and form. These re-draftings stand in the tradition of Anglo-Catholic scholarship, and they illustrate the changing stance of the

Church of England under Archbishop Ramsey's primacy. Most of the pressures against disestablishment have come from those who see Parliament as the potential protector of the 1662 Prayer Book.

During the 1960s the Church of England as a whole, or rather the wide Broad Church centre, moved noticeably towards the Catholic pole, in that Holy Communion became accepted in a very large number of parishes as the central service on Sunday. Commonly called the Parish Communion or Family Communion, it reflected the high value placed on sacramental worship in the Anglo-Catholic tradition married to the concept of the family as the unit which should pray and praise together. In many cases, but not all, children withdrew from the service for a minor Sunday School on their own before rejoining the congregation to receive the priest's blessing at the altar rails.

This shift towards a more Anglo-Catholic position has led to pressure for changes in practice over baptism and confirmation. The Broad Church view, articulated most powerfully in the theology of F. D. Maurice, that baptism was a sacrament or sign of the Kingdom of God and therefore to be given freely whether or not the recipient was aware of his status in it, gave way to the opinion that the sacrament was an act of initiation into the Church. As such, it was not a big step to argue that baptism should be the only necessary condition for receiving Holy Communion. The High Church clergy had always favoured the confirmation of children at about 12 years of age or less, compared to the more common age of 14 or 15 years before 1960, thus making light of any intellectual preparation or freedom of choice in the adult sense. Like the Catholics they believed that the sooner a child had access to the sacramental Body and Blood of Christ the better for him or her.

In February 1974 the General Synod of the Church of England considered a motion which proposed that baptized children should be admitted to Holy Communion, and then trained within the life of the Church for confirmation at 17 years or afterwards. An amendment to rule out Holy Communion for babies and very young children was defeated, although this did not mean that the Orthodox Church's custom of giving Holy Communion to babes in arms was being accepted. The resolution of the Bishop of Durham ultimately prevailed, by which each diocese was asked to consider 'if they would support a reordering of initiation practice' according to the principle that 'full sacramental participation may precede a mature profession of faith'.

As the Religious Affairs correspondent of *The Times,* who attended the synodical debate, observed: 'Behind these deliberations was a fear that the church was losing its hold. Confirmation was described by one speaker as the ceremony at which the church said goodbye to its children. Although inadequate religious education was blamed for part of that loss, there was considerable feeling that the fault also lay with the way the church formally initiated young people into Christian life. The system of baptism in infancy, confirmation in the early teens, then admission to communion, was criticized on psychological and theological grounds.'

The delay of confirmation until late adolescence, however, would place it in a time when many young people are passing through an intellectual and emotional crisis of belief about God, the Church, and life itself. Therefore it is more likely that confirmation would be sought in the years of early adulthood. In this context many believers would not feel that they needed the extra strength conferred by the laying on of a bishop's hands, especially if they are already receiving Holy Communion. Thus confirmation may be heading for virtual extinction, like the Churching of Women after childbirth.

Thus there are two factors which influence children's work in the Church of England. First, the numbers attending the traditional Sunday School to which local parents sent their children have dropped by 50% over the last twelve years. A 1973 survey in Worcester Diocese, for example, showed that 12,154 children attended Sunday Schools in 1960 compared to 5,536 in 1972. The Sunday School has been replaced in many parishes by lessons in the context of Parish Communion attended by believing families. Therefore a significant number of children from secularized Christian or non-Christian homes will no longer come to church on Sunday, a loss to the mission of the Church unless something is done about it. Confirmations in the whole Church of England also have fallen steadily from a rate of 34·2 per 1,000 people aged 12–20 years in 1960 to 19·7 in 1970. In round figures, the peak year of 1960 saw some 191,000 confirmations, compared with 109,658 in 1972. By comparison, in 1764 there were 23,946 candidates in the Devon archdeaconeries of Exeter Diocese alone, and 41,642, in the Cornish ones. In 1743 Archbishop Herring claimed that he had confirmed over 30,000 children, and Archbishop Drummond put his figure at 41,600 in 1768–9. Confirmations in the small diocese of Worcester numbered 8,945 in 1792, compared to 1,216 in 1976 some 184 years later.

Secondly, the practice of removing the step of confirmation between baptism and Holy Communion will certainly not increase the number who seek religious education in the parish church or from the clergy. It may be that the more Catholic shift in worship contains a deeper assumption that it is the grace of the sacraments and membership in the corporate community of the Church which educates, not the exercise of a child's mind. Thus Christianity is to be 'caught, not taught'. Behind it there may be also an emphasis upon the educational value of a Christian worshipping community and the Christian family rather than upon the individual as a lone searcher for truth.

Taken together, these factors spell a smaller number of children out of the national age group being involved in worship or religious education, and a smaller amount of time among those who do attend church going on activities specifically designed for children. Optimists could argue that religious education and Christian worship in the schools more than makes up for these trends. But the march of secularization tends to shorten the worship element in school assemblies, and to change religious education into a purely academic subject. No Christian can afford to be too optimistic about the state or impact of religious education for children either within the parishes or inside the schools. Not until the 1980s will we be able to evaluate the consequences of these social and ecclesiastical changes but it is likely that they will add up to a growing gap between the Church and the nation. Fortunately, the Church's mission at present still touches the lives of children in countless ways: the quality of family life, school education, medicine, social work and reform, and the parochial ministry of clergy and laity. It is not yet too late to reverse the trends described above. Moreover, children will always have their mission in the Church, contributing to its faith, hope, and joy.

SOCIAL RESPONSIBILITY

Social responsibility as a phrase became popular in the 1920s. It reflected the growing awareness of the moral value of society, especially among businessmen. The term became fashionable in the Church of England about the time the Church Assembly set up a Board of Social Responsibility in January 1958 to promote and co-ordinate the thought and action of the Church in matters affecting family, social, and industrial life. At its inception the Board was charged by the Church Assembly with the supervision of the work previously done by the Moral Welfare Council and the Social and Industrial Council, which became its Committee for Social Work and the Social Services, and the Industrial Committee under various constitutional revisions by 1971. A third, the Committee on International Affairs and Migration, came into being in 1964 and the Council for Commonwealth Settlement was merged into it.

The usual sense of the phrase 'social work' means a response to those whose needs are caused more by social factors than by either nature or sin. In practice, especially in a period which has tended to exaggerate the power of society as the source of all good and evil, it is difficult if not impossible to make such distinctions. In this aspect of its mission the Church is disposed to help those in 'trouble, sorrow, affliction, or any other necessity'; to do it in partnership with the State may strike many as the very essence of the idea of a national church. The fact that in a social capitalist society the State is willing to take on the major share of social work in this sense should be a cause for thanksgiving. Moreover, it should lead to a freedom for the Church to get on with other aspects of its mission in relation to society. But it cannot avail itself of that freedom unless it is sustaining, supporting, and supplementing the social work of the State. There can be a sharing of responsibility, but never a withdrawal from it.

One step beyond helping the needy individual by direct action lies the labour of giving guidance to professional groups who are involved with them. In the 1960s the Secretary of the Board of Social Responsibility, the Reverend G. R. Dunstan (now F. D. Maurice Professor of Social Ethics at King's College, London) made significant contributions to the evolving ethics of the medical profession on issues like abortion and euthanasia. Other individuals, such as Bishop Ian Ramsey and groups formed by clergymen—for example, the Institute of Religion and Medicine (1964)—made their mark in this important field, and their common work continues.

Chiefly through such places as William Temple College and St George's House at Windsor, this principle of stimulating decision on professional ethics was extended into the spheres of industry and commerce at a national level in the late 1960s. The founder of St George's House, now Bishop of Worcester, became the Chairman of the Industrial Committee of the Board of Social Responsibility in 1972. Thus it becomes possible that the fruits of these explorations will be made available to the diocesan staff specialists in this area. The activities of Canon Michael Mann (the present Dean of Windsor) in Norwich Diocese in the early 1970s in stimulating conferences on a regional basis between clergy, managers, and trade union officials illustrated what can be done. Obviously this work is clearly related to the direct ministry of the clergy in factories and offices, which is known as Industrial Mission.

Social responsibility includes not only the values of society and the individual as ends, but also the values of nature and the environment. At parish level these concerns include 'Wildlife Conservation in the Care of Churches and Churchyards', to quote the title of one Board of Social Responsibility pamphlet. At the national level, the use of the Church of England's power as a shareholder and landowner in a social capitalist society is bound to cause debate. The tragic thalidomide case in the early 1970s demonstrated that a small group of shareholders could swing the institutional investors to support a particular course of action in a big company. In 1973 there were pressures in the General Synod for the Church to use its shares in South African companies as a lever against *apartheid*. But that case involved politics in a way that the thalidomide issue did not.

In England there is a tacit agreement that the Established Church as a whole—like its Supreme Governor, the Queen—is above party politics. Of course this limitation does not apply to individual lay members of the Church, although clergymen are still debarred from election to the House of Commons. But the fact of Establishment, symbolized by the presence of 25 bishops in the House of Lords, implies the State's continuing recognition that the Church can and should speak to the spiritual and moral issues of the day.

Those who dislike this exclusion from party politics can argue that in effect the Church of England has been aligned with the Tory Party since the Restoration of Charles II, while the Nonconformist churches have been natural allies of the Left in politics since the English Civil War. Just as the Tory Party was converted to social capitalism in the decades after the First World War, so was the Church of England. Meanwhile the centre of Socialist movement (and Non-conformity) moved politically more towards the centre. These changes made the traditional Tory stance of the Church of England more defensible in social terms, and even allowed some episcopal supporters of social capitalism (such as Archbishop William Temple and Bishop Stockwood of Southwark) to proclaim themselves in public as socialists. But many suspected that the Church of England as a whole, while maintaining its concordat of non-interference in party politics, implicitly and unofficially continued to be the reformed 'Tory Party at prayer'.

Certainly the Tory interpretation of the role of the national church in society has been the dominant one. From its inception the Church

Assembly set its face against being anything more than a grand parochial church council and concerned itself with making church by-laws and relatively minor financial decisions. In 1921 the Bishop of London informed its members that they had yet to touch the imagination of the people of England, and they would fail as a national Assembly if they did nothing in response to the social and moral needs of the country. Lord Hugh Cecil replied that the Assembly should stick to legislation and finance, and his view of its role obviously prevailed. In 1935 the editor of *Crockford's Clerical Dictionary* declared that criticism of the Assembly for so restricting itself was unjust:

> This has been described as The Triumph of the Legalists. We do not know what title the critics claim for themselves. We can understand that there are some people who would like to induce the Assembly to endorse their favourite social, economic, or political theories.

The General Synod has continued the tradition of debates on social and moral issues. Many saw them as a contribution to the wider discussion of these issues. But, as a *Church Times* editorial in November 1975 perceptively commented:

> Here the doubt must be expressed whether the Church, in its present state, can really expect to exert much influence on the secular world. Many people think that the right way is for it to concentrate on its spiritual mission so that more and more converted individuals may make their Christian impact on secular life.

The real division, however, was well exemplified by the two positions taken by the Archbishop of Canterbury and Bishop Stockwood during the former's 'Call to the Nation' in 1975. Bishop Stockwood argued that changes in society must happen before individuals could be converted. It was a classic expression of the old social gospel hope, namely that better housing, less poverty, and improved education would prepare the way for a new social order in which the main deterrents to Christian belief would be removed. The movement in favour of this theory, with its corollary that the churches should involve themselves in political action to change society, not only in South Africa but also at home, made headway in the ecumenical movement up to the Nairobi Assembly (1975) of the World Council of Churches, but the conservative majority succeeded in heading it off. Certainly those who advocated that the churches could forward their spiritual mission by changing society rather than the individual have yet to see their case proved. Thus the Church of England retained its identity as essentially middle-class and conservative, a buttress to the established order rather than a ram laid against its foundations.

Indeed in terms of the theory of mission, the Church of England adopted a compromise position similar to that occupied by the modern Conservative Party in its attitude to social change, namely that *both* changes in society *and* the individual lot were necessary, but the former should be done slowly and on a pragmatic basis. The political activity implicit in the first proposition was to be carried out by Christian individuals, not the Church of England as a whole.

SUMMARY

The relation of churches to their contexts, the increasingly secular societies, is also changing. Societies in different parts of the world begin to resemble each other, and at the same time churches are coming to realize more how much they have in common rather than what differentiates them. Moreover, because of the two-way traffic of values between the depth or unconscious minds of the Church and society, the gap between churches and societies narrows in terms of values while paradoxically it yawns ever wider as far as intellectual belief is concerned.

This situation is common to all the churches and it poses for them both problems and opportunities. The shop-worn ideas about mission entertained in both the Protestant tradition of individualist conversion and the Catholic tradition of socialist change have to give ground to a new attempt to understand the sense of direction or purpose which is unfolding within secular history. The more effective service of that purpose of God for mankind, given at a cost by churches who are turning themselves into advance guards of the main body, seems to be the pattern for the future.

In the British context, the progress of social capitalism will be furthered by a Church of England which both interprets its inner spirit and exemplifies its very best practice. That is the high calling of the Church in any society. This *avant garde* position within the nation includes service to a new vision of England as a servant-leader in the development of a world social capitalist society, which in God's day will blend into the social non-capitalist systems of the communist countries. Common to these national, international, and universal aspirations is a high sense of the spiritual and moral value of society, a value which is but light refracted through the prism of the Kingdom of God.

11

An Alternative Church?

No book entitled 'The Becoming Church' would be complete without a recognition of the ecumenical movement as a phenomenon in church life today. But I must say at the outset of this chapter that I have neither been very involved in it personally, nor have I studied its history and contemporary state in depth. Indeed my own attitude is rather ambivalent towards a movement which I know has excited the enthusiasm of my contemporaries among the clergy. One part of me shares that enthusiasm, but another part questions the value of the exercise as it has now developed. Apart from attempting to clarify my own mind I can only justify this chapter on the grounds that I believe many others have come to share my ambivalence and stand in a similar need for clarity. Moreover, being relatively detached, it may be that I have some chance of seeing the wood for the trees in what has become a very tangled piece of forestry.

In order to do that, it is necessary to survey quite large tracts of history within a few sentences. For without understanding the historical background and the origins of the ecumenical movement there is little hope of seeing it in perspective. But, it must be added, the historical perspective alone and its cousin—pragmatic inter-church diplomacy—will never be sufficient. The perspectives of theology (which is to some extent at tension with history), sociology, and polity are all relevant for understanding what is happening—or not happening—and why this is so. Also, we shall not understand the ecumenical movement unless we realize that many of those engaged in it are thinking not so much in terms of these established academic disciplines—the well-trodden intellectual paths of Western man—but are viewing the situation of the churches essentially through the creative perspective. Therefore they are trying to create or actualize for the first time something which is unknown to them, something belonging to the future that by its nature must therefore be impossible to describe in perspectives that are trained like telescopes upon various aspects of the past or present.

The central problem of any large organization is to establish a satisfactory relation between its parts and the whole. The early Church solved it to some extent by the development of the parish system, in which local congregations in town and country were grouped together in dioceses throughout the Roman Empire. The bishop was responsible for keeping the part in step with the whole in terms of doctrine and practice. That meant that he attended conferences or general councils called for that purpose. In time the rival Bishops of Rome and the New Rome of Constantinople advanced their rights to be primates of the whole Church in the Western and Eastern Roman Empires respectively, so that for example they exercised some control over who should be made bishop in each diocese. Their quarrel was institutionalized after the Great Schism of 1054.

Geographical distance and poor communications, coupled with racial or national characteristics and the proliferation of theological speculations, led to differences among the churches which erupted into dissensions and conflict. The same factors and their results favoured the evolution of different species of churches over long periods of time. If we compare the Coptic Church of Ethiopia with the Church of England, for example, we can only explain the contrast upon social Darwinian principles, that they simply evolved in their closed environments without real contact with each other.

The Roman genius for order in the West struggled with this natural organic tendency for the parts to grow and to develop a distinctive life and style of their own. It tolerated provincial differences but maintained order by the common imperial language of Latin, and by steadily developing the institution of the Papacy. It fought against heresy as the source of disunity, but failed to contain the Reformation. The fight for national independence became intermixed with the struggle for religious freedom from Rome and Catholicism. The Pope and the remaining parts of the Catholic system reacted violently against the secessions but failed in the sixteenth century and in the Thirty Years War during the early seventeenth century to reverse them. Long after the actual fighting had subsided the hostile attitudes of the Catholic and Protestant churches remained virulent, giving rise to persecution, exclusion, discrimination, fear, and suspicion. The natural monopoly of the Catholic parish system had been broken; henceforth the churches saw themselves as competitors for the souls of men. The doctrine of the end justifying the means gave all of them licence, or so they thought, to use various forms of 'unfair competition', such as burning their opponents. As late as 1641 Archbishop Laud seriously contemplated burning a heretic.

Laud also apparently at one time considered accepting a cardinal's hat. The particular position of the Church of England made many think that it could be the first erstwhile province to return to the Roman fold. The English Civil War, topped up by the Glorious Revolution of 1688, put an end to that possibility in politics. The English parliament ensured that a combination of High Church bishops and a Catholic-minded monarch would never repeat the history of Queen Mary's reign, and seek to undo the national independence of the Church of England.

The following centuries of secularizing influence saw the gradual un-ravelling of this compound of national politics with religion, a process which was resisted step-by-step by both Whigs and Tories in Church and State. Yet paradoxically it was the march of secularization in this sense which prepared the way for toleration and later for the more friendly relations between Protestant and Catholic churches. The divorce of Rome from the civil imperial idea and the growing separation of Protestant churches from the national state slowly created a new situation.

The origins of one important strand of the modern ecumenical move-ment can be traced back to the Protestant missionary movement of the nineteenth century. The missionaries came to see that their denominational differences seemed incongrous in the new environments of Africa and Asia, and the appearance of strife amongst themselves did not commend their gospel. Some of them came to the conclusion that it would be impossible to convert the world to Christ without a reunited Church speaking with a single voice. The Edinburgh Conference of 1910 is usually taken to be the starting line for their attempts to bring the churches together again.

After the Great War it became increasingly apparent in the West that the churches were making little or no further impact on the working classes and beginning very gradually (although this was not so com-monly realized) to lose their middle-class members. In the aftermath of the Second World War, with the sudden advance towards a bright materialist bounty after years of economic depression followed by a long war, these trends speeded up. By the early 1950s some daring Christian writers were toying with the idea that such countries as France and England must be regarded as the new mission fields. Thus the need for mission and its apparent corollary, the reunification of the churches, had suddenly come home.

The High Street in Slough, where I grew up as a boy in the 1940s and early 1950s, personified this bright materialist coming society. For

Slough was ten years ahead of its time. With its light industrial trading estate it had attracted waves of immigrants from Wales in the 1930s, soon to be succeeded by coloured immigrants from the Commonwealth. In 1945 it was still possible to see a horse being shod in a blacksmith's shop just off the High Street, but the rapid post-war development of shops soon earned the town the doubtful notoriety of being the subject of one of Sir John Betjeman's poems: 'Come, friendly bombs, drop on Slough/It is not fit for humans now /There isn't room to milk a cow/Come, friendly bombs, drop on Slough.' (Having survived one or two near misses in my Slough cellar during the blitz, it is not my favourite poem.)

The parish church and its two daughter churches were staffed by men who were at loggerheads with each other for much of the time; clashing personalities and the fact that the former church was very High and the others Middle or Low doubtless contributed to that internal ecumenical problem. As far as I could see there was no communication with the Methodist Central Hall next door to our house, whose large Boys Brigade used our street as their noisy parade ground on Sunday mornings, nor with the Salvation Army who invaded the High Street on Sunday evenings. The various chapels which lined the backstreets always remained a mystery to me, though I did once attend a service in the newly-built Presbyterian Church. The Roman Catholics ran two convent schools in the town, which my sister attended, and they seemed to operate entirely in a world of their own. Relations between the churches were therefore non-existent, and occasionally the mutual indifference flared into some brisk skirmishing in the local correspondence columns on such contentious issues as the validity of Anglican Orders.

As mentioned earlier, I served in 1954 as adjutant of a Bedouin regiment of the Arab Legion. We were then the garrison regiment in Jerusalem, and I lived on the Mount of Olives. Warm relationships existed between our tolerant and broad-minded regiment, very predominantly Muslim, and various Orthodox and Catholic monasteries in or near the city. But the tattered building of the Church of the Holy Sepulchre, still supported in those days by British scaffolding, exemplified the divisions of Christendom, each denomination occupying its own space with the Egyptian Copts on the roof. At times the Arab Legion would have to stand by in order to quell interchurch riots in that church or the Via Dolorosa. The Bedouin soldiers merely shook their heads and smiled, for Islam was not plagued by such disunity.

Generalizing from these particular situations I can see why it was plausible in the 1950s to ascribe the apparent symptoms of a failure to convert England at least partly to the unedifying sight of different churches hawking their wares in the market-place, denigrating each other in public or private, and stealing each other's sheep whenever opportunity presented itself. Slough in the 1940s, in other words, presented a good microcosm of the state of church relations in general.

In the context of this new 'missionary' situation, which was largely blamed upon the Industrial Revolution, the churches at national level began to be more aware of what they had in common as well as what still divided them. Partly as a result of a series of conferences, the climate of distant coldness, suspicion, and hostility became a little warmer. Some church leaders began to press much more actively for the acceptance of church unity as a goal towards which Christians in the various churches should now work.

Behind these first green shoots of action in the 1950s there lay three or four decades of conference talk. The Lambeth Conference of 1920, for example, had issued its 'Appeal to All Christian People'. In a world needing so desperately to learn the meaning of 'Fellowship' (the main theme of the Conference), the appeal was for a closer fellowship and unity of all Christians, 'that the world might believe'. So the bishops proclaimed their hope:

> The vision which rises before us is that of a Church, genuinely Catholic, loyal to all Truth, and gathering into its fellowship all who profess and call themselves Christians, within whose visible unity all the treasures of faith and order, bequeathed as a heritage by the past to the present, shall be possessed in common and made serviceable to the whole body of Christ.

Some of the 'fiery spirits' of the Church of England began to break their hearts upon the anvil of denominationalism, in the vain belief that prophetic words alone would shatter the moulds of the institutional churches. In 1927, Canon Dick Sheppard in *The Impatience of a Parson* implored the next Lambeth Conference of 1930 'to ask this one question':

> 'In the light of the tragic failure of Institutional Religion to commend the Way of Christ to mankind, can there be in the mind of God an *alternative Church* to any that now exists; to attain to which it is our duty to bend, if needs be to the breaking point, our own denomina-

tion, and may not that Church be for the world of this day the rightful and orthodox outcome of the faith once delivered to the Saints?' . . . Dare I say that I hope other Churches, whatever their denomination, may be willing also to meet together within their own Communion to ask exactly the same question? If only the Churches were not so inflexible! [The coming together of the churches, however,] would be no end in itself but an earnest of the Churches' fitness to Fellowship and *to commend the Gospel to the world.*

These last words I have set in italics because they emphasize a general point in all the early discussions about church unity. Authors such as Dick Sheppard saw church unity as a means to an end, not an end in itself. They believed that a united Church alone could commend the gospel to the world. No mission without unity. No hope of converting the unchurched masses of East or West to Christianity without a common and united Church, silently preaching by its example the power of the Holy Spirit to unite man and man, and man and God.

Long before any changes could be observed in Slough, the conferences and meetings at international level had been fostering the idea that church unity between the Protestant churches, and possibly one day with the Orthodox and Catholic churches, were realistic goals, which if attained would lead to a renewed missionary power in the gospel. In 1942, Dick Sheppard's friend Archbishop William Temple could tell in his enthronement sermon in Canterbury Cathedral of a progress towards the fellowship part of that early vision:

> Almost incidentally the great world-fellowship has arisen; it is the great new fact of our era; it makes itself apparent from time to time in World Conferences such as in the last twenty years have been held at Stockholm, Lausanne, Jerusalem, Oxford, Madras, Amsterdam.

Until about 1970 it was easy to sustain a sense of progress in the ecumenical movement. The structures of the World Council of Churches and the national equivalents, such as the British Council of Churches and the National Councils of Churches in the United States (founded in 1950), had all been established. The Orthodox Churches had joined in the international series of conferences and councils. Above all, especially after the Second Vatican Council, the Catholic Church as a whole adopted the policy of *détente* which had been pioneered by a few, but it still carefully reserved its position on visible unity. The role of the 'observer' was invented, namely someone who attends a church council or conference without being committed in theology to the organization in question.

To cope with the new relationships between Christian churches in its formal and informal manifestations, there has developed in each of them the equivalents to a miniature foreign office or service. Senior clergymen find themselves in the role of inter-church ambassadors, while others act like diplomats: attending conferences overseas, writing documents and shepherding about visiting diplomats. In the multi-national churches these ambassadorial and diplomatic activities can become full-time jobs and even professions, while the sums of money spent on airline tickets, hospitality, and conference costs mounts and mounts.

But where is the ecumenical movement with its international bureaucracy going? Nobody seems to know. The original vision of creating, by a pragmatic or step-by-step type of inter-church diplomacy, a new Universal Church has gradually come to rest stuck hard upon the underwater reefs of reality. Nobody could see what such a united Church would look like, or how it would work without a vast bureaucracy. Moreover, by 1970 or 1971 many theologians and church leaders had begun to shift their ground and to discover conveniently just how much they valued *variety*. By a subtle form of ecumenical casuistry they argued that we could have both our cake and eat it. There could indeed be a 'great world-fellowship' while at the same time the churches could retain their separate identities (usually called euphemistically their 'traditions'). The individual churches suddenly looked like endangered species, which must be preserved from the threat of extinction by the imaginary ogre of a vast bureaucratic church. The general reaction towards the end of the 1960s against big organizations, and the re-emergence in the West of nationalism and regionalism, were related to this general movement of values. It could be summed up in the phrase 'Small is beautiful'. This strengthening of the values of variety and smallness effectively sank the hope of organizational church unity in the 1970s.

In 1973 two Protestant churches in England joined together to form the United Reformed Church, but the previous year saw the rejection of the Anglican-Methodist unity scheme by the Church of England which far outweighed that success. To carry out a full theological, historical, sociological, and political analysis of the reasons for the 1972 decision against that particular Anglican-Methodist unity scheme would be beyond the scope of this book. It is true that the promoters of it had failed to understand or research into the sociological problems of joining together two distinctive Christian sub-cultures. It is true that they hit upon the wrong method of splicing two large organizations, protracting the agony over too long a period. It is true that the proposed ordinal contained statements which looked to friends like wise if ambiguous compromises and to foes like cynical theological double-talk. It is true that the relatively new democratic polity of the Church of England gave the political minorities opposed to the scheme (the Anglo-Catholics and conservative Evangelicals who had survived at national level as coherent parties much more than they had done so in the dioceses) the means to unite to secure its rejection. But the main message it conveyed was the stability of the *status quo,* or the power of the conservative soul in the Church of England.

And all churches in their varying degrees gradually revealed their conservative souls. They all wanted to preserve their own souls, without venturing into that unknown which Dick Sheppard had called the 'alternative Church'. But the strength of this conservative and conservationist movement, which sprang up to check the ecumenical movement, can only be diagnosed by observing the actions of churches, what they were prepared to do at a real cost to themselves, not by their words. Church leaders found themselves riding two horses, a circus act which regards considerable political skills. They had to keep their churches or denominations together, while giving sufficient encouragement to the generation committed to the 'alternative Church'. The obvious compromise line is to say that the churches are in favour of unity, as St Augustine was once desirous of chastity, 'but not yet'. By 1976 it was clear that 'not yet' meant not in the foreseeable future. The ecumenists put their faith in the impetus of the movement and the possibility of the unexpected, while the churches in general began to plan ahead (as parts of this book illustrate) on the assumption of a continuing separate existence for the rest of this century.

In the new post-Vatican II climate of inter-church fellowship, some theologians advanced the theory that the ecumenical movement had achieved its objective, which they defined as fellowship and co-operation in various works of charity (such as Christian Aid) and 'social justice'. Others expressed the hope that at least the churches might have been able to have achieved the apparently close but tantalizingly evasive objective of full communion with each other (i.e. the right of members in any one church to receive Holy Communion in all other churches). The numbers of those who seriously believed in organic unity in the original meaning of that word had dwindled to a handful.

The change of heart in the 1970s about the desirability of regaining or creating anew the Holy Catholic Church—or the Universal Church, to use a less emotive word—left high-and-dry the organizations which had been established, like camps on the north face of Everest, heading upwards towards the goal of organic unity. The main task of all these organizations had been to consolidate the advance and to prepare the climbers for the final assault on the summit. But the climbers were packing up their gear, having decided that they were on the wrong mountain. The base camps were left behind, partly as tokens of intent, not as provisional organizations but hardening into institutions. Somehow the establishment of these base camps had to be passed off as a sufficient achievement in itself.

Thanks to a new branch of communications which emerged in the 1950s and 1960s, called Public Relations, these limited successes of the ecumenical movement were presented as substantial achievements, and so, to some extent, they were. The message conveyed in the secular and religious press was that spiritual fellowship was now enough. The vast improvement in human relationships between the churches had obviated the need for the organic unity of Christendom in one Universal Church. The present system maintained and conserved the pleasing variety of 'traditions', while the common ecumenical councils provided sufficient vehicles for common social action.

THE ECUMENICAL HYPOTHESIS RE-EXAMINED

At a deeper level it is possible that the old ecumenical hypothesis can be seen to be faulty in the conditions of the late twentieth century. Perhaps the ecumenical pioneers had been trying to construct a Church for the world environment of the 1890s. In the changed circumstances of today and tomorrow, would the reunion of churches—supposing it was theoretically possible—lead to a more effective universal mission?

It may have been true that Africans and Asians in the nineteenth century were confused by denominational differences, and that they acted as deterrents to belief. On the other hand the tribal pluralism of Africa and the intelligence of the people may well have led them to enjoy the European varieties of churches. Certainly the rapid expansion of Christianity in this century in precisely those areas proselytized by the diverse missionary societies and Western churches should give us grounds for questioning the ecumenical hypothesis. To explain the gradual decline in church membership in the West solely in terms of the internecine warfare and subsequent simmering dissension between the churches is far too simplistic.

By the mid-1970s it had become doubtful that the kind of church unity to be gained by the pragmatic diplomacy of the modern ecumenical movement, with its whole paraphernalia of standing institutions, conferences, schemes, and votes, would cause more than a stir of interest among those who were drifting away from Christianity as well as contact with organized religion. Such people, the growing majority, are not put off by the spectacle of different denominations, even when they engage in polemics against each other. The enemies of Christianity, those atheists who had once indeed made capital out of 'See how the Christians hate each other', had also disappeared in the secular fog. For even atheistic dogma had ceased to be of public interest. Indifference coupled with the rising standard of education meant that church unity was less likely to be an effective means towards a missionary end.

The Catholic group of opinion in the Church of England, however, has never looked upon the ecumenical movement (oriented towards the Orthodox and Roman Catholic churches in its case) as a means to an evangelical end, but rather as an end in itself. The heirs to the Broad Church party of the nineteenth century, tinged in this century by the aftermath of Tractarian influence, have also favoured reunion, in particular with the Methodist Church, because they saw the need for maintaining a national and comprehensive Church of England. But the idea of a national Church seems no longer to excite church politicians as it did in Dr Thomas Arnold's day. Indeed the trend appears to be away from that concept towards a kind of denominational separation. And the quest for church unity as an end-in-itself has never commanded wide support among an English laity who are still more Puritan in tradition than their clergy.

Some comments by Douglas Brown in the *Sunday Telegraph* shortly after the Anglican-Methodist unity scheme failed to reach the 75 per cent majority in the General Synod necessary for its acceptance, aptly evoke this questioning of the relevance of the ecumenical movement:

Churchy people—that is to say, professional clerics and those laymen who enjoy membership of ecclesiastical governing bodies—will be much preoccupied this Sunday with the failure of the General Synod of the Church of England to vote by the required majority of 75 per cent for reunion with the Methodists. Some will be bitterly disappointed and others considerably relieved, but their concern will be somewhat specialized. It is safe to assume that the ordinary man-in-the-pew, whatever church he attends, will regard the matter with comparative indifference.

As churchgoing declines, the faithful remnant becomes conscious more of what unites them than of what divides them. Instead of growing impatient with their formal separation, they increasingly tend to ignore it.

The professionals, however, spend a great part of their Christian lives in a highly institutional atmosphere. The details of Church government are naturally important to them. Thus their interdenominational relations sometimes become almost a branch of diplomacy. When this leads them to a laborious search for face-saving formulas, as though they were sitting on the U.N. Security Council, there are many who think they might be better employed, in an age when Christianity itself is fighting a rearguard action against secularism and indifference.

The Anglican and Methodist negotiators have been playing just this subtle game. The 'service of reconciliation' they have devised would have deliberately left in doubt whether or not the Methodist ministers taking part were being episcopally re-ordained. Some High Churchmen might fear they were not, while some Methodists might fear they were.

There is a greater ambiguity about this than about national sovereignty in the Common Market; and, because of it, the end product might have been three Churches instead of two. The official advocates of reunion talk as though the world judges the Christian faith by its ecclesiastical structures. . . .

Yet few ordinary people, one suspects, whether churchgoers or not, will be unduly perturbed. The two denominations get on very well together as it is. A recent Act of Parliament enables them to share church buildings. In new towns they run joint pastoral ministries. Working together, and sometimes praying together, they may fairly claim to have achieved a unity of the spirit.

Although the Methodists broke away from the Established Church only in the 18th-century, the doctrinal differences that separate them from High Anglicanism have been an integral part of European religious thought for 400 years. A sceptical world has grown used to these differences, and it is not particularly impressed when they are glossed over.

It does not look to the Churches for deft theological compromise. It looks for love.

These British reflections can be supported by evidence gathered in America about the changing attitudes of people towards the ecumenical ideal. In a Gallup survey of 1971, the results of which were published later under the title of *Religion in America,* a representative cross-section (by denomination) of the population were asked if they favoured or opposed a merger of the major Protestant churches, and to give their reasons. Their replies illustrate the balance of arguments working in practice towards the maintenance of the *status quo*. Some 61 per cent of Protestants in the survey were against the idea, with 32 per cent in favour.

Those in favour		*Those against*	
Would unify Protestant church, bringing all factions together	39%	Each denomination would lose its identity, character	23%
Competition adversely affects achievement of common goals	17%	Beliefs would have to be compromised	16%
One big church can exert more influence on people	15%	There is value in diversification	13%
Christ's teaching suggests unification	9%	Central control would be cumbersome, would not work	12%
Unification would mean greater efficiency and would save money	8%	A merger would create general problems	11%
Most denominations are simular now	8%	'We should be united in spirit only'	8%
Other reasons/Do not know/No answer	19%	Such a large church would be too powerful	6%
		Other reasons/Do not know/No answer	21%
	115%		110%

For and Against One Protestant Church

(Multiple responses explain the totals in excess of 100%)

On the question of church unity between Protestants and Catholics, some 56 per cent of Protestants approved, with 39 per cent disagreeing with the idea. But 94 per cent of Catholics favoured eventual unity, with only 4 per cent against.

All these Americans certainly realized the effects of secularization in the country. For 59 per cent of Protestant ministers, 61 per cent of Catholic priests, 63 per cent of Rabbis and 75 per cent of the general public (five times more than in 1957) said that organized religion was losing its influence in the United States. This overall average of 70 per cent contrasted with 14 per cent who thought that its influence was on the increase. (In 1957 the figures had been reversed: 69 per cent believing religion was increasing its influence, and 14 per cent seeing decline.) Yet obviously American ministers had abandoned the hope that church unity among the Protestant sects would counter this trend, or—if they thought it might—clearly they believed the price was too high to pay. Unity, on the other hand, emerges as a distinctively Catholic value in the sense of it being an end-in-itself.

THE FUTURE OF THE ECUMENICAL MOVEMENT

Having put into words these questions about the importance of church unity—an alternative Church to replace our present churches—as a prime means to a more effective mission, I want now to be true to my own ambivalence and to question my questions. Supposing one thinks of mission not essentially as converting individuals but as serving the purpose of God for the world in a conscious way, then unity may still have a direct relevance to mission in the coming decades. For an alternative Church to our present systems may prove to be the pattern for a new unity between races, nations, and creeds of the earth.

Such a Church would be a new creation. In the past, although it is a large generalization to make, church organization has followed in the train of the civil order. The early Catholic Church adopted an imperial system. Of course it survived long after the decline and fall of the Roman Empire, not least by helping to inaugurate in 800 A.D. the Holy Roman Empire. The first generation of Protestant churches presupposed an emergence of independent nation states. The World Council of Churches looks very much as if it was modelled on the League of Nations, while the parallels between the Anglican Communion and the Commonwealth have often been commented upon. In its organization forms Christianity seems never to have been particularly original: it borrowed from such sources as Judaism and contemporary civil politics.

On that reasoning we would expect a world church to appear some time after the emergence of world government in the next century. The true initiative, in this picture, would lie in the secular order. It would be attractive to think that perhaps the roles will be reversed, and the churches will be proactive rather than reactive. But there are no grounds for believing that the churches could lead the world towards a new unity, which combines the advantages of peace and common institutions on the one hand and the rich variety of nations and temperaments on the other. Therefore we have to conclude that in the long term the future of the ecumenical movement will be largely determined by the political events or movements in the secular order.

In the middle term, say 1990–2010, the initiative in the ecumenical movement will probably rest in the hands of the Catholic Church. By the logic of their theologies the Protestant churches will rest happily in the present state of affairs. For their initial interest in the ecumenical movement sprang from the assumption or belief that unity would forward mission, and lead for example 'Towards the Conversion of England' (to quote the title of a famous Anglican report published in 1945). Armed with their abstract theology of the Church as the 'invisible' body or congregation of all Christ's faithful people (regardless of denomination) and also pointing to the much better human relations between the churches, expressed in part by joint social agencies and national ecumenical councils, it belongs to their logic to 'call it a day'.

The Catholic Church, however, and Catholic-minded churchmen in the Anglican Communion, have a much deeper interest in organic and organizational unity as an end-in-itself. In the middle term we shall see some startling initiatives from the Catholic Church, especially as the realities of secularization begin to bite into active church membership.

These changes will depend upon the personalities of the next three popes. One of them may summon a great Ecumenical Council in Rome or Jerusalem in order to explore the possibility of expanding the primacy of the Pope within the wider Catholic Communion. In other words, the next major initiative will probably come from a pope, and will consist in part of an invitation to this great Vatican III Council. But the roots of the initiative will lie in a pattern of internal changes within the Catholic Communion which will open hitherto closed doors. What has hitherto been dogmatic—such as the infallibility of the Pope—would be put on the agenda for discussion. My own guess for the date of this council would be about the year 2000, the bi-millennial celebration of the birth of Christ.

Such a council might be called under the joint authority of all the recognized Christian Patriarchs. But I do not see a major initiative coming from within the Orthodox communion of churches. Devout and venerable they may be, but they do not stand in the mainstream of the creative European civilization. The inventive genius, shaped by a thousand years of European history, does not run in their veins. This tentative conclusion in no way denigrates the contribution the Orthodox churches may yet make to a yet-to-appear 'alternative Church'.

SUMMARY

The Christian Church divided and further subdivided like a tree during the centuries of its history. Many of those who use this holistic model unconsciously assume that the 'branches' are still related together. The ecumenical movement for them has been the rediscovery of the Church as a living tree or vine.

Others look upon the divided churches as imperfect fragments of a pitcher broken at the fountain by man's carelessness and sin. The failure of the churches to exert a converting power in society and even among their own nominal members they ascribe in part to this disordered experience of church life. They work towards piecing the bits together, or look to the day when the master Potter will melt down the hard jagged clay shards and throw a new pitcher, a more perfect 'alternative Church' to the present deformed counterparts.

The modern ecumenical movement is in fact a coalition of several movements. The Protestant movement stressed unity as instrumental to 'commending the gospel'. The Catholic movement, while not dismissing mission, sought to realize the value of unity as an end-in-itself. Both welcomed the coming of fellowship. Quite where the coalition goes from that half-way base camp on the mountain side, however, remains to be seen.

For an ambivalence towards the ecumenical movement, which was perhaps always latent, has begun to emerge in the West. The amount of time and money spent upon it mounts steadily, but its achievements in 'spreading the gospel' appear to be almost non-existent. As social and political forums for the churches, the ecumenical councils at national and internation levels have certainly established themselves, complete with their staffs. But is Christianity only about social reform and political intervention? Are these not manifestations of the secularized world-view which Christianity should be challenging? Has not the ecumenical movement, with its institutionalized forms and network of diplomacy, become a gigantic diversion from the main purpose of the Church? Of course the participants do not feel so, but then a sociologist may say that they have become part of an ecumenical sub-culture. So they may feel more at home in the ecumenical movement than in their own churches.

With the existence of very different ideas about the aims or objectives of the ecumenical movement and saddled with a number of ecumenical institutions, it is now unlikely that we shall see any progress towards an alternative Church in the next ten or fifteen years. The political problems posed within each church by any further real steps in that direction are too serious for those leaders who know themselves to be charged with maintaining historic organizations more or less intact. A generation or two must die out, and the effects of secularization become far more marked than the present very gradual decline in church membership before that happens.

When it does come, the next major step may be a third Council for the universal Church, called by the Pope of the day as part of a whole series of internal changes in the Catholic Church designed eventually to open the fold and to offer the papacy, in partnership with the episcopate, as the pastoral leadership of the whole Christian enterprise. Although the creation of a polity for the unnamed alternative Church which will stem from this council appears to be an impossible task, it is not so. A college of patriarchs, supported by the universal episcopate, might form the core of such a new Church with the laity involved at episcopal level as well. The central organizational problem of the relation of the whole and the parts (unity and variety) can and will be solved. Whether these changes follow upon a restructuring of the world national order, or in fact precede them as an earnest of the Kingdom of God already at work through the Christian enterprise, of course remains to be seen. But there is a case for the latter scenario. To follow Christ the Church must lead Man.

12

Morale

We sail a changeful sea through halcyon days and storm,
And when the ship laboureth, our steadfast purpose
Trembles like as the compass in a binnacle.
Our stability is but balance, and conduct lies
In masterful administration of the unforeseen.

ROBERT BRIDGES, *The Testament of Beauty*

The churches have certainly sailed upon turbulent seas since the Second
World War. In some quarters there has been an accompanying loss of
certainty, with not a few voices proclaiming the impending break-up of
the churches as institutions and advising us to take to the boats. Ahead
lies the next stretch of the unknown future, which promises to be as full
of change and incident as the last thirty years. What is the state of
morale in the churches today? What will happen to it in the coming
decades?

Answers to both these questions will be extremely various because
we have no scientific means of measuring either organizational morale
(or climate) or the morale of individual members. What can be done,
however, is to explore the sources of morale in the Christian Church.
These will include elements that are common to all organizations and
those which are unique.

WHAT IS MORALE?

Morale is not easy to define but it includes the sense of common purpose—or the purposive unity—of a group. This sense is not the same as
possessing neat definitions about the ends of the organization, it is more
a matter of spirit which infuses all work towards aims and objectives,
embracing them and holding them together in a common direction.
Because it is so vague and intangible I can speak about it only by
analogy, using such images as the invisible magnetism that moves the
compass, the wind that fills the sails or the current within the sea
that bears the vessel upon its way. Morale in this guise is not a fluc-
tuating optional extra in a group; it is an indicator of the power present
within it.

Intimately related to it is the group's or organization's confidence in the ultimate success of their venture. Morale can be badly affected by reverses and setbacks but it can recover naturally providing the group stays together. For the human spirit is resilient and hope springs up again. The hope in mind is that the organization will accomplish the common task in the end, despite—or perhaps because of—its early sufferings.

The relation of the morale of individuals to the corporate morale is far from simple. Sociology has shown that there can be wide discrepancies between the apparent purpose of an organization and the personal goals of individuals and their personal interpretations of corporate purpose (which may be in forms of rationalization). It is quite possible to have high morale in an organization as a whole and low morale in some of its members, and the reverse. The more the individual identifies himself with the organization the more he will experience its sorrows and joys as his own.

The hallmarks of good morale, then, are a sense of purpose and confidence about the future. It can be most clearly seen in a group or organization when things are going wrong. A strong sense of purpose will enable the organization not only to survive the shocks and storms but also to take the necessary steps to change itself—at whatever cost—into a more suitable instrument of purpose. Confidence about the future remains even when the present is full of 'fightings within and fears without'.

CHRISTIAN CONFIDENCE

In all monotheistic religions confidence about the future is bound up with confidence in God—that he is, and that he will save. Where God is seen as source and centre of a many-faceted moral value—love, goodness, truth—then the believer must believe that such value will prevail, and that conditions characterized by the absence of these values—evil, lies, hatred—will give way as darkness recedes before the growing light. Therefore a Christian is certain to be an optimist in that he will believe that goodness must ultimately prevail over evil in the universe. He will eschew those shadowy assumptions behind modern cynicism and pessimism, namely that in the last resort reality is evil, and that everything and everyone tends towards it. Nor will he accept the view that the misery of human existence outweighs the happiness in life.

When it comes to the Church he will be equally sanguine. His hope at this point transcends the shared theistic belief in the ultimate moral order of the universe. For the disciples in the storm on the Sea of Galilee their environment included the sleeping Jesus in their midst. Although some theologians and secular well-wishers have attempted to lighten the ship of the Church by throwing overboard the person of Christ, he is still with us. Indeed, Christians believe that it is because of the buoyancy of Christ that the waters of chaos and death cannot close above the head of the Church. Resource comes from *resurgere,* to rise again. Christ's presence in the Church means there are always spiritual resources, always a buoyancy which breaks the surface of apparently final constraints.

CHURCH MORALE

The churches are staffed by Christians who believe that they belong to the Church. Therefore they have sources of morale which lie outside the institutions in question. The major change in the past half century called the ecumenical movement has consisted in part of a shift of value from the particular (churches) to the general (the Church). As noted above, this shift has been corrected by another turn of the wheel backwards in favour of the values of the particular (variety, tradition, cultural identi- ty, etc.), but the direction of church life is still on a different course.

As far as morale is concerned there are pros and cons in this new situation. The emergence of a sense of the general (the Church) has strengthened morale by enabling Christians to share their corporate experience. It means that they have found wells in the desert beyond their own dwindling and sand-driven oasis. The world-wide fellowship of Christians, meditating upon and sharing in a common faith in Christ as present in their midst, is a real encouragement to those clergy and laity in organized religion who are frustrated by the obverse side of par- ticularity. On the other hand, the identification of Church unity as a goal to be pursued in space and time increases the chances of poor morale and individual frustration if the path towards that goal is firmly barred at a certain point or if—as some think more likely—the goal itself proves to be a mirage.

The sense of common purpose in particular churches *vis-à-vis* their surrounding secular environments is a comparatively recent and un- even development dating from around the middle of the last century as secularization became a more visible phenomenon, although of course it had its antecedent roots in all churches. Until then individual churches could see themselves either as the spiritual face of the secular communi- ty or as a community within the wider social community. The first stance gave them representative worship as their chief spiritual function; the second self-image, where it was not isolationist, interpreted purpose (or mission) in terms of evangelism.

Problems for morale can be identified in both assumptions and their accompanying attitudes. The representative worship model can look increasingly hollow in a secularized society, and the faithful 'remnant' experience a kind of cultural loneliness. In such an environment it also becomes increasingly harder to maintain churches as communities within the community. Without a common race behind them (like the Jews) they are likely first to become more secularized themselves, and eventually to become absorbed in society at large. As confidence in the possibility of converting mankind fades these community-type churches or denominations may well evolve into irrational sects with primary ecstatic or apocalyptic interests.

On the other hand, there is growing confidence in the churches at large in the unique contribution that Christianity has still to make to the future of man. This larger sense of vocation within God's purpose for mankind is an outside source of morale to all those who are seeking to guide and alter the churches to make them better servants of the Kingdom of God. Within the Christian context it is the too limited view of purpose or the too narrow definition of the Church which creates low morale. A true vision of purpose and a proper understanding of the Church, however, creates a climate in which the institutional churches can take their bearings in relation to each other and the world in a growing light of realism and hope. They can also face up to change of a far more radical nature than experienced hitherto.

A THEOLOGY OF CHANGE

It should not be assumed that all change leads to low morale. Change introduces an element of uncertainty which can affect morale, but whether it does or not depends upon our perception of the impending or possible change.

Confidence in God should encourage the churches to take risks and to explore, which means to accept the unknown and uncertain. A seaworthy ship must put out to sea. The harbour or haven is the familiar and the known, almost encircled by the man-built arms of the past. To exchange the predictability of the well-girt harbour for the unpredictability of the open seas: such is the vocation of the Church today.

Central to that understanding—and therefore to this book—lie the cross and resurrection of Christ, for they signify the buoyancy of God who always makes his own to surface above the waters of death. The cross was a fundamental change freely accepted through faith in the reality of God. Jesus took death by the hand before it took him by the throat, and thereby he transformed it into a voluntary act. A church with the cross as its centre, as opposed to an ornament upon altar or table, would be willing to change in fundamental ways if only the risen life of Christ could shine more fully. What is required in the first instance is a change of attitude: the willingness to see things differently, to be uprooted, changed, dissolved, or made redundant. For those who freely accept the provisional nature of all forms and structures are already part of the future. Those who make the present permanent are already children of the past.

But do the churches still so know Christ that they are willing to be conformed to his death? That is literally the crucial question. By their fruits they will be judged. Do they bare the branches with the knife so that fruit may grow? Do they dig and dung the tree? Do they graft in other strains? For what people will see or notice is change. Will the change be 'from glory to glory' or merely from expedient to expedient?

The word change covers a spectrum of meanings. It can be an essential difference often amounting to a loss of original identity. This is the aspect of change which arouses a deep fear within us. The greater our love for things or people as they are, the harder we find it to contemplate the loss of their identity. This anguish lies close to the heart of all bereavement, all parting, and all personal despair. 'Change and decay in all around I see', declares Henry Lyte's hymn. Like St Augustine before him, Lyte found repose in the changeless nature of God and the preservation of all identity in him.

In the context of this meaning of the word change, the Church can be held to rest upon the unchanged, unchanging, and unchangeable original identity of Jesus Christ. Therefore a Christian must conclude that the Church has not, is not, and will not change in that essential. But this reassuring Christian affirmation still leaves room for two other kinds of change. Although these necessary changes can be considered apart theoretically, so to speak, in practice they are inextricably woven together.

The gap between idea and reality supplies the tension or energy for the first kind of change, which is an inner one. The Church is identified with Christ in the sense that it is called to share his identity, without loss either of its humanity or his divinity. Consequently Christians believe that God is at work to change the Church more into the likeness of

Christ, using as always individuals, groups, and historical events to that end. This sort of change might be appropriately known as the *transfiguring* of the Church. The word transfigure comes from a Latin verb meaning 'to change the shape of' something or someone. The change in the appearance of Jesus Christ on the mountain of Transfiguration gives the clue: the true character or glory of Christ's identity shining through his human form. So the Church is called to be more translucent, so that it may become what it already is.

But another kind of change is necessary, which we might call the *altering* of the Church. The verb means to make otherwise or different in some respect, without changing the thing itself. Theologically, alteration should not be separated from transfiguration: the one sufficient reason for change in the Church ought to be that the identity of Christ may find a fuller expression in the world. But alteration is more tangible: in particular it covers the changes which happen in response to changes in the environment. For the Church is not static; it is afloat on the ocean of history within a yet evolving universe. Like sailors of old, the Church's helmsmen have to alter their ship's course and the set of its sails constantly. They will also have to face some more fundamental modifications, like sailors who had to cope with the transition from sail to steam.

THE CREATIVE PERSPECTIVE

Young people see change as a challenge, old people perceive it as a threat. The churches are old institutions. Have they the youthful spirit within them? At the crossroads of the present do they stand and look backwards wistfully at the past or eagerly to the future? Many factors—historical, sociological, and theological—turn them inexorably to the past: they are inclined to walk forwards with their back to the future. Yet the conservative spirit struggles in vain with the growing sense of purpose which works to restructure all church organization into the service of the future.

Above all, the conjunction of a purpose and a future taken together gives the churches a measure of discretion in what they are becoming. Today and tomorrow are fixed, but for the day after tomorrow the churches can choose what they want to do and be. How can they choose? Only by reference to purpose. For, as N. W. Chamberlain wrote in *Enterprise and Environment* (1968):

> Purpose—the individual's, or the organization's, hook in the future, toward which he draws himself by design—introduces an element of

control over future conduct. It calls attention to the human potential for rearranging activities and for reorganizing the use of the real assets at one's disposition in ways not wholly governed or dictated by the past, but growing out of inventiveness, creativeness, foresight, degrees of optimism and self-confidence, and assertions of power.

This exercise of taking bearings not only upon the surrounding horizons or landmarks but also upon the value-stars of purpose is essential for the churches as organizations. Secure in the knowledge of where they are and where they are going, with a buoyant cargo and good morale in the crew, they can set course under the most lowering skies. But how far should they listen to the weather forecasters?

There is no certain way of forecasting the future, because the latter is the domain of the unexpected. What we can do to some extent is to extrapolate from existing trends, a method we rely upon for any form of planning ahead. The longer the time-scale of the forecast, however, the more the present assumptions and values of the prophet will come into the picture. Moreover, although in theory all Christians are committed to a philosophical optimism, in practical affairs their temperaments may be far from sanguine. An individual Christian's disposition might incline him to putting a more favourable construction upon actions or happenings or else conversely towards emphasizing adverse aspects, conditions, and possibilities. He may be weighted towards hoping for the best and looking on the bright side under all circumstances, or towards the opposite viewpoint. So the optimist will anticipate the best possible outcome while the pessimist predicts the worst possible outcome: both are expressions of a cast of temperament and fit into that person's pattern of thinking about the future. There are more complex permutations. One person I know, for example, oscillates between the poles of extreme optimism and pessimism, while another consistently blends the two.

Are all forecasts then merely expressions of assumptions and values, flavoured by the temperamental bias of the speaker? By no means, for that leaves out a creative perspective. By that I mean the exercise of a kind of imagination, based upon experience, intelligence, and flair, which is able to picture with reasonable accuracy what a future situation will be like. Although it is a form of imagination, like most art it is based upon a close attention to reality.

The fact of such creative imagination does raise some awkward philosophical questions to do with determinism and free-will. Without going into them here, for they lie beyond the present scope, I would say that its existence denies both the black or white assumptions; namely, on the one hand, that the future is fixed, and we read it like a book, or on the other hand that it can be made out of nothing. To repeat an earlier point, the seeds of the future lie in the present. The art is to know which of the myriad possibilities will develop. Through a close attention to reality some of these possibilities can be perceived as the probabilities by gifted minds, and they become the materials fashioned in their creative imagination into one picture or scene of the future. Freedom comes into play, however, in that the creative picture may help to fulfil itself. Or else the image of the present seen in the mirror of the future which the prophet holds up might drive men to act while there is still time to ensure that the vision will not be the photograph of a future reality but rather the portrait of a discarded (but real) possibility.

The chief advantage of being able to picture the future accurately is that you can prepare for it. Perhaps imagining the future only becomes *creative* when it calls into play a restructuring of organizations or a redeployment of resources. One enemy of such imagination is unreal pessimism, which undoes morale and also prevents a creative response to the impending situation. The other deadly foe is a specious form of optimism. That again threatens morale because it raises false expectations and also inhibits the need for creative action on the vague grounds that all will be well or that help will come from some other quarter so that no painful changes need be made in the present.

CONCLUSION

The becoming Church cannot peer too far into the future, although it needs its lookouts and even its seers. But it should approach that unknown future with a confidence born of the morale it now experiences. It can survive any form of institutional catastrophe, but not unless it encourages those prophetic changes necessary if the Church is to do its work in the day after tomorrow. In order to be a more positive influence in the spiritually needy world of the 1980s the changes must come now. For the Church is called to be a proactive source of energy in its environment, not a reactive and obsolescent family of passive organisms.

What the world of the 1980s and 1990s will be like we do not know. In many ways it will be the world of the 1960s and 1970s all over again, but in other respects it will be *very* different. The wheat and the tares grow together. Great steps forward in science will be matched by more formidable human problems; for example, a global population racing towards the 5,000 million mark and all the tensions that that will bring. On the more positive side we shall see the progress of social capitalism, reflecting as it does a sense of moral values, throughout the non-communist world, and a greater interchange of values between social capitalist and communist countries in general. The seeds of a movement towards world government may well germinate in these decades. Perhaps in these great movements and shifts of history, exposing yet deeper crevasses of possible mutual catastrophe, the human family will grow closer together. The becoming Church may well lead the way.

Select Bibliography

Bliss, K., *We the People: A Book about Laity.* S.C.M. Press 1963.

Chadwick, W. O., *The Victorian Church.* A. & C. Black 1966 (2 vols.). *The Secularization of the European Mind in the Nineteenth Century.* C.U.P. 1975.

Chamberlain, N. W., *Enterprise and Environment.* New York, McGraw-Hill, 1968.

Congar, Y. M. J., tr. D. Attwater, *Lay People in the Church: A Study for a Theology of Laity.* Bloomsbury Publishing Co. 1957.

Denniston, R., *Partly Living.* Geoffrey Bles 1967.

Eccles, D., *Half-way to Faith.* Geoffrey Bles 1966.

Edwards, D. L., *Religion and Change.* Hodder & Stoughton 1974.

Eldridge, J. E. T. and Crombie, A. D., *A Sociology of Organisation.* George Allen & Unwin 1974.

Emmet, D., *Function, Purpose and Powers.* Macmillan 1958.

Gibbs, M. and Morton, T. R., *God's Frozen People.* Collins 1964.

Grubb, K., *Crypts of Power: An Autobiography.* Hodder & Stoughton 1971.

Harvey, A. E., *Priest or President?* S.P.C.K. 1975.

Hill, C., *Society and Puritanism in Pre-revolutionary England.* Secker & Warburg 1964.

Hunter, L. S., ed., *The English Church: A New Look.* Penguin 1966.

Iremonger, F. A., *William Temple: Archbishop of Canterbury.* O.U.P. 1963.

King, T. G., *Readers: A Pioneer Ministry.* Central Readers' Board 1973.

Kraemer, H., *A Theology of the Laity.* Lutterworth Press 1958.

Lampe, G. W. H., 'Secularization in the New Testament and the Early Church' (*Theology*, 1968, pp. 163–74).

Murdoch, I., *The Sovereignty of Good.* Routledge & Kegan Paul 1970.

Norman, E., *Church and Society in England 1770–1970.* Oxford, Clarendon Press, 1976.

Oldham, J. H., *The World and the Gospel.* United Council for Missionary Education 1916.

237

Paul, L., *A Church by Daylight: A Reappraisement of the Church of England and its Future*. Geoffrey Chapman 1973. *The Deployment and Payment of the Clergy*. Church Information Office 1964.

Prothero, R. E., *The Life and Correspondence of Arthur Penrhyn Stanley, D.D.* John Murray 1893 (2 vols.).

Rudge, P., *Ministry and Management: Studies in Ecclesiastical Administration*. Tavistock Publications 1968.

Sheppard, H. R. L., *The Impatience of a Parson: A Plea for the Recovery of Vital Christianity*. Hodder & Stoughton 1927.

Thompson, K. A., *Bureaucracy and Church Reform: The Organizational Response of the Church of England to Social Change, 1800–1965*. O.U.P. 1970.

Whiteley, D. E. H. and Martin, R., eds., *Sociology, Theology and Conflict*. Oxford, Blackwell, 1969.

Williamson, E. L., *The Liberalism of Thomas Arnold: A Study of his Religious and Political Writings*. Alabama, University of Alabama Press, 1964.

Wilson, B. R., *Religion in Secular Society: A Sociological Comment*. Watts 1966.

Wright, M. J., *New Ways for Christ*. A. R. Mowbray 1975.

Index